$\mathbf{X^0}$

X^0: A Theory of the Morphology-Syntax Interface

Yafei Li

The MIT Press
Cambridge, Massachusetts
London, England

MIT Press books may be purchased at special quantity discounts for business or sales promotional use. For information, please email special_sales@mitpress.mit.edu or write to Special Sales Department, The MIT Press, 5 Cambridge Center, Cambridge, MA 02142.

This book was set in Times New Roman on 3B2 by Asco Typesetters, Hong Kong. Printed and bound in the United States of America.

Library of Congress Cataloging-in-Publication Data

Li, Yafei.
  X^0 : a theory of the morphology-syntax interface / Yafei Li.
    p. cm.
  Includes bibliographical references and index.
  ISBN 0-262-12275-8 (alk. paper) — ISBN 0-262-62191-6 (pbk. : alk. paper)
  1. Grammar, Comparative and general—Morphosyntax. 2. Grammar, Comparative and general—World formation. 3. Lexical grammar. I. Title.
  P290.L5 2005
  415—dc22   2004055912

10 9 8 7 6 5 4 3 2 1

To Wayne O'Neil, my teacher, my mentor, and my friend

道生一，一生二，二生三，三生万物。

《老子》第四十二章

Contents

Preface

The core idea of this work, the Morphology-Syntax Mapping Hypothesis, was initially presented in the syntax seminar of fall, 1996, in the Department of Linguistics at the University of Wisconsin-Madison and later in the 1997 LSA Summer Institute. It surely has traveled a long way to become a book. On the one hand, it is such a relief to know that I can put it behind me now; on the other, the long course taken is also the primary reason that few most recent works find their place in the text—the references pretty much reflect what the first complete draft of the book looked like.

Like numerous works before it, this book tries to figure out the puzzle of the relation between word formation and sentence formation. The theme of the book is that some mutually opposing ideas regarding the puzzle not only can be reconciled into a single (and simple) theory but also should be. Though such an approach is not often taken in modern linguistics in the face of competing theories, it has repeatedly proven to be the right one in other fields of science that study complex natural systems. An example from biology is briefly mentioned in the last chapter of the book.

Ideas come and go (and, sometimes, come and go again). Few people have the privilege of finding their largely intact ideas a permanent place in the ever-evolving base of knowledge. Still, what I have argued for in this book is what I believe at the moment to be the best solution to the above-mentioned puzzle. And for this personal accomplishment, I owe my intellectual debts to the following three scholars, listed chronologically according to the time their thoughts influenced me: Jim Higginbotham, Richard Larson, and Mark Baker.

Jim's theory of thematic operations showed me the explanatory power of a simple computational system that is not intrinsically part of syntax.

This is the origin of my doubt that anything that can be accounted for syntactically is automatically a syntactic phenomenon. From Richard, I learned to dissociate the essence of a theory from the technical implementations of that theory. Ever since, I have felt blessed not to be tied unnecessarily to specific technical apparatuses while adopting or expressing an idea in my research. Mark's influence on me is everywhere. Though this book articulates a theory that disagrees with his in many fundamental ways, it is built on his numerous insights and his rich reservoir of data. Without his work in morpho-syntax, this book would not have been possible.

My special thanks go to Anne Mark. Without her superb editorial work, this book would have looked very different, and that difference would be one that I am glad no one else has the opportunity to see.

With this opportunity, I also want to share an anecdote. While trying to explain to my daughter what the title of my book means, I jokingly said $X^0 = 1$. Though the algebraic equation is no part of linguistics, it occurred to me that it does have a symbolic meaning for my book. After all, not only is the book concerned primarily with things happening at the X^0 level of the language faculty, but its central theme is to argue that at this level, the two mechanisms typically viewed as conflicting alternatives to each other, that is, head movement in syntax and lexical word-formation operations, are actually the coexisting and interactive factors of one simple interface system that could not exist without either one of them. In other words, X^0 is a place where "opposing" syntactic and lexical factors unite into a single component of language, which I call the morphology-syntax interface. In this sense, my book might be appropriately summarized as $X^0 = 1$.

Introduction

The Morphology-Syntax
Mapping Hypothesis

This book presents a theory of the morphology-syntax interface that resolves the debate over the role of syntactic head movement in word formation.

Ever since Chomsky's (1970) "Remarks on Nominalization," generative linguists have been trying to determine where and how a morphologically complex word (hereafter referred to simply as *a word* when no confusion arises) is formed in the model of Universal Grammar (UG). An instructive discussion of the early efforts to answer this question can be found in Newmeyer 1980.

Over time, it has become clear that different aspects of morphology and its relationships with syntax and phonology all bear on the question. An active area of research is the nature of inflectional affixes (see Di Sciullo and Williams 1987; Jensen 1990; Anderson 1992; Lieber 1992; Halle and Marantz 1993; Aronoff 1994). The relationship between the morphological module and the syntactic module has also been investigated extensively (see, among many others, Anderson 1982; Fabb 1984; Sadock 1985, 1991; Sproat 1985; Baker 1988, 1996; Borer 1988, 1991; Cinque 1990, 1999; Bonet 1991; Halle and Marantz 1993; Bobaljik 1995; Jackendoff 1998, 2002; Hale and Keyser 2002). The debate addressed in this book is a specific manifestation of this second area of research. In the debate, the syntactic approach argues that a substantial number of morphological phenomena result from head movement in overt syntax, whereas the lexicalist approach, named after the Lexicalist Hypothesis (Chomsky 1970; Jackendoff 1972; Lapointe 1980; also see Chapin 1967), maintains that morphological/lexical means are both necessary and sufficient for a theory of word formation.

Largely because of the impressive elegance with which Mark Baker accounts for the complex data of incorporation in the Principles-and-Parameters (P&P) model of syntax (Baker 1988), the syntactic approach has been widely adopted by researchers in recent years. Indeed, Baker's theory is so successful that the past decade and half has witnessed not only many efforts to apply his analysis to a broad range of morphological (as well as syntactic) phenomena but also the frequent adoption of the (tacit) belief that when syntactic and lexical accounts are both possible, the syntactic account is automatically preferred over the lexical one. For its part, the lexicalist approach has also offered various arguments that words are formed with lexical operations distinct from those found in the syntactic component (for examples, see Di Sciullo and Williams 1987; Rosen 1989). The debate continues to this day, often couched in more current terminology.

In essence, the theory proposed in this book attempts to resolve the debate by properly synthesizing the two conflicting approaches. On the basis of data accumulated in the literature and reported here, it is shown that *each side of the debate has an empirical foundation that cannot be encroached upon by the other side.* The hope for a unified account of all the relevant data lies *not* in continuously expanding the coverage of an exclusively lexicalist or syntactic theory at the cost of ad hocness, complexity, and even internal inconsistency, but in synthesizing the empirically advantageous portions of both sides into one simple and coherent theory.

One of the most crucial facts bearing on the lexicalist-syntactic debate comes from certain Semitic languages where both verbal and adjectival roots undergo causativization. The examples in (1) are from Arabic.[1]

(1) Ja$al-a   l-mudrris-uun$_i$ t-tulaab$_j$-a   yajlis-uun bi3aanib-i
    made-agr the-teacher-pl.nom the-students-acc sit-agr   next-gen
    ba$dihum l-ba$d-i$_{\cdot i/j}$.
    each   the-other-gen
    'The teachers made the students sit next to each other.'

(2) ?an-nisaa?-u$_i$ ja$l-an   l-banaat-i$_j$ maymuumaat-in min
    the-women-nom made-agr the-girls-acc upset-acc   from
    ba$dihin l-ba$d-i$_{\cdot i/j}$.
    each   the-other-gen
    'The women made the girls upset about each other.'

(3) ?al-mudrris-uun$_i$?ajlas-uu   t-tulaab$_j$-a   bi3aanib-i
    the-teacher-pl.nom made.sit-agr the-students-acc next-gen
    ba$dihum l-ba$d-i$_{\cdot i/j}$.
    each   the-other-gen
    'The teachers made the students sit next to each other.'

(4) ʔan-nisaaʔ-u$_i$ ʔaɣmam-na   l-banaat-i   min baʕdihin
the-women-nom made.upset-agr the-girls-acc from each
l-baʕḍ-i$_i$.
the-other-gen
'The women made the girls upset about each other.'

(1) and (2) are periphrastic causatives with an overtly represented biclausal structure.[2] Though the embedded predicate is a verb in (1) and an adjective in (2), the categorial distinction has no effect on how the anaphor picks its antecedent: in both cases, the binder must be the subject of the predicate in question because the embedded small clause is the local domain in which an anaphor must be bound (Chomsky 1981, 1986b). For morphological causatives, however, the choice of the binder is sensitive to the category of the root. In (3), the verb is derived from the same verb root as the embedded predicate in (1), namely, *jls* 'to sit'. And as in (1), the reciprocal can be coindexed only with the semantic subject of the root and not with the causer subject of the whole sentence. In contrast, though the deadjectival verb in (4) is morphologically associated with the embedded adjectival predicate in (2) through *ɣmm*, anaphor binding exhibits significantly different behavior, with the causer argument becoming the legitimate antecedent for the reciprocal. More data will be given later from Arabic and Modern Hebrew to show that in general, the syntactic behavior of a morphological causative depends on the category of its root.

Interestingly, the paradigm in (1)–(4) highlights not only the empirical bases for the competing syntactic and lexicalist theories of word formation but also their common defect. Details postponed, the fact that the verbal causative in (3) patterns with the periphrastic causatives in (1)–(2) with respect to anaphor binding argues in favor of assigning a similar biclausal structure to (3) and deriving the causativized verb by raising the embedded verb root to the matrix causative affix, as is typical of Baker's account of verb incorporation. Meanwhile, the simplest account of (4) is that it consists of only one clause and hence only one binding domain. In turn, this supports treating the deadjectival causative as a lexically derived word independently of syntax and claiming that it enters syntax like a monomorphemic verb with multiple arguments. Taken alone, (3) and (4) serve respectively as evidence for the syntactic and lexicalist theories. But together, these examples suggest that neither approach is adequate in itself to explain all the facts of word formation. If syntactic head movement in a biclausal structure were exclusively responsible for morphological causativization, (4) should not be possible, especially when compared with its syntactic counterpart in (2). The lexical theory of causativization faces the opposite version of the same problem, incorrectly expecting both (3) and (4) to exhibit monoclausal properties with respect to binding. Luckily, the same data also point at a conceptually simple solution: the right theory for word formation and its interaction with syntax should combine the insights of both approaches while avoiding their weaknesses. Specifically, this theory should be able to predict when a morphologically complex word functions like a morphologically simple lexical item and when it veils a more complex syntactic structure.

I propose that this theory consists of syntax-independent word formation in the style of the Lexicalist Hypothesis (LH), plus the following mapping principle:

(5) *The Morphology-Syntax Mapping Hypothesis (MSMH)*
    If morphological components X and Y are in a word W and there is a relation R between X and Y, then R is reflected in syntax if and only if
    a. R is thematic, and
    b. the representation of R in syntax obeys all syntactic principles.

According to (5), a word of the form X-Y may occupy a head position and project to its own phrase in syntax like a typical lexical item, or it may require a more complex syntactic structure to reflect the relation between X and Y. The choice depends solely on conditions (5a) and (5b). For instance, if there is a thematic relation between X and Y—say, X receives the internal θ-role of Y—then the syntactic structure for the word X-Y must (minimally) contain a head of category Y that takes a complement phrase of category X (i.e., the standard head-complement structure), provided that this structure violates no other syntactic principles.

Condition (5a) might be subsumed under the more general statement that R is visible to syntax. Given the common belief that only a limited amount of lexical/morphological information is visible to syntax, thematic information may well be the only aspect of the semantics of a word that has a direct structural representation in syntax. If so, requiring R to be syntactically visible may be effectively equivalent to requiring R to be thematic. For the purpose of this book, however, I am content with defining (5a) as it is. As for condition (5b), its validity should be self-evident: whatever syntactic structure X-Y corresponds to should naturally be well formed according to syntactic principles.

Functionally, (5) allows the LH to hold without automatically incurring the problems it faces in existing lexicalist theories, such as the difficulty in handling the biclausal property of the verbal causative in (3). All morphologically complex words are indeed lexically formed, as forced upon us by the LH, but some of them may have to "expand" into multiphrasal structures in syntax according to (5) and consequently demonstrate properties not found with monophrasal structures. As a result, (5) makes it possible to unify the conflicting lexicalist and syntactic approaches into a single theory of the morphology-syntax interface.

Conceptually, (5) is my counterpart of Baker's (1988) Uniformity of Theta Assignment Hypothesis (UTAH), which requires that identical thematic relations be represented by identical syntactic relations at D-Structure. In the most general sense, both the MSMH and the UTAH specify how certain lexical information maps to syntactic structures. This is no surprise. Any theory of the morphology-syntax interface must make explicit the correspondence between morphological and syntactic structures.

The MSMH and the UTAH overlap in their domains of application because the MSMH also requires the thematic relation between two morphemes to have a corresponding syntactic representation. The primary difference is whether this thematic-to-syntactic mapping is conditioned or absolutely required. And from this difference follow various significant empirical consequences that favor the MSMH over the UTAH, as will become clear in the following chapters.

At this point, a general clarification is in order. The UTAH is also used in the literature as a principle for consistent θ-role assignment in syntax. It may be credited, for instance, for guaranteeing that the θ-role Goal is assigned to an NP in a constant structural position inside VP. As a result, the UTAH seems to be motivated independently of the theory of the morphology-syntax interface. In contrast, the MSMH has only one function: to map certain morphological structures into syntax. From the perspective of theory optimization, the UTAH might appear to have an advantage over the MSMH.

The advantage would be real if the two hypotheses had identical empirical consequences. But they do not. The MSMH is much more restrictive than the UTAH in assigning multiphrasal structures to morphologically complex words and thereby offers a more accurate account of the relevant data. In fact, it will be shown that the various empirical problems with the syntactic approach can be traced precisely to taking the UTAH as the mapping principle between morphology and syntax. To the extent that it may be part of UG, the UTAH should be limited to what it really is: a principle that ensures consistent θ-role assignment to arguments in syntax.

The book is organized as follows.

In chapter 1, I demonstrate how, with the help of the MSMH in (5), a theory based on the LH can correctly account for the various morphological constructions analyzed in the literature by means of syntactic verb incorporation. The account combines the essence of the syntactic and lexicalist approaches: that is, word formation according to the LH and a (properly restricted) underlying multiphrasal structure enriched by head movement. The morphological phenomena examined in the chapter include verb incorporation, the applicative construction, and the V-V resultative compound in Chinese. I show that the theory also fits well with Chomsky's (1995) minimalist account of inflectional morphology.

In chapter 2, I examine causativization on the adjectival root, showing that the monoclausal nature of this construction, seen in (1)–(4), follows directly from the MSMH. I also compare the theory with the alternatives in Baker 1988 and Borer 1991, and evaluate the potentials of Baker's (2003) theory of lexical categories in accounting for the data in (1)–(4).

Chapter 3 focuses on noun incorporation in polysynthetic languages. Baker (1996) provides new arguments in favor of a syntactic account of the morphological phenomenon. I argue that in theory, noun incorporation *should* take place by lexical means and that in practice, a lexicalist account is capable not only of handling all the new facts Baker has discovered but also of doing so naturally and intuitively. The fact that Baker's new insight on polysynthetic languages, articulated in syntactic terms, is easily incorporated in a primarily lexicalist account is partially due to the ability of the theory in this book to synthesize the advantages of both approaches. Ultimately, however, this is because noun incorporation is a phenomenon that in itself cannot be used as empirical evidence for choosing between the syntactic and lexicalist approaches. I also examine the metatheoretic implications of this indeterminacy.

In chapter 4, I attempt to derive the word formation part of the LH, crucial in my interface theory, as a theorem from a modification of Kayne's (1994) Linear Correspondence Axiom (LCA). To the extent that this attempt succeeds, it is proven for the first time in the lexicalist-syntactic debate that the LH can be more than supported by sporadic morphological facts—it might be imposed on UG by syntax. Since

Kayne's LCA is a general theory of phrase structure, the consequences of any modification obviously reach beyond a role in the morphology-syntax interface. In the rest of chapter 4, I explore some of the immediate consequences of the modified LCA, particularly those of typological significance.

A word of clarification: The LH as it was originally conceived prevents syntactic operations of all kinds from affecting components within a word boundary. In this book, unless otherwise stated, I use the term *LH* only to refer to the word-formation-affecting capacity of the LH. In fact, the central proposal in chapter 3 relies on allowing the interpretive operations of LF to penetrate the word boundary in certain languages, against the usual sense of the LH.

It should be borne in mind throughout this book that the various directions of research bearing on the final theory of word formation, as briefly (and incompletely) listed at the beginning, are intertwined. For example, treating verb incorporation as the result of syntactic head movement as Baker does necessarily entails parallel or postsyntactic morphological operations. In this book, I take it for granted that morphology is distributive more or less in the spirit of Halle and Marantz 1993. Minimally, this position recognizes both "lexical" words that are formed independently of syntax and "PF" words that result from linear adjacency in a syntactic construction but do not necessarily reflect any syntactic or lexical constituency. Examples of PF words will be provided later, but unless stated explicitly, the term *word* in this book does not refer to the PF type. For lexical words, I will refer to their components, including inflectional affixes, as *morphemes*, a common (though not universal) practice also adopted in Halle and Marantz 1993. Where exactly such morphemes acquire morphophonological features is largely inconsequential to the discussions in this book. The primary concern of the book is derivational morphology, with a brief discussion on how inflectional affixes interact with lexical roots. Recent attempts to apply head movement to as many lexical phenomena as possible have blurred the distinction between derivational morphology and compounding. For this reason, I use the term *morphology* to refer to that component of the human linguistic faculty that generates lexical words with morphemes. And as in the case of the term *morpheme*, *morphology* is used this way mostly for convenience. There is no intrinsic conflict between the theory in the book and, for example, Halle and Marantz's Morphological Structure.

Chapter 1

Verb Incorporation

Morphological causativization on the verbal root provides the most convincing evidence that a biclausal structure underlies verb incorporation. Against this background, I wish to establish two points in this chapter. First, the interface theory based on the LH and the MSMH can easily maintain the insight and simplicity of the syntactic account of the phenomenon. Second, this theory proves desirably more restrictive than the UTAH-based alternative when applied to the applicative construction and certain forms of V-V compounding in Chinese. The very nature of this investigation, built on previous work of many scholars, blurs the boundary between compounds and derivational words. Partly for lack of an accepted cover term for all such words and partly because little relies on the traditional distinction, I will from time to time refer to all morphologically complex words as *m-complexes* unless the context calls for a more specific term.

1.1 Verb Incorporation in Syntax

In this section, I first review and provide evidence for the biclausal nature of the verb incorporation (VI) construction. Then I show how, under the LH, the MSMH correctly maintains a biclausal account of this phenomenon.

1.1.1 Anaphor Binding

Chimwiini VI exemplifies what is sometimes called the type II causative, in which the subject of the transitive verb root behaves like the accusative object. The basic Chimwiini data (Baker 1988, 211) are given in (1).

(1) a. Mi m-phik-ish-ize   ru:hu-y-a cha:kuja.
        I   agr$_s$-cook-cause-asp myself   food
        'I made myself cook food.'

  b. Mi ni-m-big-ish-ize   mwa:na ru:hu-y-e.
        I   agr$_s$-agr$_o$-hit-cause-asp child   himself
        'I made the child hit himself.'

  c. *Mi ni-m-big-ish-ize   Ałi ru:hu-y-a.
        I   agr$_s$-agr$_o$-hit-cause-asp Ali myself
        '*I made Ali hit myself.'

As Baker (1988) points out, the contrast between (1a–b) on the one hand
and (1c) on the other is the standard behavior of anaphors in an exceptional Case-marking (ECM) style structure, with the embedded VP/TP
being the binding domain for the object of the embedded verb.

Various lexicalist attempts have been made to explain anaphor binding in VI through operations on argument structure. Citing evidence from
Japanese causatives, Grimshaw (1990, 169–173) proposes a complex
argument structure for causativized verbs that consists of two argument
structure domains, each with its own external θ-role.

(2) a. Taroo-wa Hanako-ni zibun-no huku-o   ki-sase-ta.
        Taroo-top Hanako-dat self-gen   clothes-acc wear-cause-past
        'Taroo made Hanako put on his/her own clothes.'

  b. -sase 'cause' $(x)^1$
      ki 'wear'   (y (z))
      ki-sase 'put on'   [x [y (z)]]

The binding of the anaphor *zibun* 'self' can then be described by referring
to thematically prominent arguments rather than to syntactic configura-
tions. For a morphologically simple verb with only one external θ-role,
zibun is bound by the argument receiving it. In the case of (2a), there are
two such arguments to choose from, resulting in the ambiguity.

Grimshaw's theory of argument structure composition, illustrated in
(2b), will be taken for granted in this book for the simple reason that the
process is a logical necessity if all morphologically complex words are
formed in the lexicon under the LH. But applying the idea to binding
seems more problematic than beneficial.

On the empirical side, it is known now that bare reflexives like
zibun can be long-distance bound even in unequivocally multiclausal
contexts.

(3) Taroo-wa Hanako-ga   zibun-no huku-o   ki-ta-to
    Taroo-top Hanako-nom self-gen   clothes-acc wear-past-C
    omotte-iru.
    think-decl
    'Taroo thinks that Hanako wore his/her own clothes.'

The embedded tense -*ta* and complementizer -*to* exclude any possibility of compounding between *ki* 'wear' and *omotte* 'think'. Since the reflexive remains ambiguously bound, the binding of anaphors like *zibun* cannot possibly be limited to any single argument structure, complex or not.

The problem does not disappear even if we choose to put long-distance anaphors aside. For one thing, it would remain unclear why (1c) is unacceptable. After all, *big-ish* 'hit-cause' is supposed to have an argument structure similar to that of *ki-sase* 'wear-cause' in (2b), in which the external argument of *cause* should be a candidate for binding the local anaphor *ru:hu-y-a* 'myself' (see Grimshaw 1990, 173). The raising construction in English provides another argument against a lexical account of binding.

(4) Ezra and Sam seemed to each other [t to be suspiciously quiet].

The matrix subject *Ezra and Sam* is not a thematic argument of *seem* at all but clearly serves as the binder for the local anaphor *each other*. On the other hand, (1)–(4) can all be easily accounted for with a syntactically defined binding theory. The fact that the core cases of anaphor binding are based on syntax and not on thematic structures has been noted repeatedly in the literature. See Reinhart and Reuland 1993 and Runner 2002 for more discussion.

There are also theoretical complications to consider before Japanese data such as (2a) can be admitted to bear on lexical word formation. For example, Japanese is a head-final language in which a head by nature immediately follows the head of its own complement phrase, a fact to be examined more carefully in chapter 4. Therefore, that the morphemes *ki-sase* 'wear-cause' are pronounced together does not necessarily mean that they belong together structurally; they could be pronounced as a unit simply because of their linear adjacency (Kayne 1994). As a result, it is yet to be determined whether there is indeed a lexical m-complex before we can talk about complex argument structures in the language.

Another representative of the lexicalist approach is Di Sciullo and Williams 1987, where coindexation of θ-roles in the argument structure of a verb is used to account for reflexivization in Chimwiini (pp. 61–62). But because the theory there is rather sketchy, I consider a more elaborate variation of it in Williams 1994 instead. The relevant definitions are these (see Williams 1994, chap. 6):

(5) For two θ-roles X and Y, X th-commands Y if X is a coargument of Y; or if X th-commands B, B is linked to Z, and Z θ-commands Y.

(6) X is th-bound if there is a θ-role th-commanding[2] X and coindexed with X.

(7) A th-anaphor is a θ-role assigned to an anaphor.

(8) *Condition A*
A th-anaphor must be th-bound in some domain.

In plain words, the binding relation between an anaphor and its antecedent is in fact coindexation between the θ-roles assigned to them, provided that the θ-roles either are from the same lexical item or are from different lexical items one of which receives a θ-role from the other. (9) is an example from Williams 1994, 214.

(9) John saw a picture of himself.

The verb *saw* has two θ-roles, one assigned to *John* and the other to the NP *a picture of himself*, whose head N has a θ-role assigned to *himself*. By (5), the subject θ-role of *saw* th-commands the θ-role of *picture*. When the two θ-roles are coindexed, as is the case in (9) because one of them is assigned to the anaphor *himself*, they are th-bound and Condition A is satisfied.

But this thematic definition of binding does not explain the paradigm of binding in (1) if VI is a lexical process resulting in a monoclausal structure. (1a–b) are expected to be acceptable because any two of the three θ-roles in the m-complex *phik-ish* 'cook-cause' or *big-ish* 'hit-cause' can meet the th-command requirement between them. If one of the θ-roles is assigned to an anaphor, th-binding is established to satisfy Condition A. But the most crucial example, (1c), is wrongly predicted to be acceptable as well, for the simple reason that the θ-role for *mi* 'I' and the one for *ru:hu-y-a* 'myself' are by definition coarguments of the same lexical item and therefore form a default case of th-command. Since coargumenthood defines the smallest domain possible, th-binding holds for the two NPs, contrary to fact.

This thematic theory of binding cannot explain (4), either. The anaphor *each other* is a thematic argument of the matrix verb *seem*, whereas the matrix subject *Ezra and Sam* is thematically linked only to the embedded predicate *be suspiciously quiet*. Since the embedded TP is a thematic argument of *seem*, th-command holds only in one direction: from the θ-role assigned to the anaphor to the one assigned to *Ezra and Sam*. But this is exactly the opposite of what is needed to account for (4), in which the anaphor is bound by *Ezra and Sam* and not the other way around.

The Arabic examples of causativization cited in the introduction provide a decisive argument for assigning a biclausal structure to VI. The examples are repeated here with the addition of (10c), whose significance will become clear shortly.

(10) a. JaΩal-a   l-mudrris-uun$_i$ t-tulaab$_j$-a   yajlis-uun
       made-agr the-teacher-pl.nom the-students-acc sit-agr
       bi$\mathdefault{z}$aanib-i baΩdihum l-baΩd-i·$_{i/j}$.
       next-gen   each   the-other-gen
       'The teachers made the students sit next to each other.'

    b. ?al-mudrris-uun$_i$?ajlas-uu   t-tulaab$_j$-a   bi$\mathdefault{z}$aanib-i
       the-teacher-pl.nom made.sit-agr the-students-acc next-gen
       baΩdihum l-baΩd-i·$_{i/j}$.
       each   the-other-gen
       'The teachers made the students sit next to each other.'

    c. ?asqat-a   l-mudrris-uun$_i$ t-tulaab$_j$-a Ωalaa
       made.fall-agr the-teacher-pl.nom the-students-acc on
       baΩdihum l-baΩd-i·$_{i/j}$.
       each   the-other-gen
       'The teachers made the students fall on each other.'

(11) a. ?an-nisaa?-u$_i$ jaΩl-an   l-banaat-i$_j$ maγmuumaat-in min
       the-women-nom made-agr the-girls-acc upset-acc   from
       baΩdihin l-baΩd-i·$_{i/j}$.
       each   the-other-gen
       'The women made the girls upset about each other.'

    b. ?an-nisaa?-u$_i$?aγmam-na   l-banaat-i min baΩdihin
       the-women-nom made.upset-agr the-girls-acc from each
       l-baΩd-i$_i$.
       the-other-gen
       'The women made the girls upset about each other.'

As seen earlier, an anaphor A is allowed to take the causer NP as antecedent only if A is in a morphological causative construction whose lexical root is adjectival, as in (11b). Note that the preposition *min* 'from' in (11a–b) is semantically associated only with the adjectival base—if the PP headed by *min* could optionally modify the causal part of the predicate, it would be possible for the anaphor in (11a) to modify the matrix verb and therefore to be bound by the matrix subject.

This distinction between verb-based causativization and adjective-based causativization is by no means an accident. Benmamoun (1991) argues that Arabic verbal causativization must be analyzed as syntactic incorporation with a biclausal structure, whereas Borer (1991) provides several pieces of evidence that Hebrew deadjectival causatives project to monoclausal structures. Borer's arguments will be examined in chapter 2, together with more data displaying the verb-adjective contrast found in (10)–(11). The crucial point for now is that this contrast does not follow from any existing lexicalist theory.

It is of course easy to define the local binding domain (marked *bd* in (12)) for the anaphors in (10b–c) as the argument structure of the verbal root.

(12) a. make.sit $\langle$ Causer $\langle_{bd}$ Agent ... $\rangle\rangle$
     b. make.fall $\langle$ Causer $\langle_{bd}$ Theme ... $\rangle\rangle$

As along as an anaphor is semantically/thematically associated with the root, local binding in these examples can be analyzed in terms of argument structure. However, the same logic will automatically turn the argument structure of the adjectival root in (11b) into a binding domain, wrongly preventing the anaphor from being bound by the Causer argument.

(13) make.upset $\langle$ Causer $\langle_{bd}$ Experiencer ... $\rangle\rangle$

The failure to distinguish (13) from (12) cannot be remedied by referring to the content of the θ-roles in the definition of binding domain. While the labels used in these argument structures may not be accurate (see Jackendoff 1990), it is obvious that the θ-role of the verb root in (12a) is typical of an external argument whereas the one in (12b) is typical of an internal argument, with verbs meaning 'to fall' being stereotypical unaccusatives crosslinguistically. If both are qualified to turn the argument structure of the root into a binding domain, it simply would not make any sense that the θ-role of the adjective in (13) is not qualified, no matter how this θ-role is labeled.

It may be tempting to account for the data in (10)–(11) by appealing to the fact that, unlike verbal causatives, deadjectival causatives are sufficiently "lexicalized" in Arabic and therefore have the argument structure of the whole verb as the binding domain. But this does not answer the question at issue: why does the distinction have to be drawn according to the categories of the lexical base? After all, these deadjectival causatives are still semantically (and morphologically to a certain degree) decomposable. What would prevent the language from treating deadjectival causatives on a par with their verb-based counterparts when it comes to binding? Furthermore, Hebrew deadjectival causatives also exhibit monoclausal behavior even though they have "regular derivational morphological and semantic relations with adjectives" (Borer 1991, 130), as we will see in chapter 2. All things considered, while lexicalization may have taken place in Arabic deadjectival causatives, it is not the reason for the verb-adjective contrast, but one of its consequences: because adjective-based causatives must be treated like indecomposable verbs that project to monoclausal structures, they are liable to lexicalization.

In sum, the lexical theories of VI (including Semitic verbal causatives) have difficulties accommodating the Chimwiini data in (1) and are simply unable to explain the Arabic verb-adjective contrast in (10)–(11). In contrast, if VI has an underlyingly biclausal structure as Baker claims, there is a simple explanation for all the data on anaphor binding except the deadjectival causatives, to which I return in chapter 2.

1.1.2 Passivization

Passivization provides another piece of evidence for the biclausal structure of VI. (All examples in this section are from Al-Dobaian 1998.)

(14) a. Laʕʕab-a   ʔaḥmad-u   ʕalii-an l-kurat-a.
        caused.play-agr Ahmad-nom Ali-acc the-soccer-acc
        'Ahmad made Ali play soccer.'
    b. ʔar-rajul-u ʔarkab-a   l-bint-a   l-baʕiir-a.
        the-man-nom caused.ride-agr the-girl-acc the-camel-acc
        'The man made the girl ride the camel.'

Though the causatives in (14a–b) each contain two accusative NPs, only the thematic subject of the verb root can become the subject of the sentence under passivization. In the examples in (15) and (16), the passive morpheme takes the form /u ... i/.

(15) a. ſalii-un luſſib-a   l-kurat-a.
         Ali-nom was.caused.play-agr the-soccer-acc
         'Ali was made to play soccer.'

     b. *ʔal-kurat-un   luſſib-a   ſalii-a.
         the-soccer-nom was.caused.play-agr Ali-acc
         '*Soccer was made Ali to play.'

(16) a. ʔal-bint-u   ʔurkib-at   l-baſiir-a.
         the-girl-nom was.caused.ride-agr the-camel-acc
         'The girl was made to ride the camel.'

     b. *ʔal-baſiir-u   ʔurkib-a   l-bint-a.
         the-camel-nom was.caused.ride-agr the-girl-acc
         '*The camel was made the girl to ride.'

As the English translations suggest, the contrast between the (a) examples
and the (b) examples can be accounted for if Arabic verbal causatives
have an ECM-style biclausal structure. When the matrix causative verb is
passivized, only the embedded subject is affected (e.g., in terms of Case).
The embedded object remains licensed by the embedded verb and has no
motivation to raise to the matrix subject position.

But more telltale evidence for the biclausal nature of Arabic causatives
comes from comparison with double-object verbs.

(17) a. Manaḥ-a l-ʔab-u   l-ʔibn-a   l-jaaʔizat-a.
         gave-agr the-father-nom the-son-acc the-prize-acc
         'The father gave the son the prize.'

     b. ʔal-ʔibn-u   munih-a   l-jaaʔizat-a.
         the-son-nom was.given-agr the-prize-acc
         'The son was given the prize.'

     c. ʔal-jaaʔizat-u munih-at   l-ʔibn-a.
         the-prize-nom was.given-agr the-son-acc
         'The prize was given to the son.'

Both objects of the verb *manaḥa* 'gave' are marked accusative in (17a),
comparable to the two accusative NPs in the active causative in (14).
Unlike in causatives, however, either of these objects can be the subject
in a passive. Syntactically, the contrast is easy to explain. Passivization
is a local operation in Arabic as in other languages. The examples in (17)
have a monoclausal structure with only one verb in each sentence. If the
verb is passivized, either of its objects can be affected. The causatives
in (15)–(16) are different because passivizing the causative matrix verb

cannot affect the embedded object at all provided that causativization involves an underlying biclausal structure as Baker argues.

To the best of my knowledge, no lexical theory proposed so far can explain the contrast in (15)–(17) naturally. If a causativized verb like *laʕʕaba* 'caused.play' were a lexical verb and behaved as such, it should be like a double-object verb. Even if we adopted the idea that the two have somewhat different argument structures, ad hoc stipulations would still be needed to accommodate the Arabic data. In such a theory, the argument structures of *give* and *cause.play* are as follows (see (2b)):

(18) a. manaḥa 'gave' $(x (y (z)))$
     b. laʕʕaba 'caused to play' $[x [y (z)]]$

In (18a), passivization can affect the NP with either θ-role y or θ-role z in Arabic. In (18b), only the NP with y is affected (i.e., the thematic subject of the verb root). It might not be difficult for the theory to let y be the target of passivization in (18b), but as far as I can see, there is no natural way to exclude z in (18b) from passivization while including z in (18a) unless such syntactic mechanisms as (Relativized) Minimality are duplicated in the lexicon. After all, if passivization of the whole verb in (18b) can affect y inside the "inner" domain of the argument structure, why can't it affect z in the same domain given that y and z in (18a) are in the same domain and are equally subject to passivization?

To conclude, morphological causativization, whether in Chimwiini or in Arabic and whether for binding or for passivization, poses problems for a lexical theory with monoclausal structures but can be easily accounted for through biclausal structures, thus lending solid support to Baker's head movement approach.

1.1.3   Verb Incorporation under the Morphology-Syntax Mapping Hypothesis: Chimwiini and Arabic

If VI indeed has an underlying biclausal structure, a theory of the morphology-syntax interface must necessarily map the superficial m-complex to a multiphrasal structure with (minimally) two differently headed VPs. Here and in section 1.1.4, I show that together, the LH and the MSMH have exactly this quality.

According to the LH, all morphologically complex words must be formed lexically independently of syntax. It follows that VI causatives such as *phik-ish* 'cook-cause' in (1a) are lexically formed verbs, as the lexicalist approach claims them to be. In syntax, however, *phik-ish* is subject to the MSMH. The causative affix *-ish*, treated as a verb (see Williams 1981b; Baker 1988), takes the verb root *phik* as its thematic argument. Because the relation between the two morphemes is thematic, it must be represented in syntax as long as the resulting structure satisfies independently motivated UG principles.

Given the consensus that *-ish* assigns a θ-role (Event?) to the verb root *phik*, this relationship should be represented syntactically as V taking a VP complement. The structure is illustrated in (19), which temporarily omits irrelevant details such as the full Larsonian shell and the matrix TP/CP.

(19)

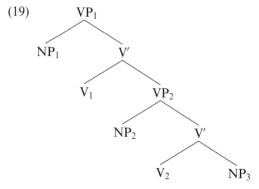

First of all, such a structure does exist in syntax for certain causative constructions, the English construction in (20) being an example.

(20) Phil made [Bill (*to) sing the song].

The obligatory absence of *to* clearly indicates that the complement of *make* is VP (see Li 1990c).

Now *phik-ish* 'cook-cause' enters syntax as a single verb because of the LH. If it is inserted in (19), a legitimate initial location is V_2, from which it can raise to adjoin to V_1 as shown in (21). (In subsequent discussions, when a non-English example is repeated, English glosses will be used provided no confusion arises.)

(21)

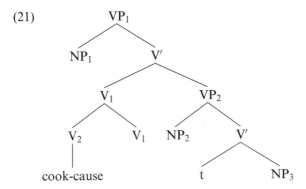

Because *cook-cause* starts in V_2, V_1 is necessarily generated as a phoneti-cally empty node. Depending on specific technical assumptions, the m-complex may either move to V_1 as an instance of substitution or adjoin to V_1. Nothing in this chapter or the next hinges on the choice. Antici-pating the derivation of the LH from a modified version of Kayne's (1994) Linear Correspondence Axiom in chapter 4, however, I adopt the adjunction structure, assuming that V_1 is generated with features partic-ular to a causative verb and that *cook-cause* adjoins to V_1 to "check them off." Specifically, I will think of the adjunction in (21) on the analogy of a biological model. In biochemistry, a receptor is part of a protein with a specific combination of amino acids; it can only "receive" another protein with the matching amino acids; and only when the two proteins bond to-gether is the received one functionally activated. In syntax, the V_1 posi-tion in (21) can be viewed as the receptor with a specific combination of features, for example, [+V, −N, +causative, . . .]. The causative m-complex carrying the same features (and others) raises to be bonded to V_1 in order for the causative morpheme to be syntactically "activated" (e.g., to assign the Causer θ-role and accusative Case, etc.) in the position of V_1. The bonding is what is called feature checking in the Minimalist Program.

In (21), all the θ-roles of *cook-cause* are assigned in the typical manner. Lexically formed, the bimorphemic word composes its argument structure from those of its components. If *cook* has $\langle x \langle y \rangle\rangle$ as its argument struc-ture and *cause* has $\langle a \langle b \rangle\rangle$, where x, y, a, and b are θ-roles and the paired brackets signal thematic hierarchy, the argument structure of *cook-cause* should be something like $\langle a \langle x \langle y \rangle\rangle\rangle$, with the θ-role b of *cause* assigned to *cook* and thus no longer available in the m-complex (see Grimshaw

1990). For more examples regarding the composition of argument structure, see Li 1990b, 1995, 1997a and the appendix to this chapter. Once *cook-cause* is inserted in V_2, x and y are assigned to NP_2 and NP_3, respectively. The remaining θ-role a is assigned to NP_1 when the verb raises to V_1.

Crucially, though the MSMH helps represent the thematic relation between *cook* and *cause* as V_1 taking VP_2 as a complement in syntax, it says nothing about how their other θ-roles are to be assigned. From the point of view of syntax, *cook-cause* is just a verb with several θ-roles. Other independently needed UG mechanisms are responsible for assigning these θ-roles properly. For instance, the thematic hierarchy encoded in the argument structure guarantees that all the θ-roles will be assigned to syntactic arguments in the right order.

The immediate consequence of (21) is the biclausal binding effect seen with type II causatives in section 1.1.2. If NP_2 is a local anaphor, its binder must be NP_1, the subject of the whole causative sentence. If NP_3 is the anaphor, however, the binding domain must be the embedded VP, restricting its binder to NP_2. This is guaranteed precisely because binding is defined syntactically so that VP_2 contains all the components (e.g., anaphor, governor, SUBJ) of a binding domain for NP_3. Hence, the crucial example supporting a biclausal analysis of VI is explained in the same way that Baker argues for. The VI verb itself is still formed lexically, but it is no longer necessary to postulate complicated and problematic lexical procedures to handle the data of anaphor binding in section 1.1.1. Also note that V-raising yields the right word order in (21), correctly accounting for (1) and other typical VI examples.

The same analysis accounts for passivization in Arabic as well. Given the commonly held assumption that passivization affects the argument structure and the Case-assigning ability of a verb, consider (15b) and (16b). When the verbal causative maps to syntax, a structure like (21) is generated with the thematic argument NP_1 suppressed (see Grimshaw 1990). Within the P&P model, there are various independently proposed means that can prevent the embedded object NP_3 from becoming the subject of the whole sentence. For instance, (21) is a typical ECM structure that has been argued for explicitly by many authors (see Postal 1974; McCawley 1988; Lasnik and Saito 1991; Zidani-Eroğlu 1997; Lasnik 1999) and implied in the Minimalist Program (Chomsky 1995) to involve raising the embedded subject NP_2 to a matrix object position such as the specifier (hereafter, Spec) of the lower copy of the matrix VP (i.e., VP_1) if

(21) were fully represented with the Larsonian structure. Details aside, this boils down to placing NP_2 inside VP_1 while keeping NP_3 inside VP_2. Then some version of Relativized Minimality (Rizzi 1990), the principle of minimal length of chain links (Baker 1996; Nakamura 1997), or the Minimal Link Condition (Chomsky 1995, 2000) can easily block A-movement of NP_3 out of VP_2.

As for the account of double-object examples in (17), it is straightforward because it contains the maximal projection(s) of only one verb. Since both NP complements are inside the same VP, either NP can be chosen to be Caseless and to become the subject of the sentence. Needless to say, it is a language-specific property for both NPs to have accusative Case and be promotable in passivization. But that is a factor independent of the concerns in this section.

Logically, the causative *phik-ish* 'cook-cause' could also take V_1 as the initial point of insertion. Then the requirement for full interpretation that triggers V-raising in (21) would force the word to lower from V_1 to V_2— otherwise *phik-ish* would not be "activated" to assign its θ-roles and Case to NP_2 and NP_3. But this would leave a trace in the position of V_1 that is not antecedent-governed by anything. Hence, such a derivation is ruled out by UG.[3] To complete the analysis, also note that in (19) and (21), VP_1 and VP_2 each in fact consist of two VPs under Larson's theory. This will not affect the proposed analysis. Once V_2 raises all the way up, all the V positions except the uppermost one (V_1 in (21)) are occupied by traces. The extra structure makes no difference to our analysis.

1.1.4   Verb Incorporation under the Morphology-Syntax Mapping Hypothesis: Chichewa

At least two types of causatives have been recognized in the literature (Gibson 1980; Marantz 1984; Baker 1988). Chimwiini and Arabic both have what is called type II, whose basic characteristic is the accusative Case on the thematic subject of the verb root. By the same logic, English also has the type II causative, minus incorporation. The other type, type I, has an "ergative" pattern in Case assignment, with oblique Case on the embedded thematic subject if the verb root is transitive and accusative Case on an NP in all other scenarios. Type I is found in Chichewa and French.[4]

The basic data are given in (22), quoted from Alsina 1992, (1)/(3), (2), (29b), (30a–b).

(22) a. Nŭngu   i-na-phík-íts-a   maûngu (kwá kádzīdzi).
        porcupine agr$_s$-past-cook-cause-asp pumpkins to   owl
        'The porcupine had the pumpkins cooked (by the owl).'
        (Alsina: (1)/(3))

     b. Chatsalĭra a-ku-nám-íts-á   (*kwá) mwăna.
        Chatsalira agr$_s$-pres-lie-cause-asp to   child
        'Chatsalira is making the child lie.'
        (Alsina: (2))

     c. Mwăna a-ku-d-éts-á   zóvâla.
        child   agr$_s$-pres-be.dirty-cause-asp clothes
        'The child is making the clothes dirty.'
        (Alsina: (29b))

     d. *mwaná áméné Chatsalirá á-ku-nám-ïts-a
        child   which Chatsalira agr$_s$-pres-lie-cause-asp
        'the child that Chatsalira is making lie'
        (Alsina: (30a))

     e. zóválá ziméné mwaná á-ku-d-ëts-a
        clothes which child   agr$_s$-pres-be.dirty-cause-asp
        'the clothes which the child is making dirty'
        (Alsina: (30b))

When the verb root is transitive (22a), its thematic subject is introduced by the oblique Case marker *kwa* and is optional. If the verb root is intransitive, be it unergative (22b) or unaccusative (22c), its thematic argument takes the form of an accusative object. With respect to *wh*-movement, however, the thematic subject of the root cannot be extracted (22d) but the thematic object can (22e). The same subject-object asymmetry holds for transitive and intransitive verb roots alike (Baker 1988, sec. 4.4.2).

Baker's (1988) analysis is based on treating (22d) as a Subjacency violation with the structure in (23), where NP$_1$ or NP$_2$ would be missing depending on whether V$_2$ is unergative or unaccusative.

(23)

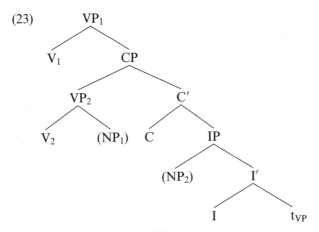

The embedded VP moves to the Spec of CP in all type I causatives. If V_2 further raises to V_1, VI takes place. The embedded internal argument, NP_1, can undergo *wh*-movement because VP_2 can be governed by V_1 (Chomsky 1986a). The embedded subject NP_2 cannot move out of CP because the Spec of CP is already occupied, a scenario comparable to a *wh*-island.

But this analysis has unsolvable problems (see Li 1990c). Since the embedded clause is a nonfinite CP, there is no way for NP_2 to receive the accusative Case in (23) unless one is willing to make utterly ad hoc stipulations. Furthermore, there is no independent evidence that the embedded C and I exist in the VI construction of any language. As a solution to these problems, I propose elsewhere (Li 1990c) that the complement of the causative affix in VI is always a VP and the difference between type I and type II results from different Case-assigning patterns of the causative morphemes. Also see Marantz 1984 and Alsina 1992 for other accounts of the phenomena.

Despite the differences among these theories, all consider the basic properties of type I VI to correlate with the fact that such languages assign only one accusative Case even in their double-object constructions with monomorphemic verbs (Kisseberth and Abasheikh 1977; Kimenyi 1980; Baker 1988). The same correlation is also found in Romance languages that have periphrastic causatives but no VI (Burzio 1986; Baker 1988). In neutral terms, this correlation boils down to the following parameter:

(24) In the domain of a canonical clause, a language may allow either
     one accusative Case or multiple accusative Cases to be assigned.

In what follows, I explore an account of the Case-marking patterns of VI
that implements (24) within the interface theory characterized by the LH
and the MSMH.

Suppose with Chomsky (1995) that a verb's ability to assign accusative
Case is enabled (activated?) only by raising it to the upper V position in a
Larsonian double-VP structure. Further suppose that when V-*cause* maps
to [V VP] under the MSMH, a language may choose between representing the VP complement either as a full Larsonian VP or as the lower
VP alone (see Collins 1997 and section A.3 of the appendix). The options
arise only when a matrix V selects a VP complement: since either option
is a VP, both are well formed structurally as long as all UG principles are
satisfied.[5] Note that when VP is not selected by a lexical head, it must be
a full VP simply because the functional head T, of which VP is the structural complement, does not select VP, with TP and CP being "extended
projections" of V (Grimshaw 1993). Without such external influence as
selection, V always projects according to the default plan, namely, to the
double-VP structure. This is similar to the ECM construction: V always
projects to the default CP structure unless a lexical head—say, *believe*—
selects TP by brute force.

As required by the LH, a morphological causative of the form V-*cause*
is formed independently of syntax. Consider a language that is parameterized under (24) to allow multiple accusative Cases in a clause. V-
cause projects to [V VP] under the MSMH, where VP may be either full
or partial. Consider the full VP option first, as illustrated in (25).

(25)

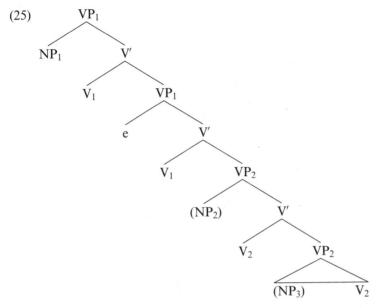

In the structure, NP$_3$ is the thematic object of V$_2$ and is absent when V$_2$ is unergative, whereas NP$_2$ is the thematic subject of V$_2$ and is absent when V$_2$ is unaccusative.

After being inserted in the lowest V$_2$ position, V-*cause* raises to the upper V$_2$ to enable an accusative Case to be assigned to NP$_3$. The verb continues to raise to the lower V$_1$ and the upper V$_1$, assigning another accusative Case to NP$_2$. NP$_2$ may have to raise to the Spec of the lower VP$_1$, marked *e*, to receive this Case if Postal's (1974) raising-to-object analysis proves to be correct (see section 1.1.3). (25) is legitimate under (24) because the parameter is set to allow multiple accusative Cases in a canonical clause. The complement of V$_1$ is only a bare VP (i.e., VP$_2$) and therefore not regarded as a canonical clause, but the whole VP$_1$ is indeed part of one. Therefore, (24) does not prevent V-*cause* from assigning more than one accusative Case while passing through the upper V$_2$ and V$_1$. The same analysis applies trivially when the verb root is unergative and there is no NP$_3$. If the verb root is unaccusative, there is no NP$_2$. Then whatever reason forces the internal argument of an unaccusative verb to move to the subject position in regular clauses (e.g., the intrinsic inability of such a verb to assign accusative Case; see Belletti 1988)[6] also raises NP$_3$ first to the Spec of the upper VP$_2$ and then to the *e* position inside VP$_1$. It follows that both the thematic subject of the unergative verb root and the thematic object of the unaccusative verb root behave like the object of the whole sentence. Obviously, (25) simply repeats the earlier analysis of type II causatives in section 1.1.3.

Next, consider the other option for representing the thematic relation in V-*cause*: namely, that VP_2 is only the lower VP of a full Larsonian structure. The structure is (26), with NP_3 representing the thematic object of the verb root (I return to NP_2 shortly).

(26)

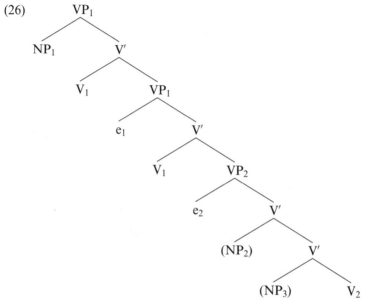

If the verb root is unaccusative (i.e., without NP_2), the structure satisfies both the θ-Criterion and the Case Filter once V-*cause* raises all the way to V_1, with NP_3 raising to the e_2 position. For all purposes, this is indistinguishable from (25) with the same unaccusative verb root.

On the other hand, the thematic subject of a transitive or unergative verb root could not be represented in an argument position owing to the absence of the upper VP_2, and the structure would violate the θ-Criterion. However, the subject θ-role has been argued to be suppressible (e.g., in passives, deverbal nouns, and the French *faire-par* construction—see Roeper 1983; Larson 1988; Grimshaw 1990; Li 1990a,c). When this happens, the NP linked to the suppressed subject θ-role is demoted to an "argument adjunct" (Grimshaw 1990, 110). Putting aside for the moment the argument structure of a morphological causative with a suppressed

θ-role from the verb root, we can syntactically represent the demoted subject of the verb root as NP_2 adjoined to V' in (26).

First, suppose that NP_3 is present (i.e., the verb root is transitive); it raises to e_2 in order to receive accusative Case from V-*cause*, which also raises to V_1. Since the language can assign multiple accusative Cases in a single clause, the suppressed subject NP_2 also receives one from the raised verb. NP_2 may also need to move up and adjoin somewhere inside VP_1 in order to be adjacent to the upper V_1 to receive its accusative Case, as we will see.

Empirical support for the option in (26) comes from the contrast between Chimwiini and Kinyarwanda, both allowing two accusative Cases in a double-object construction (Baker 1988, secs. 4.3.3.1–4.3.3.2). While Kinyarwanda causatives allow either the thematic subject or the thematic object of the verb root to become the subject in passivization, Chimwiini passivization affects only the thematic subject of the verb root. ((27a–c) and (28a–c) are from Baker 1988, (67b), (69), (74), (80), (81a–b), respectively.)

(27) *Kinyarwanda*
    a. Umugabo a-r-uubak-iish-a   abaantu inzu.
        man   agr$_s$-pres-build-cause-asp people house
        'The man is making the people build the house.'
    b. Abakozi ba-r-uubak-iish-w-a   inzu n'umugabo.
        workers agr$_s$-pres-build-cause-pass-asp house by-man
        'The workers are made to build the house by the man.'
    c. Inzu i-r-uubak-iish-w-a   abakozi n'umugabo.
        house agr$_s$-pres-build-cause-pass-asp workers by-man
        'The house is made to be built by the workers by the man.'

(28) *Chimwiini*
    a. Mwa:limu $\emptyset$-wa-andik-ish-ize   wa:na xati.
        teacher   agr$_s$-agr$_o$-write-cause-asp children letter
        'The teacher made the children write a letter.'
    b. Wa:na wa-andik-ish-iz-a: xati na mwa:limu.
        children agr$_s$-write-cause-asp/pass letter by teacher
        'The children were made to write a letter by the teacher.'
    c. *Xati a-andik-ish-iz-a: wa:na na mwa:limu.
        letter agr$_s$-write-cause-asp/pass children by teacher
        'The letter was made to be written by the children by the teacher.'

The ungrammaticality of (28c) in Chimwiini is the consequence of (25), in which the embedded object NP$_3$ cannot raise to the matrix subject position in the presence of the embedded subject NP$_2$. See section 1.1.3 for my analysis of passivization in the type II causative. In contrast, the grammaticality of (27c) in Kinyarwanda follows from (26), in which NP$_3$ raises to the Spec of the upper VP$_2$ to get Case. For all structural purposes, the raised NP$_3$ functions like the ECM subject, automatically eligible for raising to the matrix subject position in passivization. As NP$_2$ (i.e., *abaantu* 'people') precedes NP$_3$ (*inzu* 'house') in the active sentence (27a), it must have moved out of VP$_2$ and adjoined to the V$'$ in the lower VP$_1$, presumably in order to be adjacent to the raised verb for Case reasons.

The fact that (27b) is acceptable also may suggest that both languages have the structure in (25) whereas only Kinyarwanda simultaneously allows (26) as an option. This makes sense because, after all, (25) requires no subject suppression and therefore is a less marked derivation. If a language picks one option between the two, (25) is always the choice. Also see Baker's (1988) discussion of Japanese causatives, which show the same paradigm as Chimwiini in (28).

The analysis so far is based on the verb root in (26) being transitive. If the verb root is unergative, NP$_3$ is absent and NP$_2$ gets an accusative Case in the same way as with the transitive verb root. While the structure may predict that NP$_2$ will not behave like a typical argument, whether it does so or not is impossible to determine. For instance, suppose that an "argument adjunct" cannot become the subject when the morphological causative is passivized.[7] But if every language that allows (26) also allows (25), as the previous paragraphs suggest, then passivization will promote NP$_2$ to the matrix subject position on the basis of (25), in which NP$_2$ moves into VP$_1$ to get accusative Case regardless of the transitivity of the verb root. On the surface, the single argument of the intransitive verb root (unergative or unaccusative) always behaves like the object in the whole sentence, whereas the thematic object of a transitive verb root may or may not behave like an object in passivization. To my knowledge, this is indeed true of VI with multiple accusative Cases.

Next suppose that a language—say, Chichewa—opts for one accusative Case per canonical clause under (24). Again, the morphological causative of the form V-*cause* may be projected to V$_1$, taking either a full VP$_2$ or only the lower half of it. If the verb root is unergative or unaccusative, the derivation is completely identical to the multiple-accusative scenario—after all, only one NP needs an accusative Case, which can be provided once V-*cause* raises all the way to the upper V_1. With a transitive verb root, however, one of the two NP arguments must be removed to avoid a Case Filter violation. Since θ-role suppression only happens to the subject (see Grimshaw's (1990) examination of event nominals), the language is forced to utilize (26) so that the demoted subject NP_2 can receive an oblique Case in the adjunct position.

This analysis also provides a way to accommodate the optionality of NP_2 (see (22a)). Descriptively, demoted arguments marked by oblique Cases typically become optional, as seen in English passive and dative constructions.[8]

(29) a. Sam was promoted (by the company).
     b. Sam gave a lot of money (to the company).

In (29a), the demoted thematic subject is introduced by a preposition and is optional. In (29b), the Goal argument of *give* is thematically higher than the Theme argument (see Bresnan and Kanerva 1989; Grimshaw 1990; Marantz 1993; also see section 1.2); but once it is demoted, it is introduced by a preposition, *to*, and becomes optional. Whatever is the reason for this cluster of properties, it is clear that the embedded subject in Chichewa causatives patterns with the parenthesized NPs in (29): it is introduced with an oblique Case and is optional, both traits presumably resulting from demotion in a structure like (26).

As for why the thematic subject of the verb root cannot be extracted in a type I causative construction, Alsina and Mchombo (1993) and Alsina (1992) note that in Chichewa, NPs bearing a higher-than-Theme θ-role resist Ā-movement in dative constructions as well. Since the subject of the transitive or unergative verb root typically bears a θ-role higher than Theme in VI, it is expected to pattern with the dative object in Ā-movement. In other words, the ungrammaticality of (22d) may be accounted for without appealing to Subjacency as Baker proposes, thereby avoiding the problems in his analysis.

Despite differences in technical vernacular, the accounts of type I VI presented here and in Alsina 1992 have much in common. Working within the theory of Lexical-Functional Grammar (LFG), Alsina assigns various syntactic functions to thematic arguments at the level of argument structure. When a verb root is causativized, the resulting word has a composed argument structure in which the SUBJ function is assigned to the thematic subject of the causative morpheme and the single OBJ function is assigned either to the thematic subject or the object of the verb root. A simple algorithm guarantees that if the thematic object of the verb root is marked with OBJ, its thematic subject acquires no syntactic function, must be suppressed, and is optionally introduced as an oblique-Case-marked adjunct. As the SUBJ and OBJ functions in LFG correspond to the structural Cases in the P&P model, there is a straightforward conversion between Alsina's theory and mine regarding Case assignment.[9]

Finally, consider the argument structure of the type I morphological causative in Chichewa. If Chichewa syntax provides only one accusative Case per clause, the causative suffix -*its* is forced to suppress the subject θ-role of a transitive verb root so that any NP receiving a suppressed θ-role can be treated in syntax as an adjunct qualified for an oblique Case. The argument structure of such a causative word is (30), in which the suppressed θ-role is parenthesized.

(30) cause $\langle a \langle b \rangle \rangle$
       cook $\langle x \langle y \rangle \rangle$
       cook-cause $\langle a \langle (x) \langle y \rangle \rangle \rangle$

Given the thematic relation between the two morphemes (*cook* receiving θ-role *b* from *cause*), *cook-cause* should map into a multiple-VP structure. Applying the MSMH yields (26) as the only well-formed structure, with (*x*) in (30) assigned to NP_2 in the tree.

At this point, it will also be useful to consider another of Alsina's claims: that the causative morpheme in fact has three θ-roles rather than two. The "extra" θ-role is said to be Patient, which is fused (or "identified" in Higginbotham 1985 and Li 1990b) with a θ-role of the verb root. For example, (31) represents the argument structure of *phik-its* 'cook-cause' in (22a) if Alsina's claim is correct.

(31) cause $\langle a \langle b \langle c \rangle \rangle \rangle$
       cook $\langle x \langle y \rangle \rangle$
       cook-cause $\langle a \langle \underline{b} \langle (x) \langle y \rangle \rangle \rangle \rangle$

The θ-role *c* of *cause* is assigned to the root *cook*, and the Patient, *b*, is fused with *y*, the object θ-role of *cook*. The fused θ-roles are assigned to a single argument. As in (30), the θ-role *x* from *cook* is suppressed.

Whether a causative morpheme takes two or three arguments remains to be decided and may well vary from language to language or even from verb to verb. But the key principles of the theory proposed here operate at a level of abstraction higher than this specific detail. The structural representations so far are based on treating the causative morpheme as a double-argument verb. Now let us briefly examine the possible ways to map an argument structure like (31) to syntax.

Bearing in mind that Alsina's Chichewa data in (22) exemplify type I causatives, either of the structures in (32) would be legitimate, depending on whether (i) each identified θ-role is mapped to its own argument position, with a single NP moving through these positions during the derivation, or (ii) the identified θ-roles are assigned to one argument position. In both (32a) and (32b), NP_2 is the demoted subject if the verb root is transitive, while the causative m-complex is initially inserted in V_2 and moves to the topmost V_1 as before.

(32) a.

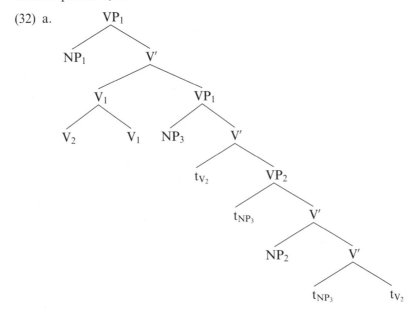

b.

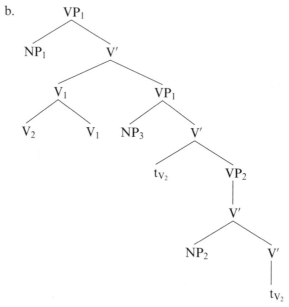

In (32a), NP$_3$ starts as the complement of V$_2$ and eventually raises to the Spec of the lower VP$_1$. Its trace inside VP$_2$ reflects the θ-role *y* in (31) and its highest position in VP$_1$ corresponds to the θ-role *b*. Together, the chain [NP$_3$, t, t] receives the identified θ-roles *b-y* from the argument structure of *cook-cause*. Technically, *b* and *y* can be regarded as the "segments" of a single θ-role assigned by the m-complex, thereby satisfying the θ-Criterion (see Higginbotham 1985). For all relevant purposes, (32a) is not distinguishable from (26), where the matrix causative verb has only two θ-roles rather than three.

Alternatively, the identified *b-y* might be assigned to a single syntactic position in a possible structure such as (32b). NP$_3$ is generated directly as an object of V$_1$ but receives *b-y*. Several authors (Baker 1989, 1996; Marantz 1993; Collins 1997) have explored the idea that when two verb morphemes share an argument, the argument is syntactically represented only in the projection of the structurally matrix verb. Accordingly, NP$_3$ incurs no trace inside VP$_2$. Syntactically, the structure amounts to treating VP$_2$ and V$_1$ as a complex predicate jointly assigning a (super) θ-role to NP$_3$.

In the P&P framework, either of (32a–b) may be developed into a legitimate representation for Alsina's causative m-complex in (31). There is a theory-internal consideration, to be examined in section 1.2, that favors the approach embodied by (32b) over the one embodied by (32a) in a different context. But to the extent that (31) can be mapped to syntax one way or another, whether the causative morpheme has two or three θ-roles is a specific issue that is not, and should not be, tied to the much more general theory of the morphology-syntax interface.

To summarize, the LH forces VI complexes to be lexically formed like any other morphologically complex words, while the MSMH guarantees that the VI construction will have biclausal properties in terms of binding and passivization. Thus, we see that there is nothing intrinsically incompatible between the lexicalist view of word formation and head movement in the derivation of complex phrasal structures.

1.1.5 Inflectional Morphology

As pointed out in the introduction, there is no intrinsic incompatibility between my theory of the morphology-syntax interface and a "post-syntactic" model of inflectional morphology. It may well be that inflectional affixes are merely morphophonological manifestations of certain features associated with lexical heads. With this in mind, I explore the consequence of my theory within a different approach, the one often found in the syntactic literature that an inflectional affix is as much a morpheme as a lexical item (see Lieber 1992). In this context, the LH and the MSMH unequivocally favor the analysis of inflectional morphology in the Minimalist Program as sketched in Chomsky 1995 over the one adopted in Government-Binding (GB) Theory in which the lexical stem and the inflectional affix merge through head movement.

Since the earliest days of transformational grammar, it has been suggested that inflectional affixes are generated in different syntactic locations from the verb root. Depending on the specific theory, either the affix "hops to" the verb or the verb joins with the affix, but always through syntactic operations such as transformation or movement. Structure (33) is a GB-style illustration of the context in which the merger takes place.

(33)

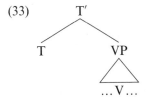

The verb form *plays*, for instance, starts with the verb root under V and
the 3rd person singular suffix -*s* under T. Moving one of them to the other
results in *plays*. Given the LH, such a structure is prohibited because, by
definition, words are never formed through syntactic operations. On the
other hand, if *play-s* is formed lexically and enters syntax as a single
verb, as shown in (34), it can adjoin to T to check whatever features -*s*
embodies.

(34)

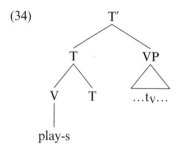

As in the case of VI, the T node is not a completely empty position because it carries a set of features (ϕ-features, tense, etc.) to be matched by
those in V-*s*.

As the relation between *play* and -*s* is not thematic, the MSMH cannot
be held responsible for generating the structure (34). I adopt the common
assumption that UG generates functional projections in syntax automatically unless there is a specific requirement for not doing so. Hence, a
typical clause must contain a TP, bare VPs being permitted only when a
lexical item such as the causative verb imposes specific requirements (and
presumably provides necessary licensing). Feature checking is of course
obligatory between the inflected verb and T because the verb is forced by
the LH to carry the T(ense)/Agr affixes when it enters syntax. But the
generation of TP (and other functional phrases) is completely independent of the MSMH.

An interesting difference between inflectional morphology and lexical
affixes such as -*cause* in VI is best illustrated with a fact noticed in Li
1990c. The examples in (35) are from Chichewa (Baker 1988, 370).

(35) a. ?Asilikali a-na-vin-its-its-a   atsikana kwa akaidi.
           soldiers agr-past-dance-cause-cause-asp girls   to   prisoners
           'The soldiers made the prisoners make the girls dance.'
      b. ?Mkango u-na-meny-ets-ets-a   mbuzi kwa anyani.
           lion   agr-past-hit-cause-cause-asp goats to   baboons
           'The lion made someone make the baboons hit the goats.'

According to Baker, these double-causative examples are "somewhat hard to process" but are judged grammatical. Marginality of the same nature is also perceived in the English translations. The processing problem aside, (35a–b) indicate that a causative affix can be embedded. In contrast, the T affix cannot be embedded, since VI is never reported to allow the verb root to carry its own T.

Another facet of the lexical-functional difference in morphology is that the verbal affixes that trigger VI are characteristically limited to causatives, modals, and certain aspectual words. This would be unexpected if all it takes in VI is for the embedded verb to raise through the embedded T (and C) to the matrix verb. After all, many verbs take clausal complements. But only a small number ever trigger VI. From these observations, the descriptive conclusion in (36) follows (see Li 1990c).

(36) A necessary condition for VI is that the complement is a bare VP, not a CP/IP.

The VI-triggering verbs are precisely those that can (optionally) take bare VP complements. The question is why (36) must hold.

In Li 1990c, I proposed that head movement resembles phrasal movement with respect to chain-internal homogeneity, measured in terms of potential θ-related positions (T-positions). For a phrasal chain C, A-positions are by definition potential θ-receiving positions and $\bar{\text{A}}$-positions are not. For a head chain C′, lexical head positions are potential θ-assigning positions and functional head positions are not. Designating both potential θ-assigning and -receiving positions as $\bar{\bar{\text{T}}}$-positions and all others as $\bar{\text{T}}$-positions, I pointed out the similarity between phrasal chains and head chains: a chain of the form [T, $\bar{\text{T}}$, T] is ill formed in both types. At the phrasal level, this is "improper movement" in a superraising context; and at the head level, this is movement from V to I/C and back to V. If such a chain is ruled out by UG (for whatever reason), then (36) follows automatically. Direct V-to-V movement creates the chain [T, T], which corresponds to an A-chain for phrases and is well formed. The same account is tentatively adopted in Baker 1996. This concept of chain homogeneity is also extended in Chomsky 1995 to constrain the set of legitimate LF elements.

Since it remains unclear why [T, $\bar{\text{T}}$, T] (or [T, $\bar{\text{T}}$] in the minimalist model) is not legitimate, however, I present below an alternative analysis that yields the same effect as (36) without the need for poorly understood stipulations.

For the purpose of representing VI syntactically under the MSMH, a verb V_1 may take either a VP complement or a clausal complement (CP or TP), both containing the verb V_2, while the latter also contains at least a functional head F_2. If any of these morphemes form a word W, the LH requires W to be formed lexically. Suppose $W = V_2\text{-}V_1$ (linear order irrelevant). When the thematic relation between V_1 and V_2 is mapped to syntax according to the MSMH, V_2 projects to its own maximal projection, namely, VP_2. For W, the syntactic complement of V_1 cannot be a CP/TP because, after all, V_1 assigns the θ-role to a verb, not to a complementizer or tense morpheme. Put differently, for V_1 to θ-mark V_2 means that V_1 selects a VP complement, not a CP/TP complement. It follows that as long as $W = V_2\text{-}V_1$, as in the actual morphological causatives, the syntactic structure of V_1 taking a clausal complement can never be generated.

Now suppose that $W = [F_2\text{-}V_2]\text{-}V_1$, with V_2 carrying its own functional affix. It is widely held that $F_2\text{-}V_2$ is of category V, not F. For example, *play-ed* is a verb, not an instance of T. It follows that W still embodies a thematic relation between two verbal morphemes V_1 and V_2. Hence, only VP_2 can be projected in syntax in order to satisfy V_1's selectional restriction. But then the morpheme F_2 cannot be licensed—there is no syntactic node FP_2 in syntax to help check the features carried by the morpheme F_2. As a result, $[F_2\text{-}V_2]\text{-}V_1$ can be formed lexically but will never have a legitimate syntactic context to occur in.

Finally, suppose that $W = F_2\text{-}V_1$. Mapped to syntax, this would mean that V_1 takes a clausal complement headed by F_2. By hypothesis, V_1 assigns a θ-role to F_2 and is the morphological head of W (Williams 1981b). The structure reflecting the thematic relation between V_1 and F_2 is (37).

(37)

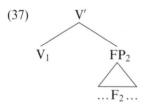

I take it as the basic rule of lexical insertion that the inserted lexical item and the syntactic location it is inserted in must be of the same category. So W cannot be inserted in the position of F_2 because of categorial mismatch. Nor can it be legitimately inserted in the position of V_1. In this position, W must move to F_2 in order to check the functional features carried by the morpheme F_2, probably because of the principle of Full Interpretation (Chomsky 1995). But this movement inevitably leaves a trace in the V_1 position that cannot be c-commanded by its antecedent, the lowered W. Thus, the derivation violates the Empty Category Principle (ECP) and/or the Proper Binding Condition (Fiengo 1977; Lasnik and Saito 1992).[10] Because W cannot be legitimately inserted in (37), there is no well-formed syntactic representation of the thematic relation between V_1 and F_2. Under the MSMH, this means F_2-V_1 can only enter syntax as a "nonexpandable" verb. Then the functional features of F_2 would never be properly checked simply because there would be no FP_2 anywhere in the syntactic structure. In sum, $W = F_2$-V_1 suffers the same fate as $W = [F_2$-$V_2]$-V_1. They can be generated morphologically but have no proper syntactic representation. Consequently, only $W = V_2$-V_1 is ever observed in actual VI, which necessarily has the structure $[V_1\ VP_2]$, and (36) follows from general UG principles given the LH and MSMH.[11]

Before ending this section, I examine Baker's (2002) recent argument against treating inflectional morphology with the lexicalist analysis in (34).

Baker starts with two parameters often found in the literature:

(38) a. The subject raises overtly or covertly to the Spec of TP.

b. The verb raises overtly or covertly to T.

The combination of these options predicts four language types, of which only three are attested (see Baker's own discussion of Julien 2000).

(39) Overt subject raising $+$ $+$ $-$ $-$
Overt verb raising $+$ $-$ $+$ $-$
                    French   English   Welsh $\varnothing$

The corresponding examples are given in (40)–(43) (quoted from Baker 2002, 321–323).

(40) *French*

a. Jean a souvent embrassé Marie.

b. Jean embrasse souvent Marie.

(41) *English*

a. John has often kissed Mary.

b. John often kisses Mary.

(42) *Welsh*
    a. Naeth y dyn brynu gar.
       did   the man buy   car
       'The man did buy the car.'
    b. Bryn-odd y dyn gar.
       buy-past the man car
       'The man bought the car.'

(43) *The language that is (wrongly) predicted to exist*
    a. Has Chris won the prize. (meaning 'Chris has won the prize.')
    b. Chris won the prize.

Since Emonds 1978 and Pollock 1989, it has been widely accepted that the data in (40)–(41) indicate the difference between English and French in whether a lexical verb raises overtly to T (irrelevant technical details are ignored). The two languages share the trait of overtly moving the subject to the Spec of TP, which is why even tense-bearing auxiliaries follow the subject in a declarative sentence. In contrast, Welsh has the same overt V-raising as French but the subject stays inside VP, resulting in the word order patterns in (42). (43) illustrates what is logically expected but seems nonexistent: neither the lexical verb nor the subject undergoes overt raising, with each component in (43a–b) occurring in the base-generated position (the auxiliary *has* is simply taken to indicate the location of a finite I).

Baker's solution to the unexpected gap is to abandon Chomsky's (1995) lexicalist implementation of Pollock's theory, in which every lexical verb is inflected in the lexicon and moves to T either overtly as in French or covertly at LF as in English—namely, the parameter in (38b). In its place, suppose that languages vary on either overtly moving the lexical verb to the inflectional affix in T or letting the two morphemes merge into a PF word through linear adjacency. If the subject raises to the Spec of TP overtly, equally overt V-raising leaves the adverb between the inflected verb and the object, yielding French. If the subject raises but the verb stays in situ, the affix in T depends on adjacency to the verb to be "hosted." This is the scenario of English, which becomes possible because the subject is no longer in the Spec of VP to intervene. Welsh is like French except that the subject is not raised, with V-raising generating the VSO word order in (42b). The language in (43) doesn't exist because the subject, remaining in the Spec of VP, necessarily separates the in-situ verb from the inflectional affix in T. That is, there is no way to create (43b).

For Baker, this explanation for the typological gap crucially relies on generating the verb and the affix in their respective positions, with inflection arising through either overt head movement or phonological merger.

While the facts in (40)–(43) definitely require explanation and Baker's work offers an insightful start, his specific conclusion against a lexicalist account of inflection, either Chomsky's or the one outlined here, is not warranted. Below, I show that even if the essence of Baker's solution is correct, no argument against a lexicalist theory of inflection can be drawn from it.

Abstracting away from the lexicalist-syntactic debate, Baker's solution is built on two assumptions, of which (44b) could be derived from a morphological theory:

(44) a. A tense affix must be under T in overt syntax.

b. A tense affix must be hosted by a verb/aux in overt syntax.

For Baker, (44a) is necessary for preventing covert movement of a tense morpheme to T as in Chomsky's analysis, and (44b) is the direct cause for the typological gap at issue: the intervening subject in (43b) prevents the affix under T from being hosted by the in-situ verb.

Now suppose that (44a–b) are part of UG and so is the LH. For languages with overt subject raising to the Spec of TP, the LH forces inflection to take place either lexically as Chomsky (1995) suggests or through phonological adjacency (see my brief discussion of Distributive Morphology in chapter 4). French chooses the lexical route. The resulting tensed verb is inserted in V but must move to T to satisfy (44a). English opts against lexical inflection, forcing the tense affix and the verb to be generated in separate positions in syntax under (44a) and relying on linear adjacency to merge them to satisfy (44b). Technical details aside, this account of the French-English pair is identical to Baker's.

Alternatively, suppose that the subject stays inside VP. Lexical inflection again results in the tensed verb moving overtly to T to satisfy (44a–b), yielding the VSO order in Welsh. The only other option that a subject-in-situ language can choose under the LH is the adjacency-dependent inflection. But because the subject intervenes between V and T, phonological merger cannot take place. Hence, the gap (more specifically, (43b)) is accounted for.

I should emphasize that the analysis I have offered here is not an endorsement of or an objection to the direction Baker takes in explaining his inflectional paradigm. Rather, I hope to show that right or wrong, his particular solution to the problem only argues against LF feature checking for T; it does not constitute an argument against a lexicalist analysis of inflection, contrary to his claim.

1.2   The Applicative Construction

Of the known morphological processes, applicative formation is among the least understood owing to the complexity of the data, which in turn has triggered many different analyses (see, e.g., Marantz 1984, 1993; Baker 1988, 1996; Alsina and Mchombo 1993; Bresnan and Moshi 1993; Foley 1997; Nakamura 1997; Hale and Keyser 2002). Since so much about the phenomenon remains unclear in terms of both facts and their theoretical implications, in this section I will take up a more modest task: to weed out an approach that is implausible both empirically and within the current theory, and to sketch a promising account of the construction found in Bantu and Iroquoian. I will not attempt to cover all the properties of the applicatives found in the literature. Instead, I will focus on demonstrating that a coherent analysis of the phenomenon can be formulated within the theoretical framework being presented here. I also argue that the UTAH is too permissive to be the mapping principle between syntax and morphology.

1.2.1   Basic Data
The examples in (45) are from the Bantu language Kichaga (Bresnan and Moshi 1993, 49), and those in (46) from the Iroquoian language Mohawk (Baker 1996, 427). Throughout this section, the applicative suffix is glossed as -*app*.

(45) a. N-a-i-ly-a   k-elya.
        foc-agr-pres-eat-fv food
        'He is eating food.'
     b. N-a-i-lyi-i-a   m-ka k-elya.
        foc-agr-pres-eat-app-fv wife   food
        'He is eating food for/on his wife.'
     c. N-a-i-lyi-i-a   njaa   k-elya.
        foc-agr-pres-eat-app-fv hunger food
        'He is eating food because of hunger.'
     d. N-a-i-lyi-i-a   ma-woko k-elya.
        foc-agr-pres-eat-app-fv hand   food
        'He is eating food with his hands.'

    e. N-a-i-lyi-i-a   m-ri-nyi   k-elya.
       foc-agr-pres-eat-app-fv homestead food
       'He is eating food at the homestead.'

(46) a. Wa-ha-natar-a-kwetar-e'.
       fact-agr_s-break-$\emptyset$-cut-punc
       'He cut the bread.'
    b. Wa-hake-natar-a-kwetar-ʌ-'.
       fact-$agr_{s/o}$-bread-$\emptyset$-cut-app-punc
       'He cut the bread for me.'

The (a) examples are the base forms. The applicative affix helps introduce an extra NP argument, shown in (45b–e) and (46b), which at least
in some languages can be optionally interpreted as Benefactive, Instrument, Locative, or Causer, depending on the verb root and/or the context
(Bresnan and Moshi 1993).

    An obvious property of the applicative affix is its location in the verbal
complex—after the verb root but before the word-final morpheme (-*a* in
(45) and -' in (46)), which has been treated as serving aspectual functions
by some scholars but simply marked as a final vowel (fv) by others. The
theoretical significance of this location is easily seen in Bantu. (47) is the
typical full schema of the Bantu morphological causative verb (see section
1.1).

(47) Agr_S-T-(Agr_O)-V-cause-asp

Morphemes to the left of V are inflectional. Starting from V, the order of
the morphemes mirrors their corresponding positions in syntax: the left-
most is the most deeply embedded, and so on (cf. Baker's (1985) Mirror
Principle). Since the applicative affix occurs after V, just like the causative
suffix, the most natural analysis is that it also corresponds to a syntactic
position higher than V.

    This conclusion immediately disfavors any treatment of the applicative
affix as a preposition, as proposed in Baker 1988 and Nakamura 1997.
From the morphological point of view, the causative sequence in (47)
clearly shows the Bantu verbal complex to be head-final, with V-*cause*
remaining a verb because the causative affix is the head and is verbal. By
the same logic, the V-*app* complex would be prepositional if the applicative affix were a P. This is implausible because the m-complex clearly
behaves like a verb, not a preposition. Exactly the same argument against
treating -*app* as P can be constructed in syntactic terms. Baker's and

Nakayama's accounts take the applicative morpheme to be a D-Structure P and raise it to a governing verb in the same way a verb root raises to the matrix causative verb in VI. A necessary condition for P-raising, however, is for P to be structurally lower than V in order for the trace of P to satisfy the ECP. But a syntactically lower P should occur to the left of the verb morpheme in the applicative cluster, not to its right. See Baker 1996 for a similar observation.

Another well-established fact about the applicative construction is the structural relation between the Theme argument of the verb root and the applicative NP. Marantz (1993) shows the Benefactive argument to be more prominent than the Theme argument in a Bantu applicative (Swahili examples from Marantz 1993, 117).

(48) a. Ni-li-m-som-e-a   kila mwandishi kitabu chake.
         agr_s-past-agr_o-read-app-fv each writer   book   his
         'I read each author his book.'
     b. *Ni-li-m-som-e-a   mwandishi wake kila kitabu.
         agr_s-past-agr_o-read-app-fv writer   its   each book
         '*I read its author each book.'

In both examples, the NP headed by *mwandishi* 'writer' is the Benefactive argument introduced by the applicative affix *e*. Given that a quantified NP must c-command a coindexed pronoun, the grammaticality of (48a) indicates that *kila mwandishi* 'each writer' c-commands the pronoun *chake* 'his' inside the Theme argument, whereas the ungrammatical (48b) shows that the quantified Theme *kila kitabu* 'each book' does not c-command the pronoun inside the Benefactive. This asymmetry follows directly if the Benefactive NP c-commands the Theme NP but not vice versa. The word order in the Chichewa examples in (49) (from Marantz 1993, 121) confirms the conclusion.

(49) a. Chitsiru chi-na-gul-ir-a   atsikana mphatso.
         fool   agr-past-buy-app-fv girls   gift
         'The fool bought a gift for the girls.'
     b. *Chitsiru chi-na-gul-ir-a   mphatso atsikana.
         fool   agr-past-buy-app-fv gift   girls

The Benefactive NP *atsikana* 'girls' must be adjacent to the verb. Signaling the typical object, this position c-commands every argument to its right. For the correlation between linear direction and c-command, see Larson 1988, Kayne 1994, and chapter 4 of this book.

But the same test on Chichewa word order suggests that a non-Benefactive applicative NP is not necessarily more prominent than the Theme NP (Marantz 1993, 122–123).

(50) a. Anyani a-ku-phwany-ir-a   mwala dengu.
     baboons agr-pres-break-app-fv stone   basket
     'The baboons are breaking the basket with a stone.'
   b. Anyani a-ku-phwany-ir-a   dengu mwala.
     baboons agr-pres-break-app-fv basket stone
     Same as (50a)

(51) a. Alenje a-ku-luk-ir-a   pamchenga mikeka.
     hunters agr-pres-weave-app-fv sand   mats
     'The hunters are weaving mats on the beach.'
   b. Alenje a-ku-luk-ir-a   mikeka pamchenga.
     hunters agr-pres-weave-app-fv mats   sand
     Same as (51a)

The Instrument argument *mwala* 'stone' in (50) and the Locative argument *pamchenga* 'sand' in (51) may occur either before or after the Theme argument. As Marantz points out, this indicates the lack of an intrinsic hierarchical relation between the Theme argument of the verb root and the added applicative argument, be it Instrument or Locative.

An implication of (50)–(51) is that the V-*app* complex in each pair cannot be invariably analyzed as a verb projecting to a simple monoclausal structure. Suppose *luk-ir* 'weave-app' in (51b) to be such a verb. It follows that the Locative argument *pamchenga* 'sand' is thematically less prominent than the Theme *mikeka* 'mats', a reasonable conclusion widely adopted in the literature. But logically, this means that the same derived verb in (51a) must not be projected to a monoclausal structure: the single verb in the clause cannot have the alternative argument structures in which the Locative is either higher than the Theme or lower than it. There is no known monomorphemic verb with such flexibility in thematic hierarchy. Put differently, in at least one of the sentences in each pair, the V-*app* complex must be treated as more than a verb projecting to its own VP. Note that this conclusion constitutes yet another argument that a pure lexicalist theory of word formation as seen in Di Sciullo and Williams 1987 is insufficient for all morphological phenomena.

1.2.2   The Morphology-Syntax Mapping Hypothesis and Syntactic Incorporation

Next, let us consider how the proposed interface theory accounts for the aforementioned properties of Bantu applicatives. To begin with, consider the following schematic scenario. Let W be a morphologically complex word composed of morphemes Y-X (linear order irrelevant for the moment) and a thematic relation between X and Y. In particular, Y assigns an internal θ-role to X.[12] Abstractly speaking, there are only two alternatives to consider: either X = Y in category or X $\neq$ Y in category. VI is an instance of the first option, mapping successfully to a structure such as (25) with an embedded binding domain. This much can be accomplished, empirically correctly, within both Baker's theory of syntactic incorporation and the one proposed here.

The second option is exemplified in (37), illustrating the impossible case of "downward" inflection. In that example, one of the morphemes is a functional affix. Now let us consider the scenario where both morphological components of the word W are lexical. The LH and the MSMH force X and Y to form W lexically and subject the syntactic representation of W to all UG principles. Since Y assigns a θ-role to X, Y is the head of W and determines its category, making W = Y in category. Furthermore, the thematic relation between the two morphemes would have the structural representation shown in (52) in syntax.

(52)

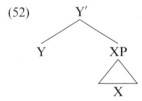

As in (37), W is prevented from being inserted initially under X as the two do not match in category. W can be legitimately inserted in the Y position, but must be lowered to X in order for X and its maximal projection to be properly interpreted; minimally, all the local thematic relations inside XP would require X to be filled by a lexical item capable of assigning (relevant) θ-roles. However, lowering W from Y to X creates a trace in Y that is not c-commanded by the antecedent.

That syntax generally forbids downward movement is widely assumed and made to follow from various UG principles—after all, all well-established overt movements target a landing site that c-commands the original site. The only solid case of lowering comes from LF reconstruction. But reconstruction presumes initial raising so that the reconstructed constituent has a trace position to fall back to. This very property underlies the copy theory of traces, according to which a trace is simply an unpronounced copy of the moved constituent and LF reconstruction amounts to interpreting the copy in the original site rather than the one in the landing site (Chomsky 1995). Since the lowering of W to X in (52) is not reconstruction, it would be a "genuine" case of downward movement and is prohibited by UG. In conclusion, W cannot be inserted either in X or in Y, leaving no well-formed syntactic structure to represent the thematic relation between X and Y. Consequently, W, of category Y, can only project to one YP and nothing more.

Once X is replaced with P and Y with V, W corresponds to the Bantu V-*app* with -*app* treated as P. We thus conclude, correctly given the morpheme order discussed with respect to (45)–(47), that it is impossible in my theory for such a V-P cluster to be mapped to a multiphrasal structure in which one of the heads is P and the other is V as is found in Baker's preposition incorporation (PI) analysis. In contrast, the structure is permitted by the UTAH-based theory, as evidenced by the fact that Baker (1988) indeed offered such an analysis. In conclusion, when used as the mapping principle between morphology and syntax, the UTAH is overly permissive, allowing syntactic derivations that do not exist.

An alternative proposal to syntactic PI is that -*app* is a verb. Marantz (1993) and Baker (1996) both treat the applicative affix as the matrix verb taking a VP complement headed by the verb root. Because this approach amounts to another instance of VI, it is intrinsically adaptable to my theory.

Taking Marantz's and Baker's analyses of the Benefactive applicative as an example, suppose that the applicative affix is a verb with two internal arguments, a Benefactive/Goal (B/G hereafter) and one that I provisionally call Theme, the latter being assigned to a verbal projection (see Baker 1996). Note that the applicative affix must somehow share the subject with the verb root: the subjects in (45b) and (46b) are clearly interpreted as the thematic subjects of the corresponding verb roots.[13] Details aside, such an analysis entails a tree structure like (53).

(53)   VP$_1$

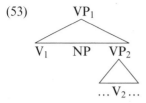

...V$_2$...

V$_1$ is the applicative morpheme, NP the Benefactive argument introduced by V$_1$, and V$_2$ the verb root. "..." stands for other constituents inside V$_2$. Raising V$_2$ to V$_1$ yields the sequence [V$_2$-V$_1$ NP ...] as seen in the typical applicative examples in (45)–(46).

The conversion from this analysis of syntactic incorporation to mine is straightforward. By the LH, the verb root and *-app* must form a word in the lexicon. The word is a verb because *-app* is a verb. The relation between the two morphemes is thematic by hypothesis, so it is subject to the syntactic representation where V$_1$ takes a VP complement, namely, (53). The word can be inserted in V$_2$ and raised to V$_1$ to satisfy all syntactic requirements.

Certain details of such an analysis deserve careful examination, however. First of all, since V$_1$ provides two internal arguments, B/G and Theme, the relative hierarchy of the two must be specified. Carrier-Duncan (1985), Larson (1988), and Baker (1989, 1996) place the Goal lower than the Theme, whereas Kiparsky (1988), Aoun and Li (1989), Grimshaw (1990), Li (1990b), Bresnan and Moshi (1993), and Jung (1999) place the Goal higher than the Theme. Marantz's Bantu examples in (48)–(49) support the latter ranking.

The starting assumption is that the thematic hierarchy is asymmetric: either the B/G role is more prominent than the Theme role or vice versa. Mapped to a binary-branching structure in syntax, this means that either NP in (53) c-commands VP$_2$ or VP$_2$ c-commands NP, but the two never c-command each other. Now in (48)–(49), the Theme NP belongs to the verb root, corresponding to V$_2$ in (53), whereas the B/G NP comes from *-app*, namely, V$_1$. Since the latter NP c-commands the former NP, it must be the case that in (53), NP c-commands VP$_2$ and thereby c-commands everything inside VP$_2$. Hence Marantz's assumption that the B/G is higher than the Theme.

The next detail to be figured out regarding (53) is how to represent the subject sharing in (45)–(46). Baker (1996) proposes to identify the subject θ-roles of the two verbs. Since θ-identification counts as a way to discharge a θ-role (see Higginbotham 1985), the verb root (i.e., V_2 in (53)) no longer needs its own subject. Adapting this proposal to the thematic hierarchy just established, we have (54) as the D-Structure representation for Benefactive applicatives.

(54)

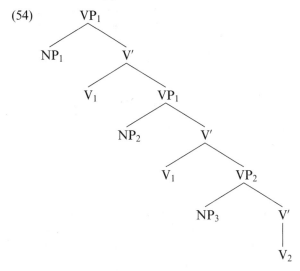

NP_1 is the subject receiving the identified θ-roles from both V_1 and V_2; NP_2 is the Benefactive argument of V_1; VP_2 receives the Theme role from V_1; and NP_3 is V_2's own internal argument. The tree assumes a Larsonian structure. Since V_2 has no subject of its own, the upper VP_2 is not needed and thus not projected.[14] Following conventional practice, I place the internal argument of V_2 in the Spec of the lower (and only) VP_2, though its precise location has no consequence for the current discussion.

Since (54) is simply a more elaborate version of (53), it is equally adaptable to my interface theory. The derived verb in (45b), for instance, is lexically formed with the following argument structure:

(55) eat ⟨x ⟨y⟩⟩
  -app ⟨a ⟨b ⟨c⟩⟩⟩
  eat-app ⟨a ⟨b ⟨x ⟨y⟩⟩⟩⟩

The innermost θ-role of the applicative morpheme, c, is assigned to the verb root *eat*. The subject θ-roles a and x of the two verbs are identified (or fused; see section 1.1.4). The thematic relation between *-app* and *eat*, via the Theme role, is eligible for syntactic representation under the

MSMH. Hence, we have (54), under the assumption that the identified θ-role of the verb root (i.e., x) is no longer assigned to a separate NP argument.

A potential complication of such a structure—both Baker's and my adaptation of it—arises when it is compared with the causative VI. Recall Alsina's (1992) claim that Bantu causative morphemes have two internal arguments (section 1.1.4) and that one of them is identified with a θ-role of the verb root (see (31)–(32)). If this indeed is the case for even a portion of the languages with morphological causativization, the general question arises of how to represent in syntax the identified θ-roles from the verb root and the derivational morpheme. For lack of known empirical evidence bearing on the issue, I will tentatively adopt the simplest strategy, as follows:

(56) Represent θ-identification with the minimal syntactic structure possible.

For applicatives, the subject θ-roles of the two verbal morphemes are identified. Assuming that the identified θ-roles can be assigned as one, as Higginbotham (1985) originally proposed, the minimal structure is to project only the subject argument in the matrix VP_1 while totally omitting the upper VP_2, the latter consisting of nothing but the embedded subject position and a base-generated empty V. Since no known UG principle is violated by doing so, we have the legitimate (54). On the other hand, if the object θ-role of a verb root is identified, as in Alsina's causatives in (31), it is impossible to omit the lower VP_2 altogether. For one thing, not projecting the lower VP_2 means there is no syntactic projection for the verb root at all, which would violate the MSMH. For another, if the demoted thematic subject of the verb root still needs to be positioned somewhere inside a projection of V_2, at least the lower VP_2 must be projected to serve as the hosting context. Hence, we have (32b) for the causative construction.

There might be theory-internal support for (56) too. In section 1.1.4, we explored the possibility that identified θ-roles might be mapped to multiple syntactic positions. Applying this to the applicative (55) yields (57).

(57)

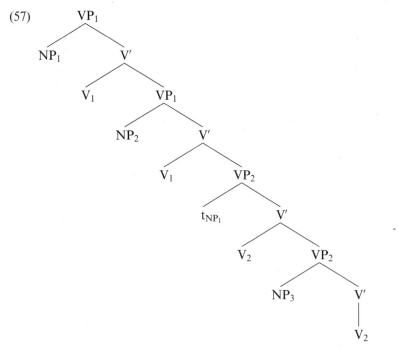

The upper VP₂ becomes necessary if the subject θ-role of the verb root must be separately represented. NP₁ originates in the Spec of the upper VP₂ and raises to that of the upper VP₁, forming an argument chain. By normal (but possibly simple-minded) standards, (57) is more complex than (54) and thus is incompatible with (56). In addition, (57) also faces the potential problem that the raising of NP₁ seems to violate Relativized Minimality (or the Minimal Link Condition in the Minimalist Program) because it must cross the intervening NP₂. For these reasons, I will adopt (54) as the structure for the Benefactive applicatives.[15]

It is worth pointing out that, though both consist of a lexical verb root plus a derivational affix, the applicative (54) and the type II causative in (25) are predicted to have different binding properties. We saw in section 1.1.4 that a full VP₂ functions as the binding domain for a nonsubject anaphor inside VP₂. On the other hand, given the definition of binding domain along the line of Chomsky's (1986b) complete functional complex (also see chapter 2 and Li 1999 for an extension of the complete functional complex in the context of crosslinguistic resultative constructions), we predict that the applicative construction in (54) will act like a monoclausal structure for binding. This is so because NP₁ is now the recipient of the subject θ-role of V_2 owing to θ-identification, making the upper VP_1 the smallest phrase containing all the thematic arguments of V_2. So an anaphor in the position of NP_3 would be able to take NP_1 as the binder. To my knowledge, this prediction is correct, as no evidence has been reported of applicatives behaving like biclausal constructions with respect to anaphor binding.

Related to this (or any) theory of the Benefactive applicative is the general question of how double-object verbs are to be analyzed. In section 1.1.2, the biclausal nature of Arabic verbal causatives was contrasted with the double-object verb *manaḥ* 'gave', which I assumed to be a single verb heading a monoclausal construction. If Benefactive applicatives can be analyzed as consisting of a matrix verb taking an embedded VP in syntax, it seems natural to subsume monomorphemic double-object verbs under the same account. This is especially tempting when a structure like (54) can even produce binding properties indistinguishable from those of a monoclausal construction. Technically, such an implementation is easy to carry out in my theory, as one can always appeal to phonetically empty zero morphemes (see Pesetsky 1995) to represent the applicative affix overtly seen in Bantu and Iroquoian. Furthermore, a syntactically decompositional analysis of double-object verbs will not affect the validity of the discussion in section 1.1.2 because, as noted in the previous paragraph, verbal causatives still have an embedded binding domain.

Nonetheless, I am inclined to take a more cautious position on the issue. A piece of wisdom obtained through the practice of Generative Semantics is that the existence of morphologically decomposable *die-cause* in one language does not automatically justify a similar analysis of *kill* in another language. In fact, crosslinguistic generalizations of this kind not only can be misleading but in fact can easily run out of control. To avoid the potential pitfall, I assume that zero morphemes participate in syntactic computation only when a given language displays an explicit morphological and/or syntactic clue to their existence. One example is a contrastive morphological paradigm (see Saussure 1974) such as the phonetically null morpheme indicating non-3rd-person-singular present tense in English. In the case of monomorphemic ditransitive *give* in English or Arabic, there is no morphological or syntactic evidence for a zero applicative morpheme. Hence, this ditransitive verb is regarded as an indecomposable word that maps to a structure different from (54). After all, languages do appear to vary with respect to which lexicosemantic concepts are lexicalized into a single morpheme and which are represented separately.

1.2.3 Non-Benefactive Applicatives

Now consider the Kichaga applicatives in (45). The applicative suffix -*i* can introduce not only a Benefactive argument but also Instrument, Locative, and Causer. A similar inventory of added arguments is also found with other Bantu languages. The consistent location of the affix determines that it must be analyzed as a verb. As mentioned earlier, Bantu words are clearly head-final. To the extent that V-*app* behaves like a verb, the suffix is the head of the cluster and therefore must be verbal in category. Then one faces the inevitable task of figuring out the argument structures of the applicative suffix in these non-Benefactive usages, a problem that has triggered everlasting debates in its own right. See the references at the beginning of section 1.2.2 and in Dowty 1987, Jackendoff 1987, Zaenen 1988, and Mohanan 1989, among many other works.

If the θ-role assigned to the verb root were simply the lowest in the thematic hierarchy, V-*app* would have (55) as its argument structure whether the added argument was Benefactive or Instrument or Locative, and the syntactic structure in (54) would be sufficient for all the examples in (45). But we have seen in (50)–(51) that the Theme argument may c-command the applicative argument as well, an option not available to the Benefactive argument in (48)–(49). How is this contrast between the Benefactive and the rest to be explained?

One of the keys to answering this question is the nature of the θ-role assigned to the verb root. So far, I have referred to it as a Theme, more or less following Baker's theory of the phenomenon. But this is not obviously correct. After all, the canonical form of a Theme argument is nominal and not verbal (Grimshaw 1979). One possibility is that the θ-role is a semantically "bleached" Theme. If one chooses to regard it as a θ-role with depleted content, its very semantic emptiness places it at the bottom of the thematic hierarchy, lower than the Instrument and Locative. Then the V-*app* compound will have the following argument structure, where *c* is the bleached θ-role assigned to V and *b* is the Instrument/Locative:

(58) V $\langle x \ldots \rangle$
     -app $\langle a \langle b \langle c \rangle\rangle\rangle$
     V-app $\langle a \langle b \langle x \ldots \rangle\rangle\rangle$

The MSMH will then map this compound to a syntactic tree identical to (54), the one for the Benefactive applicative. It follows that the Instrument/Locative NP occurs to the left of any overt argument of the verb root, as in (50a) and (51a).

On the other hand, one may choose to treat the bleached Theme still as a Theme, which is thematically less prominent than B/G but more prominent than all other internal θ-roles. The argument structure of such a compound is (59), where c is the Instrument/Locative and b is the Theme assigned to V.

(59) V $\langle x \dots \rangle$
     -app $\langle a \langle b \langle c \rangle\rangle\rangle$
     V-app $\langle a \langle \underline{x \dots} \langle c \rangle\rangle\rangle$

Since V is regarded as receiving the Theme role from *-app*, the relation is potentially subject to a syntactic representation like (60) under the MSMH.

(60)

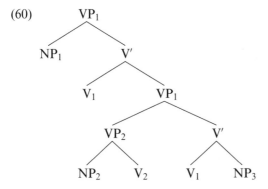

In the tree, VP_2 is higher than NP_3 to reflect the thematic hierarchy in which the Theme is more prominent than the Instrument/Locative. NP_2 is the internal argument of the verb root. But such a structure is ungrammatical for syntactic reasons. If V-*app* is inserted initially in V_2, it cannot lower to V_1 without violating the ECP or the Proper Binding Condition. If it is inserted in V_1 first, it cannot move to V_2, again for lack of c-command. Either way, there is no grammatical derivation whereby the V-*app* complex can land in all the head positions it is expected to. Hence, the MSMH determines that V-*app* must be treated like an indecomposable monomorphemic verb in syntax. The argument of the root, NP_2, is perceived as the (true) Theme argument in the sentence and precedes the Instrument/Locative NP_3, yielding (50b) and (51b).

Note that the same options of treating the bleached Theme either as Theme or as a semantically depleted θ-role should also be available when -*app* introduces the B/G argument. However, such options produce no detectable effect in this case because B/G is more prominent than Theme, bleached or not. Consequently, the scenario in (59)–(60) never exists for the Benefactive -*app*, preventing the B/G NP from ever occurring below and after the Theme. See (48)–(49). In summary, (58) is really the argument structure for all applicative verbs that ultimately project to a syntactic structure like (54), regardless of the semantic content of the applicative θ-role. If -*app* adds a non-B/G θ-role, the resulting compound may also have (59) as its argument structure, which inevitably forces the verb to be treated as syntactically indecomposable.

The two optional interpretations of the bleached Theme, as well as their syntactic consequences under the MSMH, help avoid the problem noted at the end of section 1.2.1, namely, the difficulty of keeping a consistent thematic hierarchy while accounting for the alternative word orders in non-Benefactive applicatives.[16] As a verb heading a single-VP structure, V-*app* has a consistent argument structure in which the Theme role (inherited from the verb root) is ranked higher than the Instrument/Locative role (from -*app*). When the Theme role appears lower than the Instrument/Locative, however, the construction involves a different argument structure on the part of the applicative morpheme as well as a multiple-VP structure in syntax. In terms of mapping θ-roles to syntactic positions, the two non-Benefactive V-*app* alternatives are not directly comparable because they correspond to very different syntactic structures. Hence, the inconsistency with the thematic hierarchy disappears.

1.2.4 Concluding Remarks on Applicatives

Many questions remain about applicatives. For instance, Gunwinjguan languages are reported to have the structure Agr-app-N-V-asp (Evans 1991). If morpheme order is taken seriously, such a compound certainly cannot be analyzed as VI or my adaptation of it. Baker (1996, sec. 9.3) treats it as a real instance of PI but does not elaborate on it. In my theory, syntactic derivation of the complex is ruled out as a matter of principle. If this string does not result from PF word formation owing to linear adjacency in syntax,[17] then it must be formed lexically. Furthermore, the difference in category among all the lexical morphemes involved (P, N, V) prevents it from projecting to anything more than a single VP headed by the verbal cluster. Since the prediction is clear, I leave its verification to scholars with sufficient access to the language. What I consider significant in this section is that the interface theory proposed here correctly predicts that the Bantu and Iroquoian applicatives are not the result of syntactic PI, and that it demonstrates the potential for permitting an analysis that can account for rather complicated properties of the phenomenon. Given the complexity of data beyond the scope of this book, it is expected that the analysis sketched in this section needs revision. The interface theory leaves enough room for that because it is by nature a high-level protocol in UG.

1.3   Resultative Compounds in Chinese

The interface theory presented so far indicates that there is nothing wrong in matching a multiphrasal structure with certain morphological data and applying head movement to it; indeed, the various properties of causatives and applicatives depend on such syntactic mechanisms. Rather, it is the improper and/or uncontrolled use of such mechanisms that results in wrong predictions. Resultative constructions in Chinese provide further evidence against the syntactic theory of word formation based on the UTAH. In particular, (i) that a construction *can* be derived syntactically under the UTAH does not mean that it *is* derived syntactically, indicating that a UTAH-based syntactic theory is not sufficiently restricted in its domain of application; and (ii) lexical word formation rules are empirically necessary. Only those properties of the resultatives directly bearing on the theme of this chapter are discussed in the text. More details can be found in the appendix and the references therein.

1.3.1   The Plausibility of a Syntactic Derivation
Chinese has two resultative constructions, one a compound and the other biclausal.

(61) a. Li Kui gan-zou-le   guan-bing.
        Li Kui chase-leave-asp government-soldier
        'Li Kui chased off the soldiers.'
     b. Yan Qing chang-lei-le.
        Yan Qing sing-be.tired-asp
        'Yan Qing was tired from singing.'
     c. Xiao chuan piao-yuan-le.
        small boat   float-be.distant-asp
        'The small boat floated away.'

(62) a. Li Kui gan-de   guan-bing   sichu   bentao.
    Li Kui chase-DE government-soldier everywhere ran.away
    'Li Kui chased the soldiers off to all directions.'

   b. Yan Qing chang-de jinpilijin.
    Yan Qing sing-DE be.totally.exhausted
    'Yan Qing was totally exhausted from singing.'

   c. Xiao chuan piao-de   yuelaiyue   yuan.
    small boat   float-DE more.and.more be.distant
    'The small boat floated farther and farther away.'

The compounds in (61) are composed of two verbal morphemes, the one on the left representing the causing event (hereafter referred to as V_c) and the one on the right the resulting event (V_r). Together, V_c and V_r form a single verb of the accomplishment type (Vendler 1967). In contrast, in the examples in (62) the verb of the causing event is followed by a suffix -*de*, which in turn is followed by a verb phrase indicating the resulting event. As with the compounds, V_c and V_r will be used to denote the two verbal heads of this construction. To facilitate discussion, (62) will be called the *V-de construction*.

An obvious difference between the two constructions is that the compound is predominantly bisyllabic, forcing both V_c and V_r to be monosyllabic in typical cases.[18] On the other hand, since Modern Chinese generally disfavors monosyllabic words, the monosyllabic V_r found in compounds is rarely phonologically heavy enough for the V_r predicate in the V-*de* construction. This is why the V_r phrases in (62) look more elaborate than the corresponding V_r morphemes in the compounds in (61). To the best of my knowledge, this difference has no effect on the content of this section.

There is clear evidence that in the V-*de* construction, V_r is the lexical head of a phrasal constituent in the complement position of V_c. To begin with, topicalization and relative clauses in Chinese respect the Subjacency Condition, as (63) and (64) illustrate.

(63) a. *Topicalization*
    Neishou xiaoqu,   Yan Qing chang-guo t.
    that   folk.song Yan Qing sing-asp
    'That folk song, Yan Qing sang (before).'

   b. *Relative clause*
    [Yan Qing chang-guo t] de   neishou xiaoqu
     Yan Qing sing-asp   DE that   folk.song
    'the folk song that Yan Qing sang (before)'

(64) a. *Topicalization*

   *Neishou xiaoqu,   Li Kui [zai [Yan Qing chang t] de   shihou]
   that   folk.song Li Kui at   Yan Qing sing   DE time
   dakeshui.
   doze.off
   'That folk song, Li Kui dozed off at the time when Yan Qing
   was singing.'

   b. *Relative clause*

   *[Li Kui [zai [Yan Qing chang t] de   shihou] dakeshui] de
    Li Kui at   Yan Qing sing   DE time   doze.off DE
   neishou xiaoqu
   that   folk.song
   'the folk song that Li Kui dozed off at the time when Yan Qing
   was singing'

In (64a), the topicalized NP *that folk song* is meant to be interpreted
inside the temporal adverbial *at the time when Yan Qing was singing*,
and the sentence is marginal at best. (64b) is analyzed in the same way,
under the assumption that a phonologically empty *wh*-operator undergoes movement to form relative clauses. In contrast, movement out of the
embedded V_r constituent in the V-*de* construction has no effect on its
grammaticality.

(65) a. Neifeng xin,   Yan Qing chang-de [Song Jiang mei-you xinsi
   that   letter Yan Qing sing-DE   Song Jiang not-have mood
   du   t].
   read
   'That letter, Yan Qing's singing made Song Jiang not in the
   mood to read.'

   b. [Yan Qing chang-de [Song Jiang mei-you xinsi   du   t]] de
      Yan Qing sing-DE   Song Jiang not-have mood read   's
   neifeng xin
   that   letter
   'the letter that Yan Qing's singing made Song Jiang not in the
   mood to read'

   c. Neiba bao-dao,   Li Kui xia-de   qiangdao [reng   zai
   that   sharp-knife Li Kui frighten-DE bandit   throw at
   di-shang   t].
   ground-on
   'That sharp knife, Li Kui frightened the bandit into dropping to
   the ground.'

d. [Li Kui xia-de   qiangdao [reng   zai di-shang   t]] de neiba
   Li Kui frighten-DE bandit   throw at ground-on   's that
   bao-dao
   sharp-knife
   'the sharp knife that Li Kui frightened the bandit into dropping
   to the ground'

Therefore, we conclude that in a V-*de* construction, V_c is the matrix verb
and the V_r constituent, which both Huang (1988) and I (Li 1997a) have
treated as a clause, is structurally represented as the complement of V_c.

Because the two resultative constructions can easily paraphrase each
other, it is only natural that many scholars have argued for a derivational
relation between them. Such a derivation is especially easy within Baker's
theory of incorporation given the facts in (63)–(65). Suppose that the D-
Structure forms of the two constructions have much in common, in the
sense that the result phrase containing V_r, be it a clause or less, is consistently placed in the complement of V_c. If Vr stays in situ, the expression
takes the overt biclausal form, that is, the V-*de* construction. If V_r incorporates to V_c, the compound is derived, as (66) illustrates schematically.

(66)

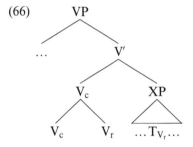

Certainly, the UTAH-based theory of the morphology-syntax interface
does not force the compound to be derived syntactically as in (66). There
is no thematic relation between V_c and V_r (e.g., between *chang* 'sing' and
lei 'be.tired' in (61b)) that is to be syntactically represented under the
UTAH. But the theory does not prevent such an analysis either. After all,
head movement out of the complement phrase is known to be legitimate.
As a result, the syntactic derivation is generally believed to be favored by
Occam's razor.

1.3.2 Evidence against a Syntactic Derivation
More careful comparison of the compounds with V-*de*, however, indicates otherwise. In this section, I examine a difference between them with
respect to postverbal adverbials, leaving more to the appendix.

While most adverbials must occur preverbally in Chinese, some of those indicating duration and frequency are allowed to follow the verb (see Huang 1982; Kung 1993; Soh 1998). The basic examples are given in (67).

(67) a. Yan Qing yilian   xiao-le   liangge shichen.
         Yan Qing continuously laugh-asp two   two.hour
         'Yan Qing kept laughing for four hours.'
     b. Li Kui ku-le   haojitian.
         Li Kui cry-asp several.day
         'Li Kui cried for several days.'

Relevant to the current discussion are the semantic/aspectual properties of the duration adverbials that provide evidence from a different perspective for the lexical nature of the resultative compounds.

In brief, duration adverbials can occur freely inside the embedded clause of the V-*de* construction but are completely unacceptable with resultative compounds. To avoid unnecessary complications from an independent restriction on the number of postverbal nominal phrases in Chinese (see Huang's (1982) Postverbal Constraint), the (b) examples in (68)–(69) are in the passive form to illustrate a transitive V_c.

(68) a. Li Kui lei-de   [ku-le   liang-tian].
         Li Kui tired-asp cry-asp two-day
         'Li Kui was so tired he wept for two days.'
     b. Lu Zhishen bei   dou-de   [xiao-le   yige shichen].
         Lu Zhishen passive amuse-DE laugh-asp one two.hour
         'Lu Zhishen was so amused that he laughed for two full hours.'

(69) a. Li Kui lei-ku-le   (*liang-tian).
         Li Kui tired-cry-asp   two-day
         Intended reading: same as (68a)
     b. Lu Zhishen bei   dou-xiao-le   (*yige shichen).
         Lu Zhishen passive amuse-laugh-asp   one two.hour
         Intended reading: same as (68b)

The sharp contrast would not be expected if the compounds in (69) were derived by raising V_r out of a resultative phrase, because the duration phrase can certainly modify a syntactically projected V_r that denotes an action, as the examples in (68) indicate. On the other hand, if the compounds are treated as lexical verbs, the unacceptability of (69a–b) is easy to explain. A resultative compound is necessarily an accomplishment verb with an intrinsic endpoint to the event it describes. Such verbs are by nature incompatible with duration adverbials (Smith 1991; Tenny 1994) regardless of their word-internal morphological structure. That is, (69a–b) are directly comparable with monomorphemic verbs of the accomplishment/achievement type.

(70) Qiangdao bei   sha-le   (*yige shichen).
     bandit   passive kill-asp   one hour
     'The bandit was killed (*for an hour).'

Crucially, because the compounds in (69) are not syntactically decomposable, the adverbial cannot operate only on the action verb V_r as it does in the V-*de* examples in (68). In conclusion, while the interface theory built on the UTAH allows the resultative compound to be formed syntactically (i.e., to have a minimally double-VP structure), such an option does not exist in the actual grammar of Chinese. The compound is simply treated like a single lexical item in syntax and projects only to one VP.

1.3.3   Resultative Compounds under the Morphology-Syntax Mapping Hypothesis

Isolated from intricate behaviors in subtle contexts, resultative compounds in Chinese could be derived either lexically or syntactically "for free," hence presenting a typical instance of the syntactic versus lexicalist debate. However, the evidence we have examined points at lexical formation.

This conclusion further confirms the need for lexical word formation mechanisms even when syntax can "do the job." Putting aside the issue of redundancy among different components of UG, which I address later, this conclusion highlights the nature of the lexicalist-syntactic debate: for want of understanding all the necessary and sufficient conditions for constituent movement to take place, showing that a specific instance of movement can happen is not enough to justify that it does happen—there may be undiscovered constraints and/or factors that end up barring the claimed movement. As long as head movement is maintained as part of syntax, caution is called for when it is invoked to explain linguistic data. At the same time, efforts must be made to uncover all the constraints on the operation. In the case of Chinese resultative compounds, head movement can indeed be properly constrained so as not to produce empirically wrong predictions. In particular, while the proposed interface theory allows VI to map to a biclausal structure, it correctly assigns only a single-VP structure to resultative compounds, a distinction that the UTAH-based interface theory fails to make.

It is straightforward to enforce the single-VP representation for a resultative compound. That the compound, like any other morphologically complex word, enters syntax as a lexical item is guaranteed by the LH. So it is up to the MSMH to prevent the bimorphemic compound from mapping to a multiple-VP structure. While the relation between the two morphemes of a VI compound is thematic, the one between V_c and V_r of a resultative compound is not. For instance, in the compound *chang-lei* 'sing-be.tired', neither *chang* nor *lei* can be said to take the other as a thematic argument. It follows that at least one of the basic requirements of the MSMH is not met, and the resultative compound can only be mapped to the monoclausal structure in syntax. Put differently, from the viewpoint of syntax, a resultative compound is simply an indecomposable verb without any internal structure—from which fact all of its monoclausal properties follow.

1.4 Concluding Remarks

Like the MSMH, the UTAH is defined to map word-internal thematic relations to corresponding syntactic structures; but these hypotheses differ in two ways. First, when a thematic relation is present word-internally, the UTAH requires it to be represented in syntax. According to the MSMH, however, the thematic relation is syntactically represented if and only if the representation is legitimate. With respect to VI, the two mapping hypotheses yield identical consequences. But as we saw in the presumed case of PI in section 1.2, not every word-internal thematic relation can be manifested in syntax. More direct evidence for the same conclusion will be provided in chapter 2. Crucially, this selective syntactic representation of a given word-internal thematic relation is predicted by the MSMH but not by the UTAH.

The second difference between the two hypotheses comes to light when there is no thematic relation between two components of a word. The MSMH forbids any word-internal nonthematic relation to be represented in syntax, as we saw in the case of Chinese resultative compounds. The UTAH, on the other hand, offers no restriction of any kind here, presumably leaving the decision to other UG principles. In the case of the resultatives, this proves to be problematic because no UG principle stops movement out of a complement (see (65)), leaving open the undesirable option to derive the compound via head-to-head movement. Note that the task at hand is to map a morphologically complex word to a proper syntactic structure. If any part of UG is responsible for the task, it is the morphology-syntax interface. Since the UTAH is designed to be the mapping principle for this purpose, it fails to constrain the results correctly and thus is empirically inferior to the MSMH.

The investigation of resultative compounds has another implication. If the compounds appear as lexical words and indeed exist independently of syntax, one naturally wonders how much of language is WYSIWYG— what you see is what you get. Obviously there is no a priori answer to this question, but it is nonetheless a legitimate question that researchers should always bear in mind. In the past few decades, much progress has been made in discovering the "hidden" mechanisms in the human linguistic faculty. The approach has been so fruitful that it is easy to detect a rampant belief in the field that a "deeper" solution is automatically preferred. This is why, for instance, researchers continuously try to subsume resultative compounds under syntax before even bothering to prove that the data cannot be accounted for by lexical means in spite of their obvious lexical appearance. A historical fact is worth remembering: when Chomsky proposed deep structure, it was only because at the time, a single layer of structural representation could not adequately account for the intrinsic relations among certain syntactic constructions, and not simply because deep structure was more abstract than surface structure. It is obviously not my intention to claim that WYSIWYG is always correct— VI and the applicative clearly argue against such a take on morphological data. Still, given a word with internal structure, anyone who wants to derive it syntactically should bear the burden to prove that the superficial form does *not* reflect its true nature. After all, to the extent that modern linguistics is an empirical field, research should be driven only by discovering how language actually works. Without this as the constant guideline, the intention to "explore the potential of a given theory" could even prove to be misleading.

Appendix

Resultative Constructions in Chinese

A.1 The Structural Properties of the V-*de* Construction

The biclausal nature of the Chinese V-*de* construction is discussed extensively in Huang 1988, 1989 and Li 1997a, 1999. It is clearly illustrated in (1).

(1) a. Song Jiang mei-you xinsi du   bing-shu.
Song Jiang not-have mood read strategy-book
'Song Jiang was in no mood to read strategy books.'

    b. Yan Qing chang-de [$_{CP}$ Song Jiang mei-you xinsi du
Yan Qing sing-DE   Song Jiang not-have mood read
bing-shu].
strategy-book
'Yan Qing's singing made Song Jiang not in the mood to read strategy books.'

(1b) is formed by directly embedding a full clause, (1a), into the post-V_c position. The structure adopted in (1b) can be further substantiated. First, since V_c *chang* 'sing' in (1b) is used as an unergative, the post-V_c NP *Song Jiang* must be the thematic subject of the embedded clause. Second, Chinese has a discontinuous focus marker *lian ... dou* 'even' that can target only preverbal phrases in a clause (see Zhu 1982).[1] The examples in (2) demonstrate how it works with NP arguments.

(2) a.   Lian Song Jiang dou   chang-le yishou xiaoqu.
LIAN Song Jiang DOU sing-asp a   folk.song
'Even Song Jiang sang a folk song.'

    b.   Wu Yong gaosu dajia   [lian   Song Jiang dou   zou-le].
Wu Yong tell   everyone LIAN Song Jiang DOU leave-asp
'Wu Yong told everyone that even Song Jiang left.'

    c. *Wu Yong gaosu lian   Song Jiang (dou) [dajia   (dou)
       Wu Yong tell   LIAN Song Jiang DOU everyone DOU
       zou-le].
       leave-asp
       Intended reading: 'Wu Yong told even Song Jiang that everyone
       left.'

Either the matrix subject or the embedded subject can be focused, as
shown in (2a–b), respectively. But there is no acceptable way to use *lian
... dou* with the postverbal matrix object in (2c).

    Meanwhile, the thematic subject of V_r in (1b) can be focused with *lian
... dou*, confirming that the NP is also the structural subject of the embedded clause.

(3) Yan Qing chang-de [lian   Song Jiang dou   mei-you xinsi du
    Yan Qing sing-DE   LIAN Song Jiang DOU not-have mood read
    neifeng xin].
    that   letter
    'Yan Qing's singing made even Song Jiang not in the mood to read
    that letter.'

When the embedded subject is coreferential with an argument of V_c, however, speakers strongly prefer that it take a phonologically empty form,
which Huang (1989) has analyzed as a pro controlled by a c-commanding
NP.

(4) a. Yan Qing$_i$ chang-de [pro$_i$ mei-you xinsi du   neifeng xin].
      Yan Qing sing-DE   not-have mood read that   letter
      'Yan Qing's singing made himself not in the mood to read that
      letter.'
    b. Li Kui xia-de   guan-bing$_i$ [pro$_i$ bu-gan
      Li Kui frighten-DE government-soldier   not-dare
      chu-zhan].
      come.out-fight
      'Li Kui scared the soldiers so much that they dared not come out
      to fight.'

    That the subject of V_c indeed c-commands into the V_r clause is proven
in Huang 1988. When a pronoun is used as the possessive of the subject
NP in Chinese, neither the object nor the embedded subject can be its
antecedent.

(5) a. *Tade$_i$ gege   bu xinren Wu Song$_i$.
      his   brother not trust   Wu Song
      'His$_i$ brother didn't trust Wu Song$_i$.'

   b. *Tade$_i$ gege   xiangxin Wu Song$_i$ neng shasi laohu.
      his   brother believe   Wu Song can   kill   tiger
      'His$_i$ brother believed that Wu Song$_i$ could kill a tiger.'

This contrasts with acceptable backward anaphora when a possessive pronoun is inside an adverbial clause. This usage is not preferred, but is detectably better than (5).

(6) Tade$_i$ gege   gang likai jia,   Wu Song$_i$ jiu   gen   saozi
     his   brother just   leave home Wu Song   then   with sister.in.law
     zhengchao-qilai.
     start.to.quarrel
     'As soon as his$_i$ brother left home, Wu Song$_i$ started quarreling with his sister-in-law.'

The generalization is that a pronoun X cannot be backward coindexed with an r-expression Y if X is immediately dominated by a phrase Z that c-commands Y.[2] Given this fact, the subject of V_c clearly c-commands everything in the V_r clause.

(7) *Tade$_i$ gege   chang-de [Wu Song$_i$ mei-you xinsi du   neifeng
     his   brother sing-DE   Wu Song   not-have mood read that
     xin].
     letter
     'His$_i$ brother's singing made Wu Song$_i$ not in the mood to read that letter.'

In other words, the clause containing V_c is structurally represented as the matrix clause and the V_r clause is embedded. See section 1.3.1 for evidence that the embedded V_r clause is in the complement position.

     In sum, the V-*de* construction has a biclausal structure with V_r serving as the predicate of an embedded clause in the complement position. If the embedded subject has a c-commanding antecedent in the construction, it takes the form of pro. Otherwise, it is an overt NP. For corresponding structural analyses of English resultative small clauses, see Hoekstra 1988, Carrier and Randall 1992, Levin and Rappaport Hovav 1995, and Li 1999.

A.2   More Differences between V-*de* and the Compound

In section 1.3.2, I showed how the compound and the V-*de* construction
behave differently with regard to postverbal adverbials. In this section,
I consider more differences between the two, all arguing against an
incorporation-style syntactic derivation of the compound and favoring a
lexicalist account. The comparisons are not meant to be exhaustive. See
Li 1999 for more.

A.2.1   Anaphor Binding

The following Chimwiini examples are repeated from (1) in chapter 1.

(8) a.   Mi m-phik-ish-ize   ru:hu-y-a cha:kuja.
         I   agr$_s$-cook-cause-asp myself   food
         'I made myself cook food.'
     b.   Mi ni-m-big-ish-ize   mwa:na ru:hu-y-e.
         I   agr$_s$-agr$_o$-hit-cause-asp child   himself
         'I made the child hit himself.'
     c.   *Mi ni-m-big-ish-ize   Ali ru:hu-y-a.
         I   agr$_s$-agr$_o$-hit-cause-asp Ali myself
         '*I made Ali hit myself.'

As mentioned there, the contrast between the grammatical (8a–b) and
the ungrammatical (8c) follows from the underlying biclausal structure
in (9), which forms the empirical base for the syntactic theory of word
formation.

(9) $[_{S_1}$ NP$_1$ cause $[_{S_2}$ NP$_2$ V NP$_3]]$

In theory, then, anaphor binding provides a way to test whether the
resultative compound and the V-*de* construction have similar syntactic
structures: because the V-*de* construction is biclausal, an anaphor serving
as the object of V$_r$ should be locally bound by the embedded subject and
reject coreference with the matrix subject when the two subjects are not
coindexed. If the compound has a comparable structure, then it should
not be possible to coindex the semantic argument of V$_r$ with the semantic
subject of V$_c$ in a similar context. Such minimal pairs can indeed be constructed. Before we examine them, however, a few words of warning are
in order. The nature of the test requires that V$_r$ be transitive. Since transitive verbs generally do not serve as the V$_r$ of the compound, examples
are not easy to come by. Furthermore, Chinese anaphors of the *them-*

selves-type do not always yield results as clean as their English counterparts because *ta-ziji* '3rd.sg-self', for instance, can be treated either as a
typical anaphor or as a pronoun *ta* '3rd.sg' plus an emphatic *ziji* 'self'.
With these difficulties in mind, consider the examples in (10) using the
reciprocal *gezi* 'each.self'.

(10) a. Fashi-men$_i$ (nian zhou) ba^3 zhongren$_j$ nian-wang-le
        priest-s   recite spell BA people   recite-forget-asp
        [gezi$_{i/j}$-de   chengnuo].
        each.own-'s promise
        'By reciting spells, the priests made people forget their own
        promises.'

    b. Fashi-men$_i$ (nian zhou) ba zhongren$_j$ nian-de   wangdiao-le
       priest-s   recite spell BA people   recite-DE forget-asp
       [gezi$_{*i/j}$-de   chengnuo].
       each.own-'s promise
       Same as (10a) without ambiguity

(11) a. ?Li Kui he   Lin Chong$_i$ ba tufei-men$_j$ da-li-le
        Li Kui and Lin Chong BA bandit-s   beat-leave-asp
        [gezi$_{i/j}$-de   jia].
        each.own-'s home
        'Li Kui and Lin Chong beat the bandits out of their own
        homes.'

    b. Li Kui he   Lin Chong$_i$ ba tufei-men$_j$ da-de   likai-le
       Li Kui and Lin Chong BA bandit-s   beat-DE leave-asp
       [gezi$_{??i/j}$-de   jia].
       each.own-'s home
       Same as (11a) without ambiguity

(12) a. Tamen$_i$ ba yahuan-men$_j$ gan-hui-le   [gezi$_{i/j}$-de
        they   BA maid-s   chase-return.to-asp each.own-'s
        wofang].
        bedroom
        'They chased the maids back to their own bedrooms.'

    b. Tamen$_i$ ba yahuan-men$_j$ gan-de   tao-hui-le
       they   BA maid-s   chase-DE run-return.to-asp
       [gezi$_{*i/j}$-de   wofang].
       each.own-'s bedroom
       Same as (12a) without ambiguity

For some informants, the contrast in certain pairs is not sharp enough. This is partially because the resultative compound generally deteriorates in acceptability when V_r is a transitive such as *wang* 'forget' and *li* 'leave'. Taking this into consideration, there is a consensus that the starred coindexation is harder to obtain.[4]

This contrast is not compatible with a typical syntactic derivation of the compound. Take (10) for example. Since the NP *zhongren* 'people' is the semantic subject of V_r *wang* 'forget' and is not thematically related to V_c *nian* 'recite', (10b) can be represented as follows:

(13) [$_{S_1}$ priests$_i$ (recite spell) BA people$_j$ recite-DE [$_{S_2}$ e$_j$ forget [their
own$_{*i/j}$ promise]]]

Whether the null subject *e* of S_2 is a pro controlled by the base-generated NP *people* after *ba*, or is the trace of that NP after overt raising, S_2 is the binding domain for the anaphor and the lack of ambiguity follows from Condition A.

Suppose that the compound in (10a) is syntactically derived by raising V_r to V_c in a similar context. The D-Structure representation of the sentence should be (14).

(14) [$_S$ priests (recite spell) BA people recite [$_\alpha$ e forget [their own
promise]]]

Minimally, α is a VP headed by *forget*. A phonologically null constituent *e* functions as the subject of α, given the by-now widely accepted analysis that the subject argument is generated inside VP (Fukui and Speas 1986; Kitagawa 1986; Kuroda 1988; Larson 1988; Koopman and Sportiche 1991; Bowers 1993; Huang 1993). For binding purposes, (14) is identical to (13), α being the binding domain for the anaphor. But this conclusion fails to explain why *gezi* 'each own' in (10a) can be optionally bound by the subject of V_c, namely, *fashi-men* 'priests'. On the other hand, if the compound enters syntax as a single lexical word, the contrast has a simple explanation.

(15) [$_S$ priests (recite spell) BA people recite-forget [their own promise]]

A single verb means a monoclausal structure, which is also the binding domain for the anaphor inside the object NP. It follows that both the subject *priests* and the other argument of the compound, *people*, are qualified as antecedent.

Note that V-raising in the syntactic derivation of the compound cannot alter the binding domain for the anaphor in (14). It has been proposed that when a head moves, its original domain is extended accordingly. Chomsky (1995) explores such an extension of a head's licensing domains, while Baker (1988) proposes the Government Transparency Corollary, which allows the head in the landing site of X^0-movement to govern into the domain of the moved head. Following this line of thought, it is conceivable that raising V_r to V_c turns the whole sentence into the binding domain for the deeply embedded anaphor in (14) and thereby explains the possible coindexation between the matrix subject and the anaphor. However, this is not desirable for the syntactic analysis because exactly the same logic would fail to account for the biclausal behavior of true VI in Baker 1988. For example, if raising the embedded V to the matrix verb *cause* in (9) could extend the binding domain of the embedded object to the whole sentence, the syntactic approach would be unable to explain the contrast in (1) of chapter 1. And this in turn would destroy one of the few crucial arguments in favor of the syntactic approach.

A.2.2 Transitive V_c and V_r

While most resultative compounds can find direct counterparts in V-*de* sentences, there is a remarkable exception: when a compound is formed with V_c and V_r that are both transitive and share the same subject and object, there is no acceptable V-*de* counterpart. Consider compounds first.

(16) a. Le He chang-hui-le   neishou xiaoqu.
      Le He sing-know-asp that   folk.song
      'Le He learned that song through singing it.'
  b. Wu Yong xia-ying-le   neipan qi.
      Wu Yong play-win-asp that   chess.game
      'Wu Yong played that chess game and won it as a result.'
  c. Li Kui ting-dong-le   Song Jiang de gushi.
      Li Kui listen.to-understand-asp Song Jiang 's story
      'Li Kui listened to Song Jiang's story and (finally) understood it.'

For V-*de* examples with the same (or similar) verbs and the same overt NP arguments, there are two logical alternative forms with respect to linear order:

(17) a. NP_1 V_c-*de* NP_2 V_r
  b. NP_1 V_c-*de* V_r NP

Examples of the (17a) type are clearly unacceptable. In each sentence in (18), either a multisyllabic V_r is provided as an option or an adverbial is added so as to exclude the factor of heaviness.

(18) a. *Le He chang-de neishou xiaoqu   hui-le/jizhu-le.
Le He sing-DE that   folk.song know-asp/remember-asp
Intended reading (cf. (16a)): 'Le He learned/remembered that song through singing it.'

b. *Wu Yong xia-de   neipan qi   (qingqingsongsongde)
Wu Yong play-DE that   chess.game easily
ying-le.
win-asp
Intended reading (cf. (16b)): 'Wu Yong played that chess game and (easily) won it as a result.'

c. *Li Kui ting-de   Song Jiang de gushi dong-le/mingbai-le.
Li Kui listen.to-DE Song Jiang 's story understand-asp
Intended reading (cf. (16c)): 'Li Kui listened to Song Jiang's story and understood it.'

In general, sentences of the (17b) type are less awkward, but still very marginal.

(19) a. ??Le He chang-de hui-le/jizhu-le   neishou xiaoqu.
Le He sing-DE know-asp/remember-asp that   folk.song
Intended reading: same as (18a)

b. ??Wu Yong xia-de   (qingqingsongsongde) ying-le neipan
Wu Yong play-DE easily   win-asp that
qi.
chess.game
Intended reading: same as (18b)

c. ??Li Kui ting-de   dong-le/mingbai-le Song Jiang de gushi.
Li Kui listen.to-DE understand-asp   Song Jiang 's story
Intended reading: same as (18c)

The ungrammatical and marginal natures of (18)–(19) are easy to explain in syntax. With both V_c and V_r interpreted transitively and an NP argument between V_c and V_r, there are only two possible structures for the examples in (18):

(20) a. NP_{1i} V_c-*de* NP_{2j} [$_{CP}$ Op_j pro_i V_r t_j]
  b. NP_{1i} V_c-*de* NP_{2j} [$_{CP}$ pro_i V_r e_j]

(20a) is excluded simply because there is no evidence that the embedded CP in the V-*de* construction contains a null operator Op. For one thing, this CP has the options of containing no gap (see (3)) or, more commonly, of having a gap in the subject position (as in most V-*de* examples so far). This contrasts with constructions with an established Op such as parasitic gaps and *tough*-movement, where the existence of the gap in the complement position is a definitive trait. Furthermore, recall from section 1.3.1 that Ā-movement takes place freely out of the embedded CP. An Op in the Spec of CP, however, would create the context for a *wh*-island.

As for (20b), there are at least two reasons for its unacceptability. First, the phonologically empty *e* in the embedded object position is neither a trace, for lack of any moved constituent, nor a pro/PRO, because empty pronominals are generally banned from complement positions. So *e* cannot be licensed in that position. Second, the embedded pro/PRO subject characteristically picks the closest c-commanding NP as its binder (see Huang's (1989) Generalized Control).

(21) a. Le He chang-de nashou xiaoqu$_i$ [pro$_i$ jiayuhuxiao].
    Le He sing-DE that   folk.song   known.to.everyone
    'Le He's singing of that folk song made it known to everyone.'

   b. *Le He$_i$ chang-de nashou xiaoqu [pro$_i$ kouganshezao].
    Le He sing-DE that   folk.song   mouth.dry
    Intended reading: 'Le He's singing of that folk song made his mouth dry.'

Whatever is the ultimate reason for this contrast, it applies straightforwardly to (20b) and prevents the embedded pro subject from being bound by the matrix subject across the matrix object. In sum, the sentences in (18) are unacceptable because there exists no good structural representation for them.

(19a–c) are easy to rule out too. They all have the structure in (22).

(22) NP$_{1i}$ V$_c$-*de* e$_j$ [$_{CP}$ pro$_i$ V$_r$ NP$_{2j}$]

As the matrix object *e* cannot be a pro/PRO or a trace (see the previous paragraph), it is sufficient to make (22) ungrammatical. However, there is a marginal alternative structural representation that can serve as a last resort to salvage these sentences. If an intransitive reading is forced on V$_c$, (22) is replaced by (23).

(23) NP$_{1i}$ V$_c$-*de* [pro$_i$ V$_r$ NP$_2$]

(23) is structurally well formed, with pro locally bound by NP_1. In fact, this is the same structure that (4) has. Because V_c is treated as an intransitive, the semantic relation between this verb and NP_2 is understood only through pragmatics, in the sense of Hoekstra's (1988) "shadow interpretation." Take (19a) for example. If Le He learned a folk song by singing, then it is only plausible that he sang that folk song. The grammatical structure (23) plus this shadow interpretation makes the examples in (19) understandable. Nonetheless, (23) is obtained by forcing intransitive interpretations on transitive verbs; the fact that such an "intransitive" verb actually has a transitive reading through shadow interpretation makes the structural status of V_c even more confusing. Hence, the sentences are perceived as highly marginal.

Presumably, the same marginal alternative is available to the V_r in (20b). But it cannot reduce the ungrammaticality of the construction because the pro subject is not locally controlled regardless of the transitivity of V_r.

To the extent that the syntactic analyses above explain the grammatical status of the V-*de* examples in (18)–(19), they already provide an argument against treating the corresponding well-formed compounds in (16) as syntactically derived. Otherwise, the contrast between the two groups of data would be unexpected. Furthermore, there already is a lexical account of all the resultative compounds in which (21) is expected. In Li 1990b, 1993, 1995, 1999, I have provided evidence that the very complex semantic/thematic properties of Chinese resultative compounds all follow from a simple lexical procedure of random θ-role coindexation. When two predicative morphemes X and Y combine to form a compound and neither one can be treated as a thematic argument of the other, the θ-roles of X can be randomly coindexed with those of Y and the coindexed pairs of θ-roles are randomly assigned to syntactic arguments. Whether a particular sentence resulting from such a random thematic operation is grammatical or not is solely determined by general linguistic principles such as the θ-Criterion, the Case Filter, and the morphological and aspectual structures of the compound. As a result, if V_c has the argument structure $\langle \theta_1 \langle \theta_2 \rangle\rangle$ and V_r has $\langle \theta_a \langle \theta_b \rangle\rangle$, one of the possibilities will be to coindex θ_1 with θ_a and θ_2 with θ_b. And this result happens to obey all the linguistic principles known in the P&P model. As a concrete example, *listen.to* is V_c in (16c) and *understand* is V_r. The two verbs have their subject θ-roles coindexed and assigned to the subject of the sentence, and their object θ-roles coindexed and assigned to the object of the sentence, yielding the actual reading of the sentence. (For details, see the works mentioned above.) For present purposes, it is sufficient to note that the facts in (16) are already accounted for in a lexical theory, further strengthening the earlier conclusion that the data should not be represented with decomposed syntactic structures comparable to the V-*de* construction.

A.2.3 The Number of Postverbal NPs

Like many languages, Chinese has verbs that can take two postverbal NP objects.

(24) a. Wu Yong gei-le   Dai Zong yi-feng xin.
        Wu Yong give-asp Dai Zong a-clitic letter
        'Wu Yong gave Dai Zong a letter.'
    b. Lin Chong dai-gei   furen yi-zhi   yu   shouzhuo.
        Lin Chong bring-give wife   a-clitic jade bracelet
        'Lin Chong brought his wife a jade bracelet.'

In this context, consider the following contrast between the V-*de* construction and the resultative compound:

(25) a. Li Kui xia-de   dianxiaoer   wang-le   yao shuo de hua.
        Li Kui scare-DE store.assistant forget-asp want say   DE words
        'Li Kui scared the store assistant so much that he forgot what he
        wanted to say.'
    b. Li Kui ba dianxiaoer   xia-de   wang-le   yao shuo de
        Li Kui BA store.assistant scare-DE forget-asp want say   DE
        hua.
        words
        Same as (25a)

(26) a. *Li Kui xia-wang-le   dianxiaoer   yao shuo de hua.
        Li Kui scare-forget-asp store.assistant want say   DE words
        Intended reading: same as (25a)
    b. (?)Li Kui ba dianxiaoer   xia-wang-le   yao shuo de
        Li Kui BA store.assistant scare-forget-asp want say   DE
        hua.
        words
        Same as (25a)

The example in (25a) is expected to be good given the biclausal account of the construction in section A.1. In (25b), *ba* is used to introduce the affected object, again a common option we have seen for resultatives. With the compounds in (26), however, the use of *ba* becomes obligatory.

The data above present a three-way contrast. First, (26a) differs from (25a) in acceptability. The two are comparable both because they are resultatives and because the compound has been suggested to have an underlying double-VP structure (see (66) of chapter 1). In such an analysis, raising V_r to V_c would result in (27), where *t* is the trace of *forget*.

(27) Li Kui scare-forget store-assistant [pro/PRO t what he want to say]

The question is why (26a) is not acceptable even though both *scare* and *forget* are transitive and therefore each capable of taking an NP object. (26a) also contrasts with the double-object verbs in (24), which obviously have no problem with two postverbal NPs.

The explanation is simple if the resultative compound is formed lexically rather than through a structure like (27). Suppose that double-object verbs such as *gei* 'give' in Chinese assign one accusative Case and one inherent Case (say, dative), as is commonly found in other languages. The grammaticality of (24) follows directly. When two transitive verbs are put together to form a compound, however, neither one has an inherent Case; so the compound cannot obtain an inherent Case from anywhere. Meanwhile, because the lexically formed compound is treated as a single verb in syntax, the only Case available is the structural accusative Case. Hence the ungrammaticality of (26a). The structure can be salvaged with an extra Case assigner, and there is ample evidence (see Li 1990b) that *ba* has this function provided that the NP it helps introduce also meets its semantic requirement. Note that the double-object verb in (24b) is also a compound. What sets it apart from the one in (26) is that its second morpheme is *gei* 'give', which itself has an inherent Case so that the compound can "inherit" it.

A.3   VP or "Less Than" VP?

The Ewe examples in (28) (from Collins 1997, 461) illustrate the so-called serial verb construction (SVC), characterized as multiple verbs with a single tense marker (if there is any) and without overt conjunctives.

(28) a. Me nya ɖevi-ɛ dzo.
         I   chase child-def leave
         'I chased the child away.'

b. Wo ḍa   fufu ḍu.
   they cook fufu eat
   'They cooked fufu and ate it.'

For reasons largely irrelevant to this discussion, scholars generally treat the SVC as a monoclausal structure in which one of the verbs is the matrix verb while the other heads an embedded phrase. Under this general treatment, one particular idea has been repeatedly implemented albeit with different technical mechanisms: the embedded phrase is not a full VP but a projection less than VP. In Baker 1989, it is argued to be V′; in Collins 1997, it is the lower VP in the Larson-style double-VP structure.

Given that a subset of SVCs express the resultative meaning and resultative compounds are also composed of two verbal morphemes, Nishiyama (1998) extends Collins's analysis of SVCs to resultatives. His theory is primarily built on Japanese and extended to Chinese as "a case study" (p. 204). In this section, only Chinese resultative compounds are compared with SVCs. The lower-VP analysis is assumed for convenience. The choice has no effect on the content of this section, but it may have other implications.[5]

A.3.1 The Lower-VP Analysis of Resultative Compounds

Nishiyama applies Collins's structural representation of the Ewe SVC in (28a) to Chinese resultative compounds like the one in (29a). The relevant part of the tree structure is given in (29b). Following Collins and Thráinsson (1996), Nishiyama uses TrP for the upper VP. While the upper V head is usually considered to be an empty position, Tr assigns an external θ-role to the subject if it is active; an inactive Tr is associated with unaccusative verbs and is thematically inert. Nishiyama also marks the covert argument of V_r as PRO rather than pro, a difference from Collins 1997 that is not significant here.

(29) a. Li Kui gan-zou-le   guan-bing.
        Li Kui chase-leave-asp government-soldier
        'Li Kui chased the government soldiers away.'

b.

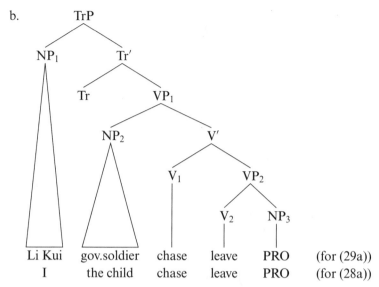

Li Kui	gov.soldier	chase	leave	PRO	(for (29a))
I	the child	chase	leave	PRO	(for (28a))

When used independently, *leave* would also have its own TrP, headed by an inactive Tr to reflect the verb's unaccusativity. PRO is controlled by the closest c-commanding NP, that is, the object of the matrix verb *chase* marked as NP_2 in the tree. The resultative compound in (29a) is formed by raising V_2 to V_1. The compound further raises to Tr to yield the right word order. Alternatively, keeping V_2 in situ and raising V_1 alone to Tr produces the Ewe SVC in (28a).

In addition to providing a unified account of resultative constructions in Chinese and Ewe, this analysis may seem to have the potential to handle some of the differences between the compound and the V-*de* construction investigated in section A.2 simply because the embedded verbal projection is "incomplete." Take (10a), for example, repeated here.

(30) Fashi-men (nian zhou) ba zhongren$_j$ nian-wang-le   gezi$_{i/j}$-de
     priest-s   recite spell BA people   recite-forget-asp each.own-'s
     chengnuo.
     promise
     'By reciting spells, the priests made people forget their own
     promises.'

Since V_r presumably does not have its own Tr in such a structure, it is possible to define TrP as the binding domain for anaphors. As a result, (30) has only one binding domain, the matrix TrP, and the reciprocal *gezi* 'each own' is expected to be optionally bound by either the matrix object or the matrix subject. In contrast, the corresponding V-*de* example in (10b) has an embedded clause with a separate TrP for V_r, forcing the reciprocal to be bound in it.

A.3.2 Problems with the Lower-VP Analysis

As attractive as it appears, the lower-VP analysis is not a viable syntactic account for the resultative compound. For one thing, there is really no way to avoid representing the projection of V_r *wang* 'forget' in (30) as anything less than TrP. This is so because *forget* has its own thematic subject *zhongren* 'people', which bears no thematic relation to V_c *nian* 'recite' at all. As a result, *people* can only be represented as an argument of V_r. If the maximal projection of *forget* contains both the thematic subject and the thematic object, however, that projection should be the binding domain by anyone's definition for the anaphor *gezi* 'each own' in the object NP, wrongly predicting *each own* in (30) to exhibit biclausal behavior.[6]

Binding is not the only place where the embedded TrP incurs problems with the lower-VP theory of resultative compounds. Recall from section 1.3.2 that resultative compounds are not compatible with postverbal duration phrases. The example in (31) illustrates the same restriction with an unergative V_r.

(31) Yan Qing (chang xiaoqur) ba Li Kui chang-ku-le (*liangge
     Yan Qing sing   folk.song BA Li Kui sing-cry-asp   two
     shichen).
     hour
     'Yan Qing's singing of folk songs made Li Kui cry (for two hours).'

Since V_c *chang* 'sing' has no thematic relation with *Li Kui*, the latter can only be the Agent argument of the V_r *ku* 'cry', making the embedded TrP necessary. Structurally, then, (31) would be practically indistinguishable from the regular causative sentence in (32).

(32) Yan Qing de xiaoqur rang Li Kui ku-le   liangge shichen.
     Yan Qing DE folk.song make Li Kui cry-asp two   hour
     'Yan Qing's folk songs made Li Kui cry for two hours.'

Both (31) and (32) would have a matrix verb and an embedded (and fully projected) TrP in the complement position. The fact that a duration phrase is well formed in the embedded TrP of (32) is natural—after all, a TrP represents a complete (type of) event. But why would the duration phrase in (31) be disallowed if it had the same syntactic structure (and otherwise identical semantics)?

Another insurmountable problem with the lower-VP analysis has to do with object sharing. All works on SVCs in the P&P model are based on a well-established fact: that SVCs are characteristic of internal argument sharing (see, e.g., Foley and Olson 1985; Déchaine 1986; Baker 1989; Collins 1997). In (28a), the object of the matrix verb *chase* is also understood as the single (internal) argument of the embedded unaccusative verb *leave*. In (28b), both *cook* and *eat* take *fufu* as the understood object. For Collins's Ewe examples, the structure in (29b) is motivated precisely by this fact, as the Minimal Distance Principle guarantees the PRO/pro argument of *leave* to be bound only by the matrix object and never by the subject.

But Chinese resultative compounds are known to have no respect for internal argument sharing (see Li 1999). (30) and (32) are cases where V_c and V_r share no argument at all. (33a–b) illustrate another type of failure to share objects.

(33) a. Yan Qing chang-fan-le   xiaoqur, you jiezhe   lian
       Yan Qing sing-fed.up-asp folk.song then continue practice
       wushu.
       martial.arts
       'After Yan Qing got fed up from singing folk songs, he resumed
       practicing martial arts.'
    b. Lu Zhishen da-lei-le   nage popi, jiu   huijia-le.
       Lu Zhishen beat-tired-asp that rascal then go.home-asp
       'Once Lu Zhishen got exhausted from beating that rascal, he
       went home.'

In these examples, V_c is transitive and V_r is intransitive (unaccusative or stative). But unlike what happens in most examples seen so far, V_r is predicated of the subject. In fact, it is precisely this ability of V_r to be thematically linked to the subject that underlies the well-documented ambiguity of compounds like *qi-lei* 'ride-tired'.

(34) Jia qi-lei   yi.
     A ride-tired B
     a. 'A rode B and A got tired as a result.'
     b. 'A rode B and B got tired as a result.'

See Li 1990b, 1995 for this well-known ambiguity and for the references cited therein.

The data in (33)–(34) pose a straightforward problem for the structure in (29b). If (29b) is the correct structure for Ewe SVCs with internal argument sharing, the embedded PRO must obey the Minimal Distance Principle and be bound by the object. Then the structure cannot be used to account for the thematic relation between the subject and V_r in (33)–(34). On the other hand, if PRO is allowed to choose between the matrix subject and object as its antecedent, the Chinese data are explained at the cost of failing to accommodate one of the defining characteristics of SVCs: internal argument sharing. Either way, the lower-VP structure fails to provide a uniform account of all the data in question. A quick fix would be to postulate a difference between Chinese and Ewe in the way antecedents for PRO/pro are identified. But this is implausible, because Chinese and languages with SVCs clearly belong to the same type for the purpose of licensing empty pronominal arguments, none of them having the rich inflectional morphology seen in Romance (Rizzi 1982, 1986).

It may also seem that the lower-VP analysis can be maintained if (33)–(34) are assigned a different structure than (29b) to avoid obligatory sharing of internal arguments. But this suggestion proves invalid as well. As long as V_c heads the matrix VP, the only way for the PRO argument of V_r to be controlled by the matrix subject without violating the Minimal Distance Principle is for V_r's projection to be adjoined higher than the matrix object. The tree in (35) illustrates the needed structure for (33a), with V_1 and V_2 replaced by V_c and V_r, respectively.

(35)

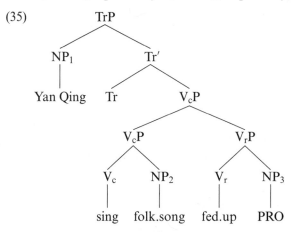

Whether V_rP actually adjoins to V_cP or to Tr' is not significant here, as long as NP_3 is not c-commanded by the matrix object NP_2.

In (35), V_r *fed.up* can be predicated of the subject NP_1 through the binding of PRO, but new problems arise. First, V_r and V_c can no longer move together to take the form of a compound. The empirical validity of head movement rests on the claim that a head can raise only out of a complement phrase and never out of an adjunct. This is the very core of Travis's (1984) Head Movement Constraint and Baker's (1988) theory of incorporation. Since V_rP is an adjunct, moving V_r to V_c is forbidden as a matter of principle. Treating V_cP as an adjunct to V_rP (as Nishiyama (1998) actually does) is not viable for the same reason. The second problem with (35) or any similar structure is that, to the best of my knowledge, it would simply be wrong to treat V_rP as anything other than the complement of V_c. That the result-denoting clause is in the complement position of the V-*de* construction was established in chapter 1 as well as in Huang 1988 and Li 1997a. Levin and Rappaport (1995) provide evidence that English resultatives consist of a verb taking a complement XP. Also see Rizzi 1990 for the structural distinctions between English resultative and depictive small clauses. In fact, if it were not for the consensus that the result phrase is in the complement position in a resultative construction, the head movement analysis of resultative compounds would not be entertainable in the first place.

The examples in (36) supply further evidence that any effort to subsume Chinese resultative compounds under a syntactic treatment of SVCs is misguided.

(36) a. Dianxiaoer   lei-ku-le.
         store.assistant tired-weep-asp
         'The store assistant was so tired he wept.'
     b. Dianxiaoer   ku-lei-le.
         store.assistant weep-tired-asp
         'The store assistant was tired from weeping.'
     c. Dianxiaoer   (chang-ger) chang-ku-le.
         store.assistant sing-song sing-weep-asp
         'The store assistant wept as a result of his singing.'
     d. Dianxiaoer   lei-si-le.
         store.assistant tired-die-asp
         'The store assistant died of exhaustion.'

In all these examples, the causal relation between V_c and V_r is unequivocal. The four examples exhaust all the combinations of unergative and unaccusative/stative verbs. Only (36d) is composed of two unaccuative/

stative verbs and therefore conforms to internal argument sharing; all others involve the sharing of at least one external argument. Given that these examples have no known counterpart in SVCs, it is only reasonable to conclude that there must be fundamental differences between SVCs and the resultative compounds in Chinese. Meanwhile, this conclusion is perfectly compatible with the point made throughout chapter 1 and this appendix: the resultative compounds are formed in the lexicon. As such, they are easily distinguished from SVCs, which clearly are syntactically formed.[7]

A.3.3   Against Phonologically Forming Resultative Compounds

Most evidence against representing the resultative compound as an underlyingly multiple-VP construction also argues against treating it as a PF word formed "postsyntactically" through linear adjacency. This is so simply because such a process presumes a syntactic structure in which each of the two verb morphemes heads its own VP, which has been shown to be untenable. Another problem arises when the object of the compound bears a thematic relation only to V_c. In such cases (see (33)), the matrix object is located linearly between V_c and V_r, effectively blocking any post-syntactic merger based on adjacency.

Chapter 2

Adjective Incorporation

In chapter 1, I demonstrated how the LH and the MSMH collaborate to guarantee that VI has biclausal properties. I highlighted the biclausal nature of VI by comparing Arabic verbal causatives and deadjectival causatives (see (10)–(11) in section 1.1.1). The point was that the difference in anaphor binding between these two types of morphological causatives cannot be explained in a lexicalist theory of word formation based on operations on argument structures, and that an underlying multiple-VP structure, accompanied by some version of head movement, is needed.

But the coin has another side: if a complex underlying structure explains the binding patterns of verbal causatives, why do deadjectival causatives in Arabic behave like monoclausal structures with respect to binding? The question is answered in this chapter. I show that "adjective incorporation" (hereafter AI) is a case where word formation through syntactic head movement based on the UTAH fails but the lexicalist approach under the LH and "enriched" by the MSMH succeeds.

2.1 Deadjectival Causatives in Arabic and Hebrew and the Morphology-Syntax Mapping Hypothesis

2.1.1 More Facts

The Arabic examples in (1) confirm what we saw in chapter 1: in the periphrastic causative construction with adjectival embedded predicates, only the complement phrase of the matrix causative verb is the binding domain for an anaphor it contains.

(1) a. Jaʕala   ʕalii-un l-bint-a   maɣmuumat-an min
       made-agr Ali-nom the-girl-acc upset-acc   from
       nafsi-ha/*nafsi-h.
       self-her/self-him
       'Ali made the girl upset about herself/*himself.'

b. Jaʕala   ʕalii$_j$-un ḥasan$_i$-an   masruur-an min   nafsi-h$_{.j/i}$.
made-agr Ali-nom Hassan-acc happy-acc   from self-him
'Ali made Hassan happy about himself.'

c. Jaʕala-t l-ʔumm-u   l-walad-a   mahmuum-an min
made-agr the-mother-nom the-boy-acc sad-acc   from
nafsi-h/*nafsi-ha.
self-him/self-her
'The mother made the boy sad about himself/*herself.'

d. Jaʕala   l-ʔustuaað$_j$-u   l-walad$_i$-a   faxuur-an bi-nafsi-h$_{.j/i}$.
made-agr the-teacher-nom the-boy-acc proud-acc with-self-him
'The teacher made the boy proud of himself.'

The morphological causatives based on the same adjectives, as we know
by now, have the whole sentence as their binding domain.

(2) a. yamm-a   ʕalii-un l-bint-a   min nafsi-h.
made.upset-agr Ali-nom the-girl-acc from self-him
'Ali made the girl upset about him.'

b. Sarr-a   ʕalii$_i$-un ḥasan-an   min nafsi-h$_i$.
made.happy-agr Ali-nom Hassan-acc from self-him
'Ali made Hassan happy about him.'

c. ʔahamm-at l-ʔumm-u   l-walad-a   min nafsi-ha.
made.sad-agr the-mother-nom the-boy-acc from self-her
'The mother made the boy sad about her.'

It should be noted that the etymological association of deadjectival
causatives with stand-alone adjectives is not productive. For instance,
there is no causative form for the adjective *faxuuran* 'proud' in (1d). But
lexicalization does not explain either why the difference in binding *has* to
coincide with the verb-adjective distinction or why it is the deadjectival
causative that is lexicalized and not the other way around. See section
1.1.1 for relevant discussion.

The contrast between verbal and deadjectival causatives is also found
in Modern Hebrew.

(3) a. Dan$_i$ xibev   'et Moshe al 'acmo$_i$.
Dan made.fond acc Moshe P himself
'Dan made Moshe fond of him.'

b. Ha-poshea'$_i$ hifxid   'et 'ish ha-asakim   me-'acmo$_i$.
the-criminal made.afraid acc the-businessman of-himself
'The criminal made the businessman afraid of him.'

   c. Hem$_i$ hisnii   'et Moshe al 'acmam$_i$.
       they   made.hateful acc Moshe P themselves
       'They made Moshe full of hate toward them.'

(4) a. Hem$_j$ hoshivue 'et ha-yeladimi$_i$ ze   al-yad ze$_{*?j/i}$.
      they made.sit acc the-children each next-to other
      'They made the children sit next to each other.'

   b. *Ha-morim hipilu   'et ha-studentim al 'acmam.
       the-teachers made.fall acc the-boys   P themselves
       'The teachers made the boys fall on themselves.'

   c. Ha-morim$_i$ hixtivu   la-yeladim$_j$ sipur al   'acmam$_{*i/j}$.
       the-teachers made.write to-the.boys a.story about themselves
       'The teachers made the boys write a story about themselves.'

In each of the deadjectival sentences in (3), the anaphor is interpreted as an argument of the adjective root but as bound by the causer subject. When the root is verbal, however, the anaphor associated with the root can only pick the thematic subject of the root as binder, as shown in (4). The unacceptability of (4b) is particularly interesting. Local binding by *hastudentim* 'the boys' is unacceptable for the pragmatic reason that it is difficult to imagine people falling on themselves. But even when this reading is not available, the informant still disliked taking the causer subject *hamorim* 'the teachers' as the antecedent for the anaphor. In the absence of pragmatic interference (as in (4a,c)), local binding is considered the only choice.[1] This contrasts with the deadjectival causatives in (3), where the informant readily accepted the binding relation between the causer subjects and the anaphors.

A different kind of argument is provided in Borer 1991 for the monoclausal nature of deadjectival causatives. Borer observes that an adjective's modifiers become unacceptable when the adjective is causativized (pp. 130–131).

(5) a. Ha-simla hayta lebana (kmo gir   /yoter me-gir).
      the-dress was white as   chalk/more than-chalk

   b. Ha-xatula hayta Smena (kmo xazir/yoter me-xazir).
      the-cat   was fat   as   pig /more than-pig

(6) a. Ha-kbisa hilbina   'et ha-simla (*kmo gir   /*yoter me-gir).
      the-wash whitened acc the-dress   as   chalk/more than-chalk

   b. Ha-zriqa hiSmina 'et ha-xatula (*kmo xazir/*yoter me-xazir).
      the-shot fattened acc the-cat   as   pig /more than-pig

The contrast between (5) and (6) can be explained if the internal structure of the deadjectival causatives is opaque to syntax. Because of this opacity, an adjective's modifiers cannot access the adjectival root in (6), making the examples ungrammatical. Borer provides a similar argument for treating English deadjectival causative verbs (e.g., *whiten* and *popularize*; pp. 128–129) in the same way.[2]

2.1.2   The Explanation under the Morphology-Syntax Mapping Hypothesis

The thematic relation between the causative morpheme and the adjectival root is the same for the periphrastic causatives in (1) and the morphological ones in (2), both having (7) as their syntactic representation according to the UTAH.

(7)

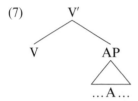

The difference lies, presumably, only in keeping A in situ or raising it to V. But then it is predicted, incorrectly, that a nonsubject anaphor inside AP should take the phrase as its binding domain in both (1) and (2).

The MSMH-based theory, on the other hand, predicts the difference. The periphrastic causatives in (1) have (7) overtly represented and therefore demonstrate the typical biclausal binding property as expected. The morphological causatives, however, are lexically formed given the LH. The thematic relation between the two morphemes would indeed be mapped to (7) if the structure proved legitimate in syntax. Now causativizing an adjectival root produces a verb, which in turn means that the word (e.g., *sarr* 'made happy' in (2b)) cannot be inserted under A. But inserting it under V also leads to an ungrammatical derivation, with UG prohibiting both lowering from V to A and generating the A-position that cannot be fully interpreted if the causative complex never lands in it. That is, the same mechanism ruling out syntactic PI also prevents AI from mapping to (7). It follows that the deadjectival causative can only enter syntax as an indecomposable lexical item and project to a single VP, thereby explaining why the anaphor semantically associated with the adjectival root can pick the causer subject as binder. This result contrasts with verbal causatives (i.e., VI) in chapter 1, for which there is a UG-sanctioned double-VP representation.

To conclude, in their syntactic behaviors, Semitic morphological causatives divide according to the categories of the lexical base. The division is not predicted by the syntactic theory of incorporation based on the UTAH, but it is predicted by the theory of the morphology-syntax interface consisting of the LH and the MSMH.

2.2 Hebrew Inchoatives

Though Borer (1991) treats the Hebrew deadjectival causative construction as monoclausal, she argues that deadjectival inchoative verbs alternate between behaving like indecomposable verbs and behaving like multiphrasal structures. In this section, I examine the effect of Borer's theory on the one proposed here and vice versa.

2.2.1 Two Types of Deadjectival Inchoatives
The crucial data for this claim (from Borer 1991, 131) are as follows:[3]

(8) a. Ha-simla hilbina   kmo gir   /yoter me-gir.
       the-dress whitened as   chalk/more than-chalk
    b. Ha-xatula hiSmina kmo xazir/yoter me-xazir.
       the-cat   fattened as   pig /more than-pig

The verbs in (8) have the same forms as those in (6), the differences between the examples being that here the verbs are used as inchoatives and, more importantly, that the modifiers unacceptable in (6) become acceptable in (8). Since the inchoative verbs are also composed of an adjectival root and a verbal morpheme, what is shown in (8) would be unexpected if the adjectival root were as opaque to syntax as it is in the deadjectival causatives.

The data in (9) (from Borer 1991, 149) further complicate the problem.

(9) a. Ha-batim hiSxiru   lahem ba-'abaq.
       the-houses blackened to.them in-the-dust
    b. ..., ha-bayit hiSxir   li.
          the-house blackened to.me
       '..., my house blackened.'

After examining the differences between Hebrew reflexive datives and possessive datives, Borer and Grodzinsky (1987) conclude that the former may only be coindexed with the external argument of a predicate whereas the latter must be associated with a VP-internal constituent. Given this conclusion, (9a) suggests that *ha-batim* 'the houses', the single argument of the inchoative verb *hiSxiru* 'blackened', is an external argument because it is coindexed with the reflexive dative *lahem* 'to them'. Meanwhile, (9b) shows the opposite: *ha-bayit* 'the house', the argument of the same inchoative verb, is associated with the possessive dative *li* 'to me' and therefore is the internal argument of the verb. Assuming the dative-based tests to be reliable, Borer (1991) concludes that (9) does not present a contradiction. Instead, it indicates what it appears to: that there are two separate syntactic representations of inchoatives, one with an internal argument and the other with the external argument. Furthermore, this distinction correlates with the use of modifiers (examples from Borer 1991, 150).

(10) a. *Ha-bayit hiSxir   lo   haki lehapli.
          the-house blackened to.it most wondrously
     b. Ha-bayit hiSxir   li   haki lehapli.
          the-house blackened to.me most wondrously

The inchoative verb can be modified only when its argument is internal, as required by the possessive dative *li* in (10b). If the argument is external, modification is prohibited (10a).

On the basis of these facts, Borer suggests that all the data on Hebrew deadjectival causatives and inchoatives are explained by the theory of parallel morphology, in which these words have the option of being derived either in the lexicon or in the syntax.

Starting with the causative, if it is formed lexically, it enters syntax as a single lexical item and forms a monoclausal structure. Lexical opacity prevents the modifiers from accessing the adjectival root, yielding the ungrammatical (6a–b). If the causative is formed in the syntax, head movement in the style of Baker's incorporation takes place to join the two morphemes, generating the tree in (11) in which V is the causative morpheme.

(11)

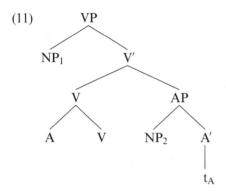

By hypothesis, the index of A percolates to V (see Lieber 1980; Di Sciullo and Williams 1987). If Spec-head agreement is obligatory and there is only one index for each constituent (Chomsky 1986b), this process of AI creates two coindexed chains, both carrying the same index: [V, t_A] and [NP$_1$, NP$_2$]. The first chain is a typical well-formed head chain; but the second is not, because it is an A-chain with two θ-positions. Hence, (11) is ungrammatical and a deadjectival causative can never be derived syntactically. As there is no adjective represented anywhere in syntax, the ungrammaticality of (6) follows.

The syntactic derivation for the inchoative is shown in (12).

(12)

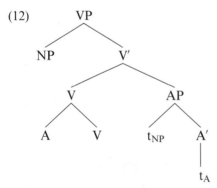

This structure differs from (11) only in that V is a raising verb approximately meaning 'to become'. As in (11), raising A to V indirectly creates a chain involving the Spec positions of VP and AP. However, this chain is legitimate because it contains only one θ-position, the one marked by t_{NP}. Since A is syntactically represented and no longer opaque, any modifier of A is automatically permitted, accounting for (8) and (10b). The possessive dative *li* 'to me' in (9b) and (10b) is associated with the NP argument of the inchoative because the latter is structurally inside VP and thus counts as VP-internal.

Alternatively, the inchoative verb can be formed lexically. The adjectival root is then opaque in syntax like its counterpart in the causative. Assuming that the single argument of the adjectival root is the external argument, Borer suggests that this external argument of A becomes the external argument of the whole verb because the inchoative morpheme, being a raising verb, has no external argument of its own (see Di Sciullo and Williams's (1987) discussion of relative heads). It follows that the reflexive dative *lahem* 'to them' can be coindexed with the argument in (9a). The ungrammatical (10a) results from a conflict of requirements: the reflexive dative *lo* 'to it' demands that the inchoative be lexically formed with an external argument, whereas the modifier forces the verb to be syntactically derived with a VP-internal argument. Thus, all the data are accounted for.

If this analysis were tenable, it would immediately pose a fatal problem for the theory articulated here because the MSMH prevents the inchoative verb from being mapped to a multiphrasal structure like (12) for the same reason that a structure like (11) is not possible for the deadjectival causative. In both cases, the categorial difference between the adjectival root and the causative/inchoative verb morpheme determines that the thematic relation between them cannot be fully expanded in syntax. While Borer's theory and mine agree on the monoclausal nature of the causative and "half of" the inchoative, an irreconcilable difference arises regarding the other half of the inchoative.

2.2.2 Syntactic Distinction versus Aspectual Distinction

Borer's analysis crucially relies on the legitimacy of the A-chain formed through adjective raising in (11)–(12), which in turn depends on the obligatory Spec-head agreement inside VP and AP. By this logic, though, VI as a syntactic process should never exist either because it would involve exactly the same structural scenario. Consider (13).

(13)

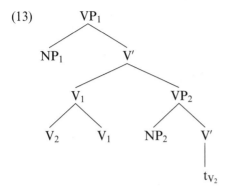

Unless V_2 is unaccusative, NP_1 and NP_2 are each necessarily the Spec of their own VPs. Since NP_1 and NP_2 would form a coindexed chain with two θ-roles, (13) would be ruled out and all verbal causative m-complexes would have to be formed lexically (which in itself is consistent with my theory) and project to a single VP just like deadjectival causatives. But we have seen in language after language that verbal causatives—namely, instances of VI—need structures like (13) and, more importantly for present purposes, that verbal causatives do not behave like deadjectival causatives (see the Arabic and Hebrew causatives in sections 1.1.1 and 2.1.1).

Needless to say, the correct account of the Hebrew data depends on a good understanding of how comparative modifiers work in syntax, and in this respect our understanding is far from sufficient. Nonetheless, plausible analyses can be thought of that do not rest on a structure like (12) to explain the differences inside inchoatives and between inchoatives and deadjectival causatives. In the rest of this section, I briefly lay out one such analysis that draws on an important insight in Borer's work.

Consider an inchoative verb like *hiSxiru* 'blacken'. If Borer is correct that (10a) and (10b) contain two different forms of the verb, there is no logical necessity that the difference must be between a lexically derived verb and a syntactically formed one. It could be due to the presence of two different inchoative morphemes—after all, the same phonological form of the morpheme can also be a causative. Consider the following English examples:

(14) a. The house became black.
     b. The house turned black.

(15) a. ?What the house did was become black.
     b. What the house did was turn black.

(16) a.   The house became black because Sam painted it.
    b.   ??The house turned black because Sam painted it.

Both sentences in (14) have the inchoative interpretation. The examples in (15) are usually employed to determine the presence of a Doer/Agent argument (Gruber 1965; Jackendoff 1972). Note that Doer/Agent does not obligatorily imply willfulness (Falk 1985; Dowty 1991). Probably Jackendoff's (1990) term *Actor* is more appropriate here. But for the purpose of this discussion, I will simply use *Agent*. By this test, *the house* qualifies as an Agent when the verb is *turn* but is less likely to be one when the verb is *become*. The contrast in (16) is even sharper. The incompatibility of *turn* with the overtly expressed external cause highlights a kind of intrinsic self-initiation in the semantics of the verb that is missing (or optionally absent) in *become*.

That *the house* in the (a) examples of (14)–(16) is not the Agent is expected. *Become* being a raising verb, the subject NP originates inside the embedded AP and therefore cannot be an Agent. As syntactic movement does not change the thematic content of an argument, *the house* remains a non-Agent throughout the syntactic derivation. But the same logic suggests that *turn* is not a raising verb (or at least does not *have to be* a raising verb). The simplest possibility is that *the house* in (14b) and (15b) is the Agent argument of *turn* and controls the PRO subject of *black*.[4]

My point here is not how to analyze *become* and *turn* accurately, nor do I intend to tackle the thorny task of sorting out θ-roles. Rather, the contrast between the two verbs suggests that the notion of inchoativity may have at least two subtly different variants. One is the "true" inchoative, in which an event happens to the participant and the participant has no control over the event. Linguistically, this variant is embodied by a raising verb like *become*. The other variant holds the participant to be somehow responsible for the event, maybe in the form of an initiator or (unwillful) actor. Linguistically, this variant is embodied by a control verb like *turn* that has its own thematic subject.

Now suppose that the Hebrew deadjectival verb *hiSxiru* 'blacken' really is three verbs: an adjective root (A) plus the causative morpheme, A plus the "control" inchoative morpheme, and A plus the "raising" inchoative morpheme. The lexical semantic representations in (17) will help illustrate the paradigm here, though I make no effort to achieve accuracy.

(17) a. Raising inchoative   [x BECOME black]
     b. Control inchoative   [x ACT [x BECOME black]]
     c. Causative   [x CAUSE [y BECOME black]]

Given the MSMH, none of these verbs can be mapped to a [V AP] structure like (11) or (12), so they all must be represented as single verbs with
single VP projections. For the causative and the control inchoative, the
subject is the external argument of the verb morpheme and therefore of
the whole verb. This immediately explains why it can be coindexed with
the reflexive dative (see (9a)). For the raising inchoative, the verb morpheme has no external θ-role; the adjectival root does not have an Agent
θ-role either. When they form a lexical verb, the most natural result
(contra Borer's claim) is for the verb's argument structure to contain no
external θ-role. But if the verb has only an internal θ-role in its argument
structure, it behaves like an unaccusative and its NP argument can only
be associated with the possessive dative (see (9b)).

The remaining question is why only the raising inchoative permits
comparative modifiers.[5] I share Borer's intuition that the grammaticality
of the modifiers hinges on the internal structure of the predicates in the
examples under investigation. But the structure does not have to be syntactic. Following Davidson (1967), Higginbotham (1985) proposes that at
the semantic level, the modifier of a predicate P operates on P's event
position. Suppose that an event, in the most general sense of the term, has
the maximal structure articulated in Grimshaw 1990, 40.

(18)   Event

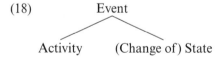

     Activity   (Change of) State

An event with only the Activity part is linguistically represented by an
action verb; an event with only the (Change of) State part is embodied by
a stative or unaccusative verb; when an event consists of both parts, the
verb is of the accomplishment/achievement type (see Vendler 1967 and
Dowty 1979 for the aspectual classification of predicates). If a modifier M
operates on the event denoted by a predicate P, it is only natural that the
relationship between M and P is sensitive to the event type.

That the modifiers in (6) are incompatible with deadjectival causatives
is expected. Since the derived verb in such examples is indecomposable
in syntax, as both Borer and I believe, it must be treated as a single verb
denoting a single event. The State part of the event is thus opaque to the

modifier phrase, which can only "see" the whole event. Provided that the modifiers in (6a–b) are exclusively about measuring the degrees of a state, the unacceptability of the examples is attributed to semantic incompatibility between the type of the event a deadjectival causativized verb describes and the type of event those modifiers can operate on. In plain words, phrases like *yoter me-gir* 'more than chalk' modify the state of being white, not the causal event of making ... white.

In contrast, the adjectival root alone represents a state, and the deadjectival "raising" inchoative, which I suggested is unaccusative, is about a change of state. There is a simple way to understand why these two apparently different types of subevents are placed under the same branch in (18). Strictly speaking, the right branch of the structure is a state, period. But the "history" of the state may vary. If a state exists throughout a given event, the predicate describing it is stative. If a state spans only part of the event, it is said to be a change of state. A change of state may be regarded as taking place by itself or as the consequence of another event. The former option is represented linguistically by inchoatives, the latter by stereotypical causatives. From this point of view, the event structure of both stative and inchoative predicates can be represented as (19).

(19) Event
       |
      State

The only difference lies in whether the state represented in the daughter node has the same time span as the event represented in the parent node. This difference is clearly reflected through different lexical items and possibly their syntactic behaviors,[6] and it may be explicitly represented in a more elaborate event or aspectual structure (cf. Smith 1991; Pustejovsky 1995). But the fact remains that neither statives nor unaccusatives have the Activity branch in their event structures.

Since the State *is* the Event in (19), it is no longer opaque to the syntactic modifiers of the predicate. When the modifiers in (8) operate on the event of the raising inchoative verb, they *are* operating on the state. In other words, the type of event denoted by the inchoative *hilbina* 'whiten' matches the type of event that *yoter me-gir* 'more than chalk' modifies, even though the state of being white does not exist at the beginning of the event. This explains why the examples in (8) are grammatical.

By the same logic, the event structure of a "control" inchoative should be (20).

(20)   Event

         Activity   State

The Activity branch is required because of the Agent argument (recall (17b)), which by definition can only be a participant of an activity (Grimshaw 1990). That is, to the extent that the subject of *The house turned black* is an actor or initiator, the sentence is to be paraphrased as 'The house acted in some way so that it became black'. Applying this logic to Hebrew inchoatives like (10a), the verb *hiSxiru* 'blacken' must have (20) as its event structure when the reflexive dative forces it to have an external Agent argument. But then (20) necessarily prevents the modifier from accessing the opaque State. The conflict of requirements renders the example ungrammatical.

In summary, there are plausible ways to account for the Hebrew data in (8)–(10) within a uniform single-VP analysis dictated by the theory of the morphology-syntax interface proposed in this book.

2.3   The Nature and Role of PredP above AP: A Brief Look at Baker 2003

Baker 2003 was published right before this book was finalized. Of particular interest is Baker's proposal that adjectives and nouns, if and only if used predicatively, are embedded in a functional PredP because it is Pred, not A, that ultimately provides the θ-role for the subject. This idea bears directly on the theme of this chapter and thus deserves special attention. (Throughout this section, bare page and section numbers all refer to Baker 2003.)

2.3.1   A Functional PredP and Its Implication for the Current Analysis

Conceptually, Baker's new proposal consists of two parts: the association of PredP with the predicative use of a nonverbal lexical category (Bowers 1993) and the functional (F) nature of Pred. I find the notion of PredP intuitively plausible but its technical justifications, both by Bowers and by Baker, too intricately entangled with other issues of an unclear nature to be sufficiently assessable. For instance, I am not convinced that some of the distributional properties of A are better accounted for with the absence of PredP as Baker claims than with some intrinsic relation between V and T. Precisely because this matter is difficult to resolve at the moment but is at the heart of Baker's theory, however, I will adopt the PredP analysis for the sake of discussion while focusing in this section on his arguments in support of treating Pred as a functional category.

A cluster of facts about the morpheme *yé* in Edo, a Nigerian language, are interpreted as "superficial evidence" for treating Pred as F (p. 43). After defending the idea that *yé* is Pred rather than a copular verb, Baker notes three differences between Edo verbs and *yé*:

(21) a. "[M]onosyllabic verbs vary in tone to show the past-nonpast distinction, whereas *yé* has an invariant high tone;

     b. *yé* cannot be nominalized or undergo predicate cleft, as true verbs in Edo typically can;

     c. *yé* plus an adjective cannot appear in a serial verb construction, as one would expect if *yé* were a stative verb."

But notice that all these only prove that *yé* is not a "true verb." There are at least two possible scenarios whereby *yé* can be lexical yet still not be a true verb. First, in Baker's theory (p. 36), Pred has the same semantic function as v in Chomsky's (1995) vP-VP system and v is taken to be a lexical head for a reason I will recount later. Logically, unless one could show that a morpheme that manifests v only (i.e., not a verb moving from V to v) had all the verbal properties in (21) that *yé* does not have, the comparison says nothing about the lexical/functional nature of *yé*. Second, since *yé* is comparable to v above VP, it could even be "a" above AP, being lexical in category (just like v) but behaving differently from verbs for categorial reasons. Therefore, I will lay (21) aside in evaluating the claimed functional nature of Pred.

The rest of the arguments for a functional Pred are more complicated, so I will simply introduce them now and examine their validity in the next section.

A common pattern among languages is that the predicative adjective needs a copula only when the tense morpheme is phonetically nonnull. The Arabic examples in (22) are from Benmamoun 2000.

(22) Omar (kan) mriḍ.
    Omar was sick
    'Omar is/was sick.'

Baker proposes to account for data like (22) with (23) (his (63), sec. 2.5).

(23) (In certain languages, certain) tenses must attach to a lexical category.

By hypothesis, the predicative use of *mṛiḍ* 'sick' requires PredP. The default present tense, one of those tenses that do not need to attach to a lexical category, allows T to take PredP directly as complement. The past tense, however, needs a lexical host, forcing the copular V to be present (i.e., a VP between TP and PredP). Crucial to this account is that Pred is functional—otherwise, it would be indistinguishable from the copular verb.

Another argument for the functional nature of Pred comes from Italian *ne*-cliticization. The examples in (24) indicate that an adjective patterns with an unergative verb rather than an unaccusative when *ne* cliticizes out of the single NP argument. ((24a–b) are from Burzio 1986 and (24c) is from Cinque 1990.)

(24) a. *Ne   telefoneranno molti.
         of.them will.telephone many
         Intended reading: 'Many of them will call.'
     b. Ne   arriveranno molti.
         of.them will.arrive   many
         'Many of them will arrive.'
     c. *Ne   sono buoni pochi.
         of.them are   good few
         Intended reading: 'Few of them are good.'

Baker suggests that the paradigm follows from a revised version of the ECP, which requires a trace to be c-commanded by and in the minimal domain of a lexical head L (p. 67, def. (98)). In the case of the unaccusative verb *arriveranno* 'will arrive' in (24b), the NP containing the trace of *ne* is the complement of the verb, making the trace of *ne* c-commanded lexically and locally. The NP argument of the unergative verb *telefoneranno* 'will call' in (24a) is base-generated in the Spec of vP. Even though v is lexical, it does not c-command the trace inside this NP. The structural context for the adjectival predicate in (24c) is the same given Baker's basic hypothesis (sec. 2.3) that the subject θ-role of an adjective relies on the presence of Pred. As a result, the subject NP must be generated in the Spec of PredP, which neither is lexical nor c-commands the *ne*-trace in the NP.

Moving to deadjectival causativization, Baker notes that there are three structural contexts to consider: (i) the complement of the causative verb is a PredP containing an AP, or it is a bare AP with the causative verb expecting either (ii) an Event argument or (iii) an Event plus a Theme.

The first context blocks the syntactic derivation by means of head movement because, under Relativized Minimality, the adjectival root would have to reach the matrix V via the intermediate Pred, which is a functional head. See (36) of chapter 1. The second context has no interfering PredP and in principle allows syntactic incorporation; but it is ruled out for violating the θ-Criterion. The Causee argument has no θ-role from the causative verb because the latter has only one internal argument, namely, the Event. Nor does the Causee receive any θ-role from the adjective; in the absence of Pred, adjectives have no θ-role for the subject. The only legitimate context is the third one, in which there is no PredP and the causative verb provides the Theme role for the causee. See my discussion of Alsina's (1992) proposal regarding three-place causative verbs in section 1.1.4.

Now consider how Baker's theory of adjectives might be used to deal with the Arabic deadjectival causatives in (2). Because the grammatical representation of such sentences necessarily involves not a PredP but a bare AP without its own subject and because the subject is taken to be a critical component of the binding domain, it seems only natural that the whole sentence, with the matrix causative verb and the embedded adjective, forms the binding domain for the anaphor inside AP. That yields the coindexation pattern in (2). On the other hand, PredP can be legitimately generated in the periphrastic causative for lack of head movement from A to V. Containing the subject for the embedded adjective, PredP serves as the binding domain and the "biclausal" pattern in (1) follows automatically. As for VI, head movement happens as before because, in place of PredP between the matrix verb and the embedded predicate, there is a vP whose head v is lexical and thus allows V-to-V movement through it without violating (36) of chapter 1. In other words, Baker appears to equip the syntactic approach to morphology with the ability to predict the crucial verb-adjective contrast in causativization just as my interface theory does. In the next section, I argue that this is not the case.

2.3.2 Why Deadjectival Causatives Remain a Problem for Syntactic Theory

The above-mentioned alternative account of (1)–(2) hinges on two assumptions: that Pred is functional and that a subjectless AP extends the binding domain to the matrix clause. In this section, I show that the first assumption is not sufficiently justified and the second empirically incorrect.

Regarding the correlation between a particular tense morpheme and the use of a copula exemplified in (22), it is unclear to me why sensitivity to the functional-lexical distinction as stipulated in (23) offers a better understanding of language, either empirically or conceptually, than reference to different lexical categories (e.g., V vs. everything else). Furthermore, if predicative adjectives in Arabic need the copula to carry a past tense morpheme merely because the Pred node between T and A is functional, then the prediction is that when AP is used without PredP, the same tense morpheme should be allowed on the adjective, which is a lexical category. In Baker's theory, this scenario in which a bare AP is used does arise, namely, when AP is used attributively. T, however, is not permitted.

An argument in Baker's theory for associating the subject θ-role with Pred rather than A is based on the fact that adjectives can directly modify N whereas verbs cannot. Since the bare A (or AP) has no subject θ-role, merging it with N does not violate the θ-Criterion. In contrast, the default projection of V contains v, which assigns the subject θ-role. When the vP is used attributively inside an NP, this θ-role has no way to be properly assigned (p. 195).

Under (23), then, the attributive use of adjectives is precisely where the schematic structure in (25) should be permitted with the interpretation 'a boy who *was* sick'.

(25) [[sick-past.tense] boy]

At least in Arabic, (25) would satisfy all the syntactic requirements in Baker's theory. The tense morpheme signals the presence of TP, but this causes no problem because the language is argued to have a null expletive (Fassi Fehri 1993; Ouhalla 1998) that can be inserted in the Spec of TP for syntactic feature checking. In reality, an Arabic adjective in the attributive context agrees with N in Case but never carries tense. In sum, it is not clear, even inside Baker's own theory, that the distribution of the copula is evidence for a functional Pred: even if Pred is lexical, it can still reject the past tense morpheme as the unequivocally lexical adjective does in (25).

Ne-cliticization in Italian does not help choose between a functional and lexical Pred either. In fact, it simply does not bear on the issue. The

structures in (26) are copied from Baker 2003, 66–68, with a few irrelevant details omitted and the transitive verb in (26c) replaced by an unergative to match the examples in (24).

(26) a.

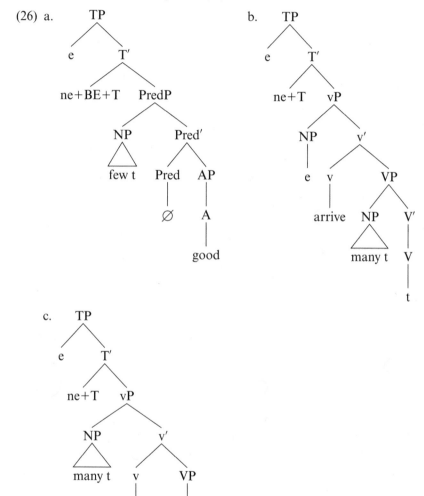

In all the structures, the *t* after the quantifier is the trace of *ne* raised
to T.

The unaccusative verb, moved to the v position, c-commands the trace of *ne* in (26b). But no such lexical c-commander is available for the clitic trace in the other two structures. This is so no matter whether the NP subject is the Spec of vP as in (26c) or the Spec of PredP as in (26a). In other words, even if Pred is as lexical as v, (26a) and (26c) have the same structural context in which there is no lexical c-commander for the trace of *ne*.[7]

Whereas there is no empirical evidence that Pred is functional, there is a conceptual reason for treating it as a lexical category given Baker's proposal that "Pred takes an . . . AP and makes a theta-marking category out of it" (p. 36). The initial insight beneath the functional-lexical distinction is that the latter group contributes toward the basic semantic content of a clause while the former is responsible for the more abstract and subtle aspects of the interpretation such as agreement and scope. In this sense, any category that performs the critical function of bringing the thematic subject into existence (rather than simply licensing an existing subject as T does) is more appropriately classified as a lexical category than a functional one. After all, the thematic subject is arguably one of the most basic pieces of a situation that a clause encodes canonically.[8] In fact, such a classification of Pred is consistent with Baker's own explicit drawing of "the general parallelism between Pred+AP and VP" (p. 36). In his theory, v must be lexical in order for syntactic VI to be allowed. And v for Baker is the syntactic component that helps bring about the subject θ-role of a verb. Since v and Pred contribute in the same way toward the thematic structure of a lexical word and v is lexical, the default conclusion is that Pred is lexical as well. But if Pred is lexical, being essentially the predicative extension of A, then moving A through Pred to V will satisfy the condition in (36) of chapter 1 in the same way that V-to-V movement via v does. It follows that even in the case of deadjectival causativization, the adjectival predicate can have its own subject after all, leaving unanswered the original question, Why do anaphors skip the semantic subject of the adjectival root in (2) but not in (1)?

But even if PredP could not be generated in the environment for AI as Baker proposes, there is evidence that the syntactic approach to morphology would still face the same question raised by (1)–(2). This involves the precise definition of the binding domain, to which I turn in the rest of this section.

In an attempt to account for certain significant differences between the resultative constructions in Chinese and English, I argue elsewhere that the English resultative AP, italicized in (27a), does not have a subject inside any projection of the adjectival head, in contrast to the typical VP with the thematic subject in its Spec (Li 1999, 466, def. (41)). My structural representation of (27a) is given in (27b).

(27) a. I wiped the table *clean*.

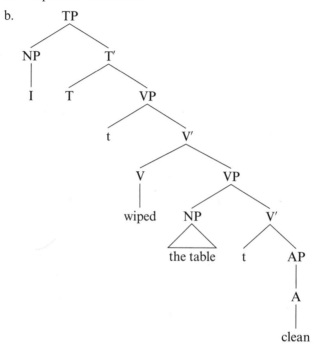

Technical details aside, this conclusion not only echoes Baker's general claim that AP is a legitimate projection of A even when the subject is not structurally represented in it, but also is very similar to his (2003, 221) treatment of the same construction, copied in (28).

(28)

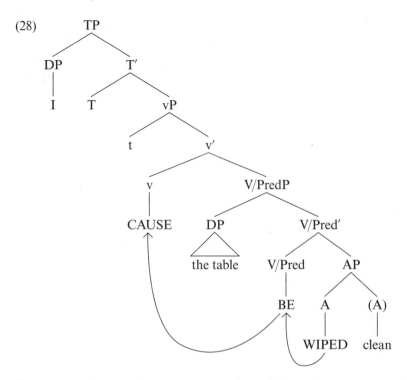

For reasons that need not concern us here, Baker adopts a generative semantic approach to verbs that are decomposed into such semantic operators as CAUSE and BE and adjectival roots such as WIPED. The resultative A (or AP) is merged with WIPED to form a kind of complex predicate. Crucially, since *clean* does not have its own PredP, it does not have a thematic subject of its own, relying on the PredP of WIPED to provide the understood subject *the table*.

Against this background, consider the following examples from Li 1999, 472:

(29) a.   John bullied his friends sick of him.
     b.   *John bullied his friends sick of himself.

The pronoun *him* in (29a) can be coindexed with the matrix subject *John* whereas the anaphor *himself* in (29b) cannot. Given the conclusion that the resultative AP does not contain its own thematic subject (i.e., there is no PRO/pro subject inside AP), (29a–b) indicate that the AP and the NP *his friends* form the binding domain even though the NP is structurally

the object of the matrix verb *bully* and is only understood as the subject of *sick*. In my account, the subject-predicate relation holds because
the adjective still has its own subject θ-role to be assigned and actually
assigns it outside AP; in Baker's, the relation is mediated through the
PredP of the matrix adjective (WIPED in (28) and whatever adjectival
root Baker would attribute to the decomposition of *bully*). What the two
accounts have in common is that *his friends* is outside the phrasal projection of *sick* but turns its combination with the adjective into a binding
domain.

A crucial detail about (28) is worth noting at this point. Double-
complement verbs like *donate* display the pattern in (30) with respect to
binding.

(30) a. Bill donated the land to himself.
     b. Sam showed the paintings to herself.

Baker's decompositional analysis of *donate* is shown in (31) (p. 81).

(31)

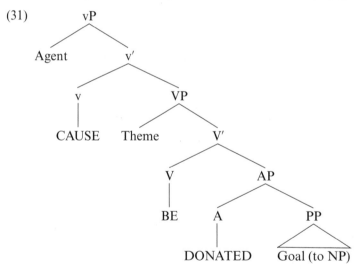

In place of the A/AP sister to the adjectival root in (28), this tree has a
PP. Otherwise, the two structures are identical, including the fact that
both the PP and the AP may contain an anaphor, as shown in (30) and
(29), respectively. However, though the anaphor in PP is bound by the
Spec of vP (see (30)), the one in AP can only pick the Spec of the BE operator as its binder (see (29)). Intuitively, it is clear what this means: unlike the Case marker *to*, *sick* is a lexical word separate from the matrix

verb/adjective. Therefore, it has the potential to define its own binding domain and will do so when its semantic subject is structurally presented, one way or another.[9]

Returning to Arabic deadjectival causatives, let us accept Baker's (2003) theory that Pred is a functional head that would block A-to-V incorporation and that the only UG-sanctioned context for AI is one in which the causative morpheme takes a bare (subjectless) AP as complement and assigns a Theme role in addition to Event. The relevant part of the structure for (2b) that accommodates these conditions is given in (32). Without knowing how Baker would represent a lexical causative verb (e.g., whether such a verb is decomposed into a root adjective plus certain lexical-semantic operators), I simply treat it as a V.

(32)

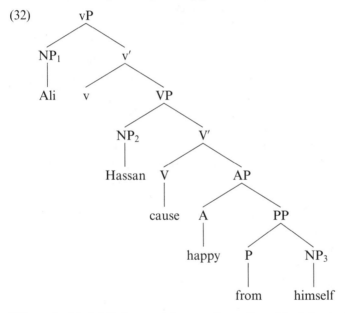

The embedded AP does not have a thematic subject for lack of its own PredP, but the interpretation is unequivocally that Hassan is happy. Under my (1999) analysis, this would be because the subject θ-role of *happy* is eventually assigned to NP_2, under the general subject-predicate relation first made structurally explicit in Williams 1980. Under Baker's (2003) analysis, this interpretation could be achieved once the matrix verb is decomposed into an A plus a Pred whose Spec is filled by the Theme argument *Hassan*. Regardless of the details, however, it is the smallest phrase that contains both *Hassan* and the AP—namely, what is called VP

in (32)—that functions as the binding domain given what we know from
(29). But this is exactly the wrong prediction that the blind use of the
UTAH produces, as we saw at the beginning of the chapter.

2.4   The Status of the Uniformity of Theta Assignment Hypothesis in Universal Grammar

In this chapter, we have examined morphological causatives and inchoatives in Arabic and Hebrew. The interface theory consisting of the LH
and the MSMH correctly predicts them to act in ways characteristic of
a monoclausal structure. On the other hand, the theory using the UTAH
as the mapping principle, though handling VI well, fails to explain why
the category of the root affects the syntactic behaviors of a morphologically complex word. As we saw in chapter 1, the lack of restriction in the
UTAH-based theory also is responsible for wrongly allowing syntactic
derivations of resultative compounds (RCs) in Chinese and PI in Bantu.
It probably is not reasonable or even desirable to make the mapping
principle responsible for ruling out all wrong analyses related to the
morphology-syntax interface. But failure to predict the basic properties
of so many nontrivial morphological phenomena should be regarded as
a clear sign that there is something fundamentally wrong with taking the
UTAH to be the core principle for the morphology-syntax interface.

Granted, any condition bearing on mapping θ-roles to syntactic positions is relevant to the morphology-syntax interface because thematic
information is one of the limited channels through which syntax and
morphology communicate. But conceptually, when to map a θ-role to a
syntactic position and where to map the θ-role to are two separate questions. If the where-question is not properly answered, an analysis may
encounter problems of a technical nature. If the when-question is not
properly answered, however, more fundamental problems arise.

The UTAH is designed to answer both questions simultaneously. The
where-question is answered by maintaining consistent mapping between
a θ-role and a syntactic position; the answer to the when-question is
"always." As we have seen throughout the first two chapters, the second
answer is incorrect, leading the UTAH-based theory of the morphology-
syntax interface to make more wrong predictions (as with AI, PI, and
RC) than right ones (as with VI). In contrast, the MSMH focuses on
providing an adequate answer to the when-question by explicitly specifying the conditions under which semantic relations among morphemes are

represented in syntax. As a result, it captures the more fundamental aspect of the morphology-syntax interface. If the UTAH or some version of it is indeed part of UG,[10] its role should be restricted to answering the where-question—namely, which syntactic position a θ-role is mapped to *if the θ-role is indeed mapped to a syntactic position.*

Chapters 1 and 2 also illustrated the problems that arise in some existing lexicalist theories. These theories interpret the lexical formation of words in an unnecessarily narrow sense, indiscriminately matching one word in the lexicon to one phrasal projection in syntax. As a result, rather complex lexical mechanisms must be developed to accommodate certain facts of binding and passivization that can be easily accounted for in a multiple-VP structure in syntax (section 1.1). More important, these theories cannot explain why the verbal root of a morphological causative is associated with a binding domain whereas the adjectival root is not (sections 1.1, 2.1). Another problem is the alternative linear order between the Theme and non-B/G arguments of an applicative verb (section 1.2.1). As long as V-*app* is treated as a lexical verb projecting to its own VP, the Theme argument of the verb root is regarded as that of the whole compound, and there is no easy way (not even through the two interpretations of the bleached Theme on the part of the -*app* morpheme) to explain this apparent problem with the thematic hierarchy. The dilemma is bypassed in my theory because, when the Theme argument from the verb root is lower than the Instrument/Locative argument from -*app*, the two arguments are eventually mapped to different VP projections in syntax. Such thematic mapping is allowed by UG for the same reason that an embedded clause may have its own Agent argument regardless of what thematic arguments the matrix verb happens to have.

Chapter 3

Noun Incorporation: A Case Study

In recent years, noun incorporation (NI) has been an active battlefield between the lexicalist and syntactic camps (Sadock 1980, 1985, 1986; Mithun 1986; Di Sciullo and Williams 1987; Li 1988; Baker 1988, 1996, 2002; Rosen 1989), each side using it to defend its own position and to encroach on the opponent's. It is not my intention in this chapter to examine all the proposed theories. Rather, I focus on Baker 1996, where new data from polysynthetic languages are introduced in favor of deriving the phenomenon through syntactic head movement. My primary goal is to demonstrate that (i) Baker's new data all have a natural account in the lexicalist theory based on the LH and enhanced by the MSMH, and that (ii) in an effort to incorporate the insight of Baker's Morphological Visibility Condition, the lexicalist theory removes the mystery from the condition. The chapter ends with a discussion of redundancy in theory formulation.

Given the nature of the issues being addressed, I must make one point at the outset even at the cost of possibly sounding cynical: while the lexicalist analysis of NI presented in the upcoming sections constitutes a serious attempt to show that no data of NI, old or new, can be used in favor of the syntactic approach to morphology, the validity of the specific claims and proposals in the analysis is not necessarily tied to the plausibility of my interface theory. Though there are alternative accounts of certain data from polysynthetic languages (e.g., Legate 2002) within the same P&P model, Baker's work on such languages in general and on NI in particular was the most comprehensive and detailed when this chapter was initially written (and in my opinion still is). As a result, the lexicalist theory of NI presented here is built around Baker's data as well as what I consider to be his insight. Inevitably, many details in my analysis depend on his work. However, I see no intrinsic problem with formulating a lexicalist alternative to any syntactic theory of NI.

3.1 Background

3.1.1 The Basic Facts and the Issue

The Mohawk examples in (1)–(2), from Baker 1996, chap. 7, illustrate a well-established asymmetry in NI.

(1) a. O-'wahr-u   i-hse-nut   ne erhar.
         pref-meat-suff ∅-agr-feed NE dog
         'Feed the dog some meat!'
     b. Se-'wahr-a-nut   ne erhar.
         agr-meat-∅-feed NE dog
         'Feed the dog some meat!'
     c. *O-'wahr-u   se-nahskw-a-nut.
         pref-meat-suff agr-pet-∅-feed
         Intended reading: 'Feed the pet some meat!'

(2) a. A'ʌn-a'   wa'-ka'-ratsu-'   ne yo-'ar-ʌ'tu.
         arrow-suff fact-agr-tear-punc NE pref-lace-hang
         'The arrow tore the curtain.'
     b. *Yo-'ar-ʌ'tu   wa-w-a'ʌn-a-ratsu-'.
         pref-lace-hang fact-agr-arrow-∅-tear-punc
         Intended reading: 'The arrow tore the curtain.'

While the Theme object can incorporate (as in (1b)), neither the Goal nor any D-Structure subject can ((1c), (2b)). In existing lexicalist work (e.g., Di Sciullo and Williams 1987), this asymmetry is accounted for by requiring that the lexical mechanism that forms the N-V compound apply only to the Theme argument. The analysis receives support from English deverbal N-V compounds ((3b) quoted from Grimshaw 1990).

(3) a. car-driving vs. *student-driving
     b. gift-giving to children vs. *child-giving of gifts

Given that *car-drive* and *gift-give* are not well-formed verbs in English, there is now a consensus on both sides of the debate that N-V-*ing* compounds are not syntactically formed. Crucially, exactly the same asymmetry is observed in such compounds between the Theme and everything else. Hence, whatever lexical rules are responsible for (3) should be sufficient to generate the data in (1) and (2).

On the other hand, Baker (1988) proposes to account for (1) and (2) with head movement restricted by the ECP. In particular, if the trace of a head must be antecedent-governed (see Chomsky 1986a), the theory can be easily formulated to guarantee that only the head trace of the Theme argument will be locally c-commanded by a coindexed head without any intervening barrier. While this is regarded by many as a successful expansion of syntax into the domain of morphology, Baker himself recognized later that given that the UTAH associates the Theme argument with a constant syntactic position and that the nature of the Theme is not at all clear, "the difference between the two approaches to NI [is not] a directly empirical one" and "the issue is not readily decidable" (Baker 1996, 294–295). Therefore, he sought new evidence for the syntactic account of NI, presenting his results in Baker 1996.

At this point, it is helpful to clarify where the interface theory in this work will side on the issue. Note first that *car-driving* is in fact a specific type of the very common N-N compound, where *car* combines with the deverbal *driving*. The only other possibility would be for *car* and *drive* to form a compound verb that is then nominalized by *-ing*. But the obligatory nominalization would be impossible to explain since no other English verb must be nominalized.

The compound must be lexically formed given the LH. Being thematic, the relation between the two noun components may qualify for syntactic representation. The structure would be (4), where N_1 corresponds to *driving* and N_2 to *car*.

(4)

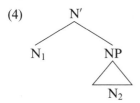

The compound would start in N_2 and raise to N_1. Since both sites are nominal, the movement itself would be legitimate for the same reason that V-to-V raising is legitimate in VI. However, (4) is ungrammatical because the complement NP has no Case, N_1 being nominal and thus incapable of assigning Case. It follows that the thematic relation between N_1 and N_2 cannot be syntactically represented, and the compound can only project to a single NP. In sum, my theory correctly predicts the "lexicalist" nature of the English N-V-*ing* compound.

Next look at Mohawk NI. The N-V compound would map to (5) in syntax.

(5)

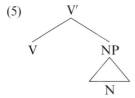

The categorial mismatch of the two head positions is sufficient to prevent such a representation: as a verb, the compound can be inserted only at V, but it cannot license the N position for Full Interpretation because lowering is prohibited. It follows that NI in Mohawk cannot be represented as (5) in syntax, again coinciding with the lexicalist analysis. But as Baker points out, it is very difficult, maybe impossible, to distinguish the lexicalist and syntactic approaches merely on the basis of (1)–(3). And such uncertainty largely explains why the debate goes on to this day.

3.1.2 Baker's New Arguments for Syntactic Noun Incorporation

Let us begin with a brief review of those properties of polysynthetic languages that are directly relevant to subsequent discussions. (Unless stated otherwise, all examples and analyses in this section are from Baker 1996, and all bare page numbers and sections refer to the same book.)

Polysynthetic languages are characterized by a productive process of NI and subject-object agreement on the verb. Note the following Mohawk paradigm (p. 21):

(6) a.   Shako-nuhwe'-s (ne owira'a).
         $agr_{s/o}$-like-hab   NE baby
         'He likes them (babies).'

 b.   Ra-wir-a-nuhwe'-s.
         agr_s-baby-$\varnothing$-like-hab
         'He likes babies.'

 c.   *Ra-nuhwe'-s ne owira'a.
         agr_s-like-hab NE baby
         'He likes babies.'

The verb must be associated with either an object *agr* (6a) or an incorporated noun (6b); ungrammaticality results if neither is present, even when an overt NP object is available (6c). Another significant fact about NI in polysynthetic languages is the apparently referential nature of the noun. In the right context, (6b) can also mean 'He likes *the* babies', where the babies are in the discourse domain set up by a previous utterance. The example in (7) illustrates this fact well (p. 321).

(7) Rabahbot wa'-k-atkatho-'   tsi yutʌhninutha' sok
    bullhead fact-agr$_s$-see-punc at-store   so
    wa'-k-its-a-hninu-'.
    fact-agr$_s$-fish-$\emptyset$-buy-punc
    'I saw a bullhead at the store and so I bought the fish.'

In contrast, it is generally agreed that in English N-V-*ing* compounds such as *car-driving*, N does not have the specific/definite reading.

Baker also argues that overt NPs in polysynthetic languages corresponding to thematic arguments in nonpolysynthetic languages are in fact adjuncts. Strong evidence comes from coreferential r-expressions (sec. 2.1.1).

(8) a. Wa-hi-'nha'-ne'   ne tsi   Sak ra-yo'tʌ-hser-iyo.
       fact-agr$_{s/o}$-hire-punc because Sak agr-work-nom-be.good
       'I hired him because Sak is a good worker.'
    b. Wa-hi-hrori-'   tsi   Sak ruwa-nuwhwe'-s.
       fact-agr$_{s/o}$-tell-punc that Sak agr$_{s/o}$-like-hab
       'I told him that she likes Sak.'

(9) a. Wa'-t-ha-ya'k-e'   ne thik Sak rao-a'share'.
       fact-dup-agr$_{s/o}$[1]-break-punc NE that Sak pref-knife
       'He broke that knife of Sak's.'
    b. Kanat-a-ku wa'-etsiseni-kʌ-'   isi   tanu Sak rao-skare'.
       town-$\emptyset$-in fact-agr$_{s/o}$-see-punc you and Sak pref-friend
       'He saw you and Sak's girlfriend in town.'

In (8a), the 3rd person singular object pro of the matrix verb -*'nha'* 'hire', signaled by the agreement -*hi*, may be optionally coreferential with the embedded subject *Sak*. But in (8b), *Sak* must be referentially disjoint from the matrix object. The contrast indicates that Mohawk, like English, obeys Binding Condition C, which requires an r-expression to be free. Inside a complement clause, *Sak* in (8b) is c-commanded by the matrix object, making coreference impossible. Since the embedded clause containing *Sak* is an adjunct in (8a), it is not c-commanded by the object and coreference between the object and *Sak* does not result in binding. But Binding Condition C seemingly is not respected in (9a–b): as a proper part of the object NP, *Sak* can refer to the 3rd person singular subject that should c-command the object in a language like English.

The problem disappears if overt NPs like *Sak* are not in argument position but rather are base-generated adjuncts adjoined to IP. Coupled with an in-situ VP-internal pro subject (p. 86), this configuration effectively places *Sak* outside the c-commanding domain of any true argument in the clause. Such a treatment of overt NPs in Mohawk also works well with the generally free word order observed in polysynthetic languages because within a clause, adjuncts typically enjoy more freedom in word order than arguments. For several more pieces of evidence pointing at the same conclusion, see Baker 1996, chap. 2.

The theoretical question is why Mohawk is so different from English. At the core of Baker's answer is the Morphological Visibility Condition (MVC).

(10) *Morphological Visibility Condition*
     A phrase X is visible for θ-role assignment from a head Y only if it is coindexed with a morpheme in the word containing Y via
     a. an agreement relationship, or
     b. a movement relationship.

The MVC is a parameter in UG that is on in Mohawk and off in English. When it is off, θ-roles are assigned in the familiar manner, directly from a lexical head to a syntactic position and generating true NP arguments in English. When the MVC is on, however, no θ-role can be assigned by a lexical head to a syntactic argument unless the latter is associated with a morpheme that forms a word with the θ-role assigner. In (6a), the crucial relaying morpheme is the object agreement morpheme (*agr* hereafter); and in (6b), it is the incorporated N. Since the verb in (6c) has neither, it cannot even "see" any NP argument, leaving its object θ-role unable to be assigned and violating the θ-Criterion.

To fully explain the adjunct nature of the overt NPs, Baker proposes another important property characteristic of polysynthetic languages (p. 86).

(11) An *agr* adjoined to a head X receives X's Case.

When NI does not take place in a polysynthetic language, *agr* is required by the MVC to help a lexical head assign all its θ-roles. If (11) is indeed true, any Case assigned by a head is already assigned to the corresponding *agr*, leaving the true argument positions Caseless. Since the Case Filter demands a Case for each overt NP argument, only phonologically empty nominals like pro are still permitted in the argument positions, driving overt NPs to adjunct positions. This is why the subject position in (9a), for instance, is occupied by a pro whereas the overt object NP is relegated to an adjunct position. On the other hand, since clauses don't need Case, (11) has no effect on them. Consequently, a clause interpreted as the thematic object stays in the complement position. This explains the contrast between (8a) and (8b), with the complement clause in (8b) c-commanded by the matrix object NP.

Now we turn to Baker's new evidence in favor of the syntactic derivation of NI.

The paradigm of Mohawk examples in (6), repeated here, needs one more example to be complete.

(12) a. Shako-nuhwe'-s (ne owira'a).
         $agr_{s/o}$-like-hab   NE baby
         'He likes them (babies).'

     b. Ra-wir-a-nuhwe'-s.
         agr_s-baby-$\emptyset$-like-hab
         'He likes babies.'

     c. *Ra-nuhwe'-s ne owira'a.
         agr_s-like-hab NE baby
         'He likes babies.'

     d. *?Shako-wir-a-nuhwe'-s.
         $agr_{s/o}$-baby-$\emptyset$-like-hab
         'He likes babies.'

The last example, (12d), shows that Agr_O cannot co-occur with NI, though either one is possible by itself (12a–b). This can be easily explained if NI is formed by raising the head N of the object NP to the verb. Thematically, the incorporated N serves as the relay for the verb to assign its internal θ-role to the object NP, satisfying the MVC. Since Agr_O is not needed for θ-role assignment, it is not permitted (see Chomsky 1995). (And without agreement, the verb can assign its Case to the object NP, even though it really makes no difference in this particular situation because the NP has no phonological content after the head N raises to V.)

On the other hand, (12d) would be problematic for Di Sciullo and Williams's (1987) lexical theory of NI. In brief, these authors treat NI as a verbal compound composed of two predicates. The θ-role of the N and the internal θ-role of the V are identified and assigned by the compound to a single syntactic argument, most often a pro. The problem: if this were the case, the N-V compound in (12d) should behave indistinguishably from any other verb (e.g., *-nuhwe'* 'like' in (12a)), leaving unexplained why the object *agr* is banned only in one case and not in both.

The second argument for syntactic NI is based on these examples (p. 321):

(13) a. Rabahbot yah tha'-te-yo-tʌhutsoni ne uhka
        bullhead   not contr-dup-agr$_s$-want NE someone
        a-ye-hninu-'.
        opt-agr$_{s/o}$-buy-punc
        'The bullhead doesn't want anyone to buy it.'
     b. Rabahbot yah tha'-te-yo-tʌhutsoni ne uhka
        bullhead   not contr-dup-agr$_s$-want NE someone
        a-ye-hninu-'.   ne kʌ-ts-u'.
        opt-agr$_{s/o}$-buy-punc NE pref-fish-suff
        'The bullhead doesn't want anyone to buy fish.'
     c. Rabahbot yah tha'-te-yo-tʌhutsoni ne uhka
        bullhead   not contr-dup-agr$_s$-want NE someone
        a-ye-ts-a-hninu-'.
        opt-agr$_{s/o}$-fish-$\emptyset$-buy-punc
        'The bullhead doesn't want anyone to buy the fish.'
     d. Rabahbot wa'-k-atkatho-'   tsi yutʌhninutha' sok
        bullhead   fact-agr$_s$-see-punc at-store   so
        wa'-k-its-a-hninu-'.
        fact-agr$_s$-fish-$\emptyset$-buy-punc
        'I saw a bullhead at the store and so I bought the fish.'

The embedded pro object in (13a) may be coreferential with the NP *rabahbot* 'bullhead' in the matrix clause. But when the pro object is re-placed by a full NP *kʌ-ts-u'* 'fish' in (13b), no coreference is possible. Nor can the incorporated N *-ts* 'fish' be understood as the bullhead in (13c), though coreference becomes possible again in (13d).

The contrast between the first two examples results directly from Bind-ing Conditions B and C. The pro object in (13a) must be free in the embedded clause but may be bound beyond it—hence the possible co-reference. The corresponding NP object in (13b) is an r-expression that must be free, imposing a disjoint reading from the matrix pro subject (which in turn is semantically associated with the NP *rabahbot* 'bull-head'). Since only a disjoint interpretation is allowed in (13c), Baker argues that there is also an r-expression, namely, the D-Structure object

NP whose head N incorporates to the embedded verb in syntax. (13d) serves as a control sentence, proving that there is no intrinsic incompatibility between NI and coreferentiality. As long as the antecedent *rabahbot* 'bullhead' doesn't c-command the object headed by -*ts* 'fish', coreference is permitted by Binding Condition C.

Again, the data pose a problem for Di Sciullo and Williams's lexicalist analysis of NI, which would treat the empty object in (13c) as a pro. As Baker notes, a pro object would satisfy Binding Condition B in (13a,c,d) alike, with or without NI, and one would not be able to explain why NI patterns with an overt NP object.

The third argument is derived from the incompatibility between NI and *wh*-questions. According to Baker, the only overt NP that can be base-generated in an argument position in polysynthetic languages is a *wh*-phrase. Given evidence that a *wh*-phrase in Mohawk raises to the Spec of CP at S-Structure (sec. 2.1.4), only a trace will be left in the argument position by the time the Case Filter applies. Since the filter only restricts NPs with phonological content, the trace is ruled grammatical even when an *agr* takes away the Case.[2] Given this context, consider the following Mohawk examples (p. 323):

(14) a.   T-ʌ-ke-wir-a-hkw-e'   ne ka-wir-iyo.
          dup-fut-agr$_s$-baby-$\emptyset$-pick.up-punc NE pref-baby-nice
          'I will pick up the nice baby.'
     b. ?*Uhka t-a-hse-wir-a-hkw-e'?
          who dup-fut-agr$_s$-baby-$\emptyset$-pick.up-punc
          'Who are you going to pick up (a baby)?'

(14a) is an example of doubling that involves both NI and an adjunct NP, each independently justified, as we have seen. The ungrammatical (14b) is easily explained if *uhka* 'who', unlike a referential NP, is generated in the argument position. Basically, (14b) is ruled out because both the *wh*-phrase and the incorporated N are competing for the single object position. If *uhka* is there at D-Structure, it is no longer possible for -*wir* 'baby' to head the same NP.

Now suppose that the incorporated N and the verb form a compound in the manner proposed by Di Sciullo and Williams (1987). Since the compound verb can take the overt NP as object in (14a), it also should be able to take the *wh*-phrase as object in (14b), wrongly predicting the latter to be grammatical.

3.2   An Alternative Analysis of Baker's Data

The MVC, summarizing Baker's insight on what separates polysynthetic languages from others, is meant to capture the old wisdom that verbs in these languages form "miniature" clauses with the agreement morphology and incorporated nouns (Jelinek 1984, 1989; Mithun 1987; Foley 1991). The theoretical question concerns the nature of such a principle and its implications for the organization of UG. In this section, I first examine the nature of the MVC and then show how it may affect our understanding of the inner workings of UG. On the basis of my conclusions, I present an alternative analysis of Baker's data that synthesizes the MVC with the interface theory I have proposed.

3.2.1   Dissecting the Morphological Visibility Condition
Technicalities aside, the MVC makes two closely intertwined yet different claims about polysynthetic languages:

(15) a. Certain morphological components are needed for θ-role
          assignment in syntax.
      b. The internal structure of a word is transparent to syntax.

If it were not for (15b), a phrase would not be able to single out a morpheme in a word and be coindexed with it. But without (15a), the examples in (12) would not be explained whether morphological structures are visible to syntax or not. While (15b) runs head on against the Lexical Integrity Hypothesis, its validity is ultimately an empirical matter. There is nothing difficult to understand in the claim itself: word-internal structure is visible to syntax in some languages but opaque in others. (15a), however, is utterly mysterious. If a θ-role can be assigned directly to a syntactic argument in some languages (like English), why is the process/ mechanism suddenly unavailable in others so that morphological aids become necessary? Baker recognizes the mystery, and tries to find a theological answer for it.

It must be noted that on the surface, only (15a) needs to be stipulated in the MVC. Given the way the parameter is positioned in Baker's theory, (15b) does not seem to demand a separate status. After all, both the *agr*s and the incorporated lexical morpheme join the θ-role assigner in syntax. Since they are generated as separate heads in syntax and the merger is accomplished through syntactic movement, they are naturally visible to syntactic operations. Whether this is indeed a trivially justifiable claim depends on what one wants to accomplish, though.

The MVC presumes by definition that syntactic incorporation exists. If it participates in establishing any part of an argument in favor of syntactic NI, the risk of logical circularity is high. Therefore, when the debate is precisely over whether incorporation is syntactic or not, the MVC's reliance on a transparent word-internal structure cannot be simply taken for granted. In neutral terms, what the MVC assumes is that the individual morphemes inside a polysynthetic compound are visible to syntactic operations such as θ-role assignment. Whether this assumption is derivable from syntactic movement of lexical heads hinges on whether syntactic incorporation in Baker's sense can be proven independently of the MVC. In chapters 1 and 2, I argued that morphologically complex words are all lexically formed and that even VI, a prime case of biclausal structures underlying morphologically complex words, does not really entail two morphemes inserted in different syntactic locations and merged via head movement. In this theory, the MVC may still hold, but the transparency of word-internal structures can no longer be attributed to syntactic merger of heads.

Assuming the MVC to be on the right track toward explaining the differences (and similarities) between polysynthetic and nonpolysynthetic languages, the following questions arise: Why do natural languages divide parametrically into two groups according to the transparency of their word-internal structures? How exactly is the setting of the parameter related to the mysterious (15a), which ties θ-role assignment to morphology? And ultimately, how should the insights embodied in the MVC be adapted to my interface theory? After all, the MVC is couched in syntactic contexts. Since the LH and the MSMH result in a largely lexicalist model of the morphology-syntax interface, one wonders how to construct a coherent theory of UG that contains both the LH and the MSMH on the one hand and what the MVC tries to tell us on the other.

The answer to all these questions starts with reconsidering the boundary of what is referred to as the lexicon. Almost all researchers assume the existence of (i) a set of operations for constructing words, and (ii) a phrase structure mechanism such as X-bar theory. In a nonpolysynthetic language, these two structure-building mechanisms are separated by the lexicon-syntax boundary, the site of what we call the morphology-syntax interface. Now suppose that the location of the boundary is not constant across languages, remotely comparable to variation in the Spell-Out point that separates overt syntax and LF. In particular, let the *m-lexicon* be the collection of morphemes in a given language, and let morphology and syntax be what they are normally assumed to be. Now suppose (16) to describe a parametric difference between polysynthetic and nonpolysynthetic languages.

(16) *The Parameter of the Lexicon (POL)*

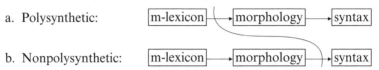

    a. Polysynthetic:

    b. Nonpolysynthetic:

To the left of the curved line is what is considered the lexicon in a given language. (16) may be somewhat idealized in the sense that even polysynthetic languages could have highly idiosyncratic compounds that belong to the m-lexicon. But productive morphological processes such as compounding and incorporation are not regarded as part of the m-lexicon in this model.

A few clarifications about the POL.[3]

1. The terms *lexical* and *morphological* have been used loosely and interchangeably so far. Given (16), *lexical* is now reserved for anything to the left of the curved line, while *morphological* refers to processes that belong to morphology regardless of the placement of the curved line. So the lexicon of a polysynthetic language is identical to its m-lexicon, but the lexicon of a nonpolysynthetic language consists of the m-lexicon plus morphology. An intuitive interpretation of this division among languages is as follows. Polysynthetic languages consider any generative process, be it morphological or phrasal, to be outside the lexicon, or "postlexical" for the purpose of this discussion. On the other hand, nonpolysynthetic languages consider anything at or below the word level to be inside the lexicon. So the POL reflects nothing more than different perspectives on forming natural classes.

2. Regardless of where the lexicon's boundary lies, the MSMH remains an interface principle between morphology and syntax—two autonomous modules of UG, each with its own unique set of operations and material to operate on. The role of the MSMH for a nonpolysynthetic language has been abundantly illustrated. For a polysynthetic language, its role is identical. Typical, morphologically complex words are mapped into either monophrasal or multiphrasal structures. In particular, an NI

compound can only be treated as a verb in syntax (see (5)). As for idiosyncratic compounds, they may not even be regarded as decomposable at all by the grammar of the language. The precise effect of the MSMH on idiosyncratic compounds can be determined only empirically, of course. But the general relation between the POL and the MSMH is straightforward.

3. I adopt the general spirit of the Minimalist Program that syntax is responsible only for building phrase structures and that interpretive mechanisms such as binding belong in LF, the conceptual-intentional interface (Chomsky 1993). In this view, there is no conceptual reason why LF can only interpret the structures formed in syntax. In fact, it is at least equally plausible that LF interprets everything not shielded by the opaque lexical boundary, that is, the curved line in (16). For a nonpolysynthetic language like English, this is identical to the standard function of LF because syntax is the only "postlexical" module. For a polysynthetic language like Mohawk, however, both morphological and syntactic structures are up for LF interpretation as both are to the right of the lexical boundary and, by hypothesis, transparent to LF. In this sense, *(16) parameterizes the portion of the LH (in its original definition; see the introduction) that protects word-internal components from interpretive operations in LF*, a component of UG that used to be considered part of syntax. Once this is made clear, however, I see no reason for confusion here; so I will continue using the LH to refer to its word-formation-affecting capacity only, as made clear in the introduction.

In sum, the POL in (16) is my answer to the question raised by (15b) about the nature of the parametric transparency of word-internal structures. The two natural ways to group morphology, with the m-lexicon or the syntax, are the basis for the division between, say, English and Mohawk (point 1). If postlexical, morphological structures become transparent for LF interpretation just like syntactic structures (point 3). Needless to say, this is also the ultimate reason why polysynthetic words have "felt" like miniature clauses: they are processed in the conceptual-intentional interface with the same mechanisms as those for clauses. Finally, the POL fits well with my interface theory because, regardless of how it is set, morphology and syntax remain mutually autonomous, with the MSMH in between (point 2).

To finally remove the mystery of the MVC, I propose the axiom in (17).

(17) Thematic operations must be carried out at the earliest possible
     level of postlexical derivation.

The intuition behind (17) is best illustrated with an analogy. The lexicon is a warehouse that stores building materials, namely, lexical items. Languages like Mohawk store these materials only in their most basic form (the m-lexicon), while languages like English also store half-assembled parts (the m-lexicon plus products of morphology). What (17) requires is that once the materials are taken out of storage, they (or at least the ones that are designed to function together as a unit) must immediately be properly assembled.[4]

Designed to hold in all languages, (17) is meant to capture the MVC's requirement for morphologically aided θ-role assignment, that is, (15a). Shortly I will provide detailed analyses demonstrating how (17) collaborates with the POL to explain all the morphological facts in Mohawk. For the moment, it is important to see how the mysteries in (15a) are solved at the conceptual level.

What is most difficult to understand about the MVC is why θ-role assignment in syntax, which clearly can be done exclusively by syntactic means in English, must depend on certain components of a morphologically complex word in Mohawk. If the POL and (17) are correct, the mystery is in fact the consequence of misrepresenting this portion of UG. In English, θ-role assignment happens in syntax because syntax is the earliest level of structure construction beyond the English lexicon. For Mohawk, however, such operations do not wait until syntax to take place, morphology being the "first" level of postlexical derivation where there are means for thematic operations. In this model, it is not the case that syntactic arguments have to rely on coindexation with a morphological component of the verbal cluster to be visible for θ-role assignment. Certain morphemes, such as N in the N-V compound and Agr, indeed participate in thematic operations, as we will soon see. But they do not do so to enhance the visibility of any syntactic argument. Rather, they participate because they are the means available to morphology to discharge the θ-roles of a verb. Their links, via coindexation, with syntactic components such as an NP are merely due to the general requirement of Full Interpretation. The links are interpretable at LF precisely because both morphological and syntactic structures are visible at LF once the value of the POL is set properly. There is nothing mysterious about polysynthetic languages because both the variations described in the POL and the universal requirement in (17) are obviously well within the natural capacities of the human mind.

3.2.2 Thematic Operations

Since (17) requires thematic operations to be carried out in the morphology of polysynthetic languages when possible, it is necessary to clarify what these operations are both in general and at the level of morphology.

Higginbotham (1985) argues for three thematic operations: θ-assignment, θ-identification, and θ-binding. θ-assignment is assumed and used widely in the P&P framework, but θ-binding, together with its relation to θ-assignment, is much less well understood. The difficulty comes from what I have elsewhere called the *characteristic θ-role* (ch-role) of certain lexical heads (Li 1988). Since a noun such as *book* specifies a set of entities, it is generally taken to have a θ-role like lexical items of other categories. Williams (1981a) calls it the *R role*, suggesting its referential function in a nominal; and I termed it the *ch-role* because, unlike "normal" θ-roles, this one ranges over entities that the noun exclusively characterizes. For instance, *Bill* is among the set of entities that run by virtue of receiving a normal θ-role from *ran* in *Bill ran*. However, this does not mean that running characterizes Bill's most basic nature; running might be an uncharacteristic thing Bill does by accident. On the other hand, an entity in the set specified by *book* does not have to be anything else, but it must have the characteristics of a book. Both the names *ch-role* and *R role* are meant to reflect the fact that this θ-role behaves differently from "normal" ones. In this work, I use *R role* to highlight its reference-related nature. The question concerning us now is what happens to the R role of a noun N when some projection of N is also a θ-recipient.

In Higginbotham 1985, it is bound by D in the typical operator-variable manner, thereby satisfying the θ-Criterion inside the nominal phrase through what Higginbotham calls θ-binding. While this view may be tacitly adopted by many linguists who deal with θ-assignment, I do not adopt it here for reasons to be discussed shortly.

Williams (1981a) lets the R role of a nominal participate directly in θ-assignment. In his theory, an NP inherits the R role from its head because determiners like *the* and *a* do not saturate it. When the NP receives a θ-role from a verb, the two roles essentially cancel each other out to satisfy the θ-Criterion. An obvious advantage of this analysis lies in accounting for examples like *They consider Bill a hero*, where the NP *a hero* with a determiner can still function as a predicate. If the NP still has the unsaturated R role, it can be assigned to *Bill*. But the analysis in turn raises a new question. *Bill a hero* is the thematic argument of the matrix verb *consider*. If the R role of *hero* goes to *Bill*, what θ-role is there to cancel out the object θ-role of *consider*? The question obviously generalizes to all verbs taking clausal complements. One may argue that all the problematic cases involve thematic arguments that do not refer like an NP. But the fact remains that θ-assignment in general does not require two θ-roles, one from the assigner and one from the recipient, in order to take place.

Heim's (1982) theory resembles Williams's in not relying on a determiner to be the structural "saturator" of the R role. In her theory, Williams's R role is interpreted as a free variable in semantics, and a determiner is just a flag for the semantic interpretation of the variable. From the syntactic point of view, however, one still wonders how the R role satisfies the θ-Criterion. The answer is not as simple as moving (the functions of) the θ-Criterion to LF, as suggested in the Minimalist Program. If a syntactically unsaturated θ-role could be mapped to a free variable at LF that in turn is bound by some operator, why can't we say *Bill always puts in the closet* with the interpretation [∀x, Bill puts x in the closet]? Obviously, the Theme role of *put* must be associated with an NP in syntax to guarantee proper semantic interpretation. Minimally, this means that normal θ-roles behave differently from the R role with respect to how they satisfy the θ-Criterion in pre-LF computation.

Some of these questions will be picked up later in the chapter. As the discussion below is largely independent of these details, I will simply adopt the general Williams-Heim approach as follows:

(18) a. Functional categories such as definite and indefinite articles do not saturate the R role of a lexical head.
   b. When a nominal X is used referentially at the derivational level L, any R role of X may *somehow* be saturated at L and interpreted as a variable subject to proper LF operations.

For ease of reference, I will refer to (18b) as *automatic saturation*. Automatic saturation happens only to an R role.

Next consider θ-identification. Technically, the process coindexes two θ-roles so that they can be assigned together. In essence, this coindexation marks one of the θ-roles with a "tag" so that it is reserved for use with the other θ-role. At the point of tagging, the θ-role is not yet assigned but is considered taken care of because its future whereabouts are already determined. This is why Higginbotham considers θ-identification a means to saturate one of the two θ-roles—the tagged one in my terms—just as θ-assignment saturates a θ-role. (For an elaboration of this idea, see Higginbotham 1985.)

By definition, θ-identification needs two separate θ-roles to operate on, and it has been used to account for various syntactic and morphological constructions (e.g., Higginbotham 1985; Li 1988, 1990; Baker 1996). But given Higginbotham's original take on the concept, made explicit when it is described as a tagging process for later use, θ-identification can be viewed as the specific implementation of a more general means of θ-saturation: *θ-reservation*. When situations arise where a θ-role cannot be assigned to an argument in the standard way, it may still be tagged as reserved, thereby satisfying the θ-Criterion at that point in the derivation. If it is reserved for assignment with another θ-role, that is θ-identification. But logically, the second θ-role is not necessary if there are other ways to assign the tagged one. I propose that this is precisely what the MVC is about: an agreement morpheme unequivocally tagging a θ-role of the lexical stem so that in the morphological structure, that θ-role is saturated through θ-reservation, as required by (17).

To complete the theoretical repertoire of my theory, I adopt Baker's (11), which lets an agreement morpheme attached to the verb root receive the corresponding Case. Apparently, (11) holds beyond polysynthetic languages. For details, see Baker 1996, sec. 2.2.

3.2.3   Revisiting Baker's Arguments for Syntactic Noun Incorporation

Baker's first argument in favor of syntactic NI and against a lexicalist account has a simple explanation now: the object *agr* and the incorporated noun exclude each other because they would be competing for a single θ-role (see (12)). The object θ-role of the verb root can be either assigned to the morphologically incorporated noun in (12a) or reserved through object *agr* in (12b), either way satisfying (17). Having neither N nor *agr* results in a θ-Criterion violation in Mohawk morphology (12c) because the language has enough mechanisms at this level of derivation to saturate a θ-role of the verb root. The θ-Criterion is also violated when both N and *agr* form a word with V, as the presence of N leaves no θ-role for *agr* to tag (12d). Logically, it is possible to reserve the object θ-role first and assign it later to the incorporated noun. But as Baker points out, there is no need for both when one of them is considered sufficient to satisfy the θ-Criterion inside morphology. Hence, the possibility is ruled out if UG is a minimalist system.

When a θ-role is reserved morphologically through *agr*, it will be eventually assigned to the designated argument in syntax (i.e., a pro in the subject or object position), for full interpretation at LF. Unlike assigning a morphologically reserved θ-role in morphology as discussed above, doing so in syntax does not incur ungrammaticality in a minimalist system because it is not part of the morphological computation. As mentioned above and listed in (19), there are three possible ways to satisfy (17) inside morphology, and it is obvious that (19c) is the most costly.

(19) a. θ-reservation with *agr*
b. θ-assignment to the incorporated noun
c. θ-reservation followed immediately by θ-assignment

θ-assignment in syntax, however, is not an alternative derivation in morphology. Nor is it the morphological continuation of, say, (19a) because the two operate on different kinds of constituents (one on morphemes and the other on phrases) in different kinds of structural contexts (word-internal vs. word-external). This contrasts with (19c), where θ-assignment to a nominal morpheme is a proper part of a morphological process that accomplishes the same goal as θ-reservation does. Put differently, whatever happens to the reserved θ-role in syntax does not interfere with the minimalist evaluation of the three alternative morphological derivations in (19), and vice versa, because operations in different components of UG cannot be compared for cost.

As for why only a pro can occupy the syntactic argument position in polysynthetic languages, Baker's insight can be directly preserved in my theory. With *agr*s receiving the available Cases as Baker proposes,[5] there is no Case left for syntactic arguments. So the latter must take phonologically empty forms. Note that the pro argument is still necessary for θ-role assignment because *agr* only reserves a θ-role. Exactly the same situation is found with θ-identification, where an identified θ-role is still to be assigned to a real argument. With pros occupying argument positions and receiving θ-roles, lexical NPs are forced into adjunct positions. Overall, Baker's theory of polysynthetic languages can be duplicated without syntactically merging various lexical and functional heads.

Baker's second piece of evidence against lexicalist theories, the r-expression-like behavior of NI, also has an explanation under the POL. To begin with, note that the Binding Condition C effect demonstrated by NI in (13c–d) is directly paralleled by bare NPs found in many languages, one of which is Chinese.

(20) a. Xiaotou$_i$ bu xiwang jingcha buzhuo zuifan$_{*i/j}$.
      thief   not want   police catch   criminal
      'The thief did not want the police to catch criminals/the
      criminal.'

    b. Jingcha kandao-le xiaotou$_i$, suoyi jueding buzhuo zuifan$_{i/j}$.
      police see-asp   thief   so   decide catch   criminal
      'The police saw the thief, so he decided to catch criminals/the
      criminal.'

The NP *zuifan* 'criminal' can be coreferential with *xiaotou* 'thief' only in
(20b), where there is no c-command relation between the two. Logically,
the identical behaviors of bare NPs and incorporated nouns may be explained in one of two ways: that NI is derived from an underlying structure containing the bare NP, or that NI does not share a structural source
with the bare NP but nonetheless acquires all the semantic properties of
the latter. Baker takes the first approach, which also seems simpler on the
surface, at the cost of a mysterious MVC. Now I show that the second
approach not only is just as simple under the POL, but also results in a
structural analysis of NI practically indistinguishable from Baker's. Consequently, all the mechanisms needed to account for the semantics of syntactic NI in Baker's theory straightforwardly apply to the incorporated
noun in a morphologically formed NI compound.

My analysis consists of two parts: (i) to argue for the plausibility of
subjecting the incorporated noun and the bare NP to the same LF mechanisms, and (ii) to prove that for all the purposes of LF interpretation, the
morphological structure of NI is indistinguishable from the structural
context of bare NPs. Indistinguishable structures interpreted by the same
LF principles automatically yield identical semantic results.

For part (i), it must be admitted that making word-internal components accessible to LF operations is not a common practice in the P&P
literature.[6] But it is important to remember that research on LF, exten-
sive as it is, has been exclusively based on nonpolysynthetic languages.
Since syntax is the only module transparent to LF in these languages (see
the POL in (16)), LF is naturally regarded as an extension to phrasal
syntax, with no access to any part of morphological structure. Given the
POL, however, it is natural for LF to see all the generated structures not
shielded by the lexicon (= anything to the left of the curved line in (16))
and to interpret them with the same principles. In fact, I claim that this
is precisely why the Mohawk NI compound *its-a-hninu* 'fish-∅-buy' in

(13d) differs from *car-driving* in a nonpolysynthetic language like English. *Its* 'fish' is interpreted at LF as a noun bearing a θ-role from *hninu* 'buy'. In contrast, the whole compound *car-driving* in English is considered by LF as an indecomposable lexical item with an internal structure that LF has no access to. A direct outcome of this model is the straightforward reflection of the common perception that a polysynthetic word feels like a clause in a nonpolysynthetic language—after all, both constructions are interpreted by the same principles at LF.

Proceeding to part (ii) of my analysis, first consider what the theory must say in order to have a parallel account of the incorporated noun and the bare NP. Under the LH, the NI compound must be formed morphologically, prior to syntax. If N in the compound is to be interpreted like a bare NP in every way, it is obligatory that no NP-internal constituent should play a decisive role in the definiteness/specificity of the bare NP, and that the saturation of the R role of the head N should not depend on the presence of a determiner. This is so because neither a determiner nor any other constituent is available to the incorporated noun in my theory. As we saw in section 3.2.2, the Williams-Heim treatment of the R role provides precisely what we need.

Now consider the corresponding part of Baker's (1996) theory of NI. Because of the MVC, the R role of N cannot be assigned unless an agreement morpheme or a lexical morpheme is part of a word that contains N. Suppose that *agr* affixes to N, which itself projects to NP and further to DP. Since *agr* absorbs Case, the recipient of the R role must be a phonologically empty pro, which Baker places in the Spec of NP like a typical thematic argument (p. 256). It follows that a separate D outside NP is irrelevant to the saturation of the R role, a conclusion Baker uses to explain why polysynthetic languages characteristically do not have true determiners and why their noun suffixes are "meaningless morphemes" —they are the semantically do-nothing determiners "attached to free-standing nouns as a formal requirement" (p. 256).

There also is the option of not using *agr* for θ-role saturation. This option arises when the noun incorporates syntactically to the verb root. With the help of a modified MVC (p. 286), the verb root not only makes the R role of the noun available for assignment, but in fact discharges the role under Williams's (1981a) theory of θ-assignment, in which two θ-roles cancel each other out. The R role is ultimately treated as a free variable at LF, in the sense of Heim 1982. Since no *agr* is needed for discharging the R role of the syntactically incorporated N, the NP generated in the complement position of the verb root contains no pro in its Spec. Furthermore, it is a fact that NI, like VI, never has the form [*aff*-N]-V, where *aff*- is a functional morpheme associated with N. Baker adopts my (1990c) theory of head movement that prevents movement from a lexical position to a functional position and back to a lexical position (see section 1.1.5). It follows that in order for NI to take place in syntax, the nominal argument of the verb root must be a bare NP and not DP. For details, see Baker 1996, sec. 7.1.

Baker's theory of NI and mine share two conclusions. First, only a bare nominal serves as the thematic argument of the verb root. In my theory, this is the direct consequence of morphological compounding. In Baker's, it is due to the way θ-roles are assigned under the MVC and the obligatory absence of D so as to allow the head N to raise to V. The incorporated noun is of course structurally different from the D-less NP, but it is not clear at all what this difference does at LF when both of them are interpreted as the thematic argument of the verb root. To my knowledge, there is no evidence that semantics change simply because X projects to a bare XP.[7] Second, the R role of the noun is not saturated inside the nominal projection. In my theory, this is so because the noun never projects in morphology. In Baker's, there isn't any constituent available in the bare NP to receive the R role. This is why both theories take a Heim-style approach to account for all the referential/semantic properties of NI at LF—there really isn't anything one can do about the R role before LF. To be sure, Baker saturates the R role of the incorporated noun by adopting Williams's theory, whereas I choose the noncommittal (18). But this difference has no consequence for the issue at hand. For one thing, (18) is a broader assumption that properly includes Williams's theory. For another, Williams only provides a syntactic means to saturate the R role, whose semantic interpretation still depends on LF operations. Since Baker's argument against the lexicalist approach is semantic (Binding Condition C, referentiality, etc.), his theory of NI is indistinguishable from mine at LF.

Also worth noting is that there is nothing in the theory presented here to prevent the LF raising of the noun morpheme in an NI compound. Within the Minimalist Program, morphological bonding is neither relevant to nor expressible in LF. So the mere fact that N and V are concatenated in Mohawk morphology cannot deter raising N out of the compound. (Recall that what shields the word-internal structure from LF operations in English is not the morphological module but the boundary

of the lexicon as parametrically defined in the POL.) As long as the chain
condition in terms of c-command and locality is respected, the noun in
the NI compound is subject to movement as much as any other LF constituent. An immediate consequence is the possibility of raising N out of
the NI compound at LF and adjoining it outside the VP boundary to
obtain a specificity reading, along the lines proposed by Diesing (1992).[8]

In conclusion, a morphologically incorporated noun is shown to be
semantically identical to a bare NP under the POL. If the latter obeys
Binding Condition C, so does the former. In addition, morphological NI
does not rely on the mysterious MVC, resulting in a more explicit theory
of UG.

Before moving on to Baker's third argument, we need to examine
another process of Mohawk NI, stranding and doubling, illustrated in
(21) and (22), respectively (pp. 308–310).

(21) a. Thikʌ ʌ-ye-nakt-a-nuhwe'-ne'.
        this   fut-agr$_s$-bed-$\varnothing$-like-punc
        'She will like this bed.'
    b. Asehtsi ʌ-ye-nakt-a-nuhwe'-ne'.
        new   fut-agr$_s$-bed-$\varnothing$-like-punc
        'She will like the new bed.'

(22) a. Uwari ʌ-ye-nakt-a-nuhwe'-ne'   ne Sak rao-nakt-a'.
        Mary fut-agr$_s$-bed-$\varnothing$-like-punc NE Sak pref-bed-suff
        'Mary likes Sak's bed.'
    b. Sha'teku ni-kuti   rabahbot wa-hʌ-tsy-a-hnihu'   ki
        eight   part-agr bullhead fact-agr$_s$-fish-$\varnothing$-buy-punc this
        rake-'niha.
        my-father
        'My father bought eight bullheads.'

Semantically, *thikʌ* 'this' and *asehtsi* 'new' in (21) modify the incorporated noun *nakt* 'bed'. They are "stranded" in the sense that if the noun
originates as the head of the complement NP and raises to V, as is typical
of syntactic incorporation, the rest of the NP is left behind. In (22a), the
incorporated noun is doubled by an overt NP headed by the same noun;
and in (22b), the incorporated noun specifies a class of which the full NP
refers to a proper subset (i.e., bullheads form a subset of fish).

Putting an overt NP (with overt modifiers and a trace in the N position) in the thematic object position in (21) satisfies the MVC in Baker's

theory because the incorporated N mediates the object θ-role of the verb to the NP argument. But the overt NP in (22) must be an adjunct because the head N of the phrase is present, excluding the possibility of its having raised to V. Baker's analysis is that the true object NP contains only the head, which raises to V. This argument NP is thematically licensed in the same way as in the case of stranding. But its presence pushes the "doubling" NP to an adjunct position. Since two separate NPs are involved, there is no necessity that they are headed by an identical N. Thus, both (22a) and (22b) are allowed.

Baker's analysis of doubling clearly resembles his treatment of overt NPs associated with *agr*s. Recall that agreement licenses (and forces) a pro argument, pushing the overt NP (if there is one) to the adjunct position. And in both cases, it is necessary to make explicit how the NP adjunct is interpreted like a semantic argument of the verb stem. Baker accomplishes this task with chains. Essentially, an adjunct NP forms an $\bar{\text{A}}$-chain with either pro or a trace in an argument position, and receives appropriate (thematic) interpretation through the chain.

The account works inside Baker's theory, but NI doubling has a property that deserves more attention. While the incorporated N does not have to be identical to the head of the doubling NP, any difference is always semantically one-directional, as schematically illustrated in (23).

(23) a. ... fish-buy eight bullheads
      b. *... bullhead-buy eight fish

Apparently, no doubling like (23b) has ever been reported (Baker 1988, 145). Descriptively, the head noun of the overt NP must be no less specific in reference than the incorporated N, which is why (23a) is also called classifier incorporation (Chafe 1970; Mithun 1984). If we adopt Baker's $\bar{\text{A}}$-chains to describe the structural relation between the c-commanded incorporated N and the c-commanding doubling NP, this means the head of the chain must be at least as referentially specific as the tail.

That something like this may be a general requirement for chains is already independently suggested. Lasnik (1991) notes the following contrast:

(24) a. John-ga   [kare-ga [zibun-ga tensai-da-to] nomotte-iru-to] itta.
          John-nom he-nom self-nom genius-is-C think-pres-C   said
          'John said that he thinks that self is a genius.'

   b. *John-ga   [zibun-ga [kare-ga tensai-da-to] omotte-iru-to] itta.
      John-nom self-nom he-nom genius-is-C think-pres-C said
      'John said that self thinks that he is a genius.'

(25) a. ?John-nun [ku-ga   [caki-ga   chenjaela-ko] sengakhanta-ko]
        John-nom he-nom self-nom genius.be-C think-C
        malhaetta.
        said
        'John said that he thinks that self is a genius.'

   b. *John-nun [caki-ga   [ku-ga   chenjaela-ko] sengakhanta-ko]
      John-nom self-nom he-nom genius.be-C think-C
      malhaetta.
      said
      'John said that self thinks that he is a genius.'

(24) is from Japanese and (25) from Korean. Both languages allow a bare
reflexive (respectively, *zibun* and *caki*) to function as the subject of an
embedded clause. Since Binding Conditions A and B are clearly satisfied,
Lasnik proposes (26) to explain the contrast in each pair.

(26) A less referential expression cannot bind a more referential one.

In (24a), the pronoun *kare* 'he' binds and is more referential than the
reflexive *zibun* 'self'. So the sentence is good. In (24b), the sequence is
reversed, leaving the less referential *zibun* binding the more referential
kare and thus violating (26). The same analysis applies to (25). Also see
Lee 1996 for extending (26) to other dependency relations in Korean and
English syntax.

   Though terms like *more referential* and *more specific in reference* are
defined differently in the cited works, it is clear what the authors are trying to express. Generally, for an A- or $\bar{\text{A}}$-chain to be well formed, the
set of individuals specified by the head of the chain must be a subset (i.e.,
$\subseteq$) of what the tail refers to. Equipped with this insight, let us return to
Baker's third argument in favor of syntactic incorporation, namely, that
wh-phrases like *uhka* 'who' are incompatible with NI. The relevant example, (14b), is repeated here.

(27) ?*Uhka t-a-hse-wir-a-hkw-e'?
     who   dup-fut-agr$_s$-baby-$\emptyset$-pick.up-punc
     'Who are you going to pick up (a baby)?'

   As elsewhere in my theory, the N-V compound is formed not by syntactic movement but by presyntactic morphological rules. Being poly-

synthetic, Mohawk requires the N to discharge the θ-role of the verb stem in morphology. This means that no NP object of any kind is permitted because there is no θ-role for that position. It follows that any overt NP corresponding to the incorporated noun must be generated as an adjunct, including *uhka* 'who' in (27). Since the *wh*-phrase is, by hypothesis, associated with *-wir* 'baby', an Ā-chain is formed at LF for full interpretation of the adjunct NP *who*.

(28) [who, baby]

The chain is made possible because the incorporated N is visible to LF operations, as was established earlier. Now in terms of referential sets, *who*, being a quantifier, ranges over all humans whereas *baby* specifies a much smaller set. This is exactly the form a chain should not take, with the head specifying a superset of the tail's reference, violating (26). In other words, (27) is ruled out not because *who* competes with the incorporated N for the D-Structure object position, but because the Ā-chain in the sentence fails to respect a basic semantic property of chains.

In contrast, the examples in (22) contain well-formed chains.

(29) a. [bed, bed]   (for (22a))
      b. [eight bullheads, fish]   (for (22b))

The two members in (29a) have identical referential sets. The chain is redundant, which is what true doubling is all about, but the subset requirement is still respected. In (29b), the head refers to a proper subset of the tail's set, generating the "classifier" interpretation. Note that even though the incorporated noun is an r-expression at LF (see (20) and the surrounding discussion), there is no Binding Condition C violation in (29) because the head of the chain is not in an A-position. See Baker 1996, chaps. 1–2.

Now consider stranding in (21a–b), the latter of which is repeated here.

(30) Asehtsi ʌ-ye-nakt-a-nuhwe'-ne'.
     new   fut-agr$_s$-bed-$\varnothing$-like-punc
     'She will like the new bed.'

As in doubling, the incorporated N receives the θ-role and the object Case, so the NP containing the modifier *asehtsi* 'new' and a phonetically empty N must be an adjunct. Given the semantics of the sentence, either the empty N results from equi-deletion in the process of derivation to avoid repetition, or an empty N position is generated at the outset and receives a copy at LF from the incorporated N, much like what happens in ellipsis (Ross 1967; Sag 1976; Williams 1977). Either way, the actual chain at LF is like (31), which clearly is well formed because the referential set of the tail *nakt* 'bed' is definitely not smaller than that of the head.

(31) [new bed, bed]

Following the same logic, we expect the modifier *new* to be replaceable by the *wh*-word *ka nikayʌ* 'which'; the latter's semantics encodes a superset-subset relation. This is clearly true (Baker 1996, 323–325).

(32) a. Ka nikayʌ t-ʌ-hse-wir-a-hkw-e'?
         which   dup-fut-agr$_s$-baby-$\emptyset$-pick.up-punc
         'Which baby are you going to pick up?'
     b. Ka nikayʌ wa-hse-ks-ohare-'?
         which   fact-agr$_s$-dish-wash-punc
         'Which dish did you wash?'

As Baker points out in the same context, *which* differs from *who/what* in its ability to take an N head.

(33) a. ??Uhka eksa'a wa-she-kʌ-'?
         who child fact-agr$_{s/o}$-see-punc
         'Who (a child) did you see?'
     b. Ka nikayʌ eksa'a wa-she-kʌ-'?
         which   child fact-agr$_{s/o}$-see-punc
         'Which child did you see?'

Hence, the bare *which* in (32) entails an NP headed by an empty N. It follows that each sentence in (32) contains a chain like (34).

(34) [which N, N]

The rest of the analysis is identical to (31) because *which* N is necessarily a subset of N.

In addition to its simplicity and intuitiveness, this account of (14)/(27) avoids a *wh*-chain that originates in an A-position without Case. Recall that Baker's analysis requires the chain [*who*, t] in which *t* is in the D-Structure complement position of the verb. Since the chain is well formed when there is no NI but the verb root carries object agreement, *t* also receives no Case. According to Baker, this is permitted because *t* has no phonological form. But *who* does. And there is no evidence that such a chain can escape the Case Filter (see note 2). The problem no longer exists in my analysis. First, well-formed chains like (34) are not subject to the Case Filter because they are not formed through movement originating in an A-position. Adjunct NPs themselves may or may not need Case, but that is a separate issue because, by definition, they do not occupy an A-position at any stage of derivation. See Larson 1985 for a possible Case-theoretic account of adjunct NPs in English.

In summary, all three new arguments that Baker uses to defend syntactic NI and counter the lexicalist theories have natural (sometimes, more natural) explanations when NI is morphologically formed under the POL. Next, I consider the more complex phenomena in Baker 1996. Again, I show that the lexicalist theory plus the POL fares at least as well as the syntactic theory.

3.2.4 More on Noun Incorporation: Coexistence with Agreement

According to Baker, the data on which his first new argument is based have exceptions: many speakers do allow NI and object agreement to coexist (p. 319).

(35) a. Uwari ye/ruwa-kstʌ-hser-ʌhaw-e'   ne   rake-'niha.
       Mary agr$_s$/agr$_{so}$-old.person-nom-carry-impf NE my-father
       'Mary is holding my father.'

   b. Ke/Ri-ksa-ht-a-nuhwe'-s   ne   tshe-'nha'-u.
      agr$_s$/agr$_{so}$-child-nom-$\emptyset$-like-hab NE agr$_{s/o}$-hire-stat
      'I like the child that you hired.'

   c. Wa'-ke/hi-kstʌ-hser-ahset-e'.
      fact-agr$_s$/agr$_{so}$-old.person-nom-hide-punc
      'I hide the old man.'

In all these examples, the (matrix) verb can agree either with the subject alone or with both the subject and object, even in the presence of an incorporated N. Even though NI without object agreement is "more common in texts" and "there are some instances ... where speakers do not seem to permit agreement," like (12d), the two options "often exist side by side in Mohawk" (pp. 319–320).

Baker suggests treating the option with object agreement as being lexically (in the traditional sense of the term) formed as in Di Sciullo and Williams 1987, an approach that would be able to explain the option's less common occurrence through lexical idiosyncrasy. It should be noted, however, that the option shown in (35) is not really rare, judging from Baker's wording and the examples found throughout his work. Furthermore, many other polysynthetic languages (Southern Tiwa of Tanoan, Mayali of Gunwinjguan, and some dialects of Ainu) apparently allow the two options quite consistently (Baker, sec. 7.4.5). Therefore, this option might as well be regarded as a productive process of NI rather than a marginal idiosyncrasy.

What is more important is a hidden problem in Di Sciullo and Williams's lexical analysis of NI that ultimately leads to failure to limit NI to the thematic object. In Baker's analysis, based on Di Sciullo and Williams 1987, the crucial point is that the verb's object θ-role remains available in the argument structure of the compound, only modified by the R role of the noun. The two merged θ-roles, now functioning like one, are associated with *agr* and eventually assigned to a pro argument in syntax. But this is θ-identification between the verb and the noun, in essence tagging the noun's R role and forcing it to be assigned together with the θ-role of the verb. The problem is that there is ample evidence that θ-identification, unlike θ-assignment, does not respect the thematic hierarchy.

Consider the Chinese resultative compounds in (36).

(36) a. Le He chang-wang-le yijian zhongyaode shiqing.
       Le He sing-forget-asp an   important   thing
       'Le He was so absorbed in singing that he forgot an important thing.'
   b. Lin Chong qi-lei-le   ma.
       Lin Chong ride-tired-asp horse
       Can mean: 'Lin Chong became tired from riding the horse.'

In (36a), the argument structure of the V_c *chang* 'sing' is $\langle a \rangle$ and that of the V_r *wang* 'forget' is $\langle x \langle y \rangle \rangle$. The compound *chang-wang* 'sing-forget' has the argument $\langle \underline{a} \langle x \langle y \rangle \rangle \rangle$, where *a* and *x* are identified and eventually assigned to the subject *Le He*. As the compound is formed in the lexicon (see the appendix to chapter 1), nothing happens yet to the object θ-role of V_r when V_r's subject θ-role is tagged for later assignment with the single θ-role of V_c. Similarly, the compound *qi-lei* in (36b) consisting of *qi* 'ride' with $\langle a \langle b \rangle \rangle$ and *lei* 'tired' with $\langle x \rangle$ has the argument structure $\langle \underline{a} \langle b \langle x \rangle \rangle \rangle$. The single θ-role of V_r, *x*, is identified with the subject θ-role *a* of V_c regardless of the thematically lower *b*.

Baker's analysis of applicatives leads to the same conclusion. Recall from section 1.2.2 that he identifies the subject θ-roles of the verb root and the *-app* affix. Since he projects each verb to its own VP, the θ-roles of a transitive verb root are discharged in accordance with the thematic hierarchy, identifying the subject θ-role after assigning the object θ-role to an argument NP. But we have seen that the syntactic analysis typical of his theory of VI is to be replaced by the lexicalist formation of applicative verbs subject to syntactic expansion under the MSMH. This means that the subject θ-roles of the two verbal morphemes are identified in the argument structure of the whole applicative verb prior to any thematic operation on the object θ-role(s).

This lack of respect for the thematic hierarchy on the part of θ-identification can be attributed to the fact that it is by nature just a reservation (see section 3.3.2). No real θ-assignment takes place yet; hence, hierarchical restrictions on assignment do not extend to reservation. But independently of why this is so, it is clear that θ-identification does not take place according to the thematic hierarchy, at least when it happens during word formation. Then why does Baker's lexical NI still demonstrate the well-known subject-object asymmetry? Whether co-occurring with *agr* or not, Mohawk NI always happens only to the (Theme?) object and never to the subject (see (2)). If the existence of *agr* indicates lexical NI through θ-identification, the asymmetry should disappear; that is, Mohawk should have lexical NI wherein the R role of N is identified with the subject θ-role of V, directly matching the resultative compound in (36b). This is clearly a wrong prediction.

One solution is to always treat the incorporated noun as receiving a θ-role from the verb root while optionally allowing it to be either a referential argument or a predicate. Under the latter option, the R role of the incorporated noun becomes part of the argument structure of the N-V compound, just like the verb root in VI. But before I spell out the details, let me outline the general aspects of this analysis. First, though Baker's syntactic analysis of NI derives the subject-object and Theme-Goal asymmetries from the ECP and other minimalist mechanisms (see Baker 1996, sec. 7.3), the same asymmetries hold for lexically formed compounds as well. The examples in (3) are repeated here.

(37) a. car-driving vs. *student-driving
      b. gift-giving to children vs. *child-giving of gifts

Therefore, some separate morphological mechanism is still necessary to generate (37). Since the nouns in (37) are generally taken to receive the object θ-role from the verb, Baker's account (as well as Di Sciullo and Williams's) would need additional means to maintain the same asymmetries if lexical NI were formed through θ-identification. On the other hand, if all instances of NI and similar compounds like those in (37) are regarded as formed morphologically, with N receiving the Theme θ-role from V, maximal consistency can be maintained. One still wonders why only the Theme argument can incorporate in morphology, but that is the question that even Baker needs to answer in the face of (37). Minimally, the theory being proposed here does not contain double mechanisms to prevent the N in NI from having the subject reading.

Another question is what prevents θ-identification from taking place between N and V in an NI compound. If the process is possible in Chinese and Bantu languages, why doesn't it take place in Mohawk as Baker and Di Sciullo and Williams suggest? Various possibilities come to mind, an obvious one making use of Grimshaw's (1979) Canonical Structural Realization. In this theory, the noun in NI is a canonical θ-role recipient of the verb and therefore is always treated as such. In contrast, V_r in a Chinese resultative compound cannot serve as the thematic object of V_c because V_c simply does not take a verbal argument. It follows that θ-identification becomes the only alternative for thematic operations between V_r and V_c.

Moving to the coexistence of NI and *agr* in (35), suppose that when N and V form a compound in morphology and N takes the object θ-role from V, either the R role of N is automatically saturated according to the Williams-Heim approach in (18), or it is left untouched, in effect treating N as an embedded predicate. The argument structure of the second option is illustrated with the compound in (35c).

(38) old.man $\langle x \rangle$
     hide $\langle a \langle b \rangle\rangle$
     old.man-hide $\langle a \langle x \rangle\rangle$ (N functions as embedded predicate)

In this usage, the R role of the noun *old.man*, marked as *x*, is used not for referential purposes but as a "normal" θ-role to be assigned to an argument (cf. the predicative use of the noun *hero* in *They considered Sam a hero*). During word formation, the object θ-role of *hide* is assigned to *old.man*, but the compound obtains a new internal θ-role, *x*, from the incorporated noun. In other words, the compound is just like an ordinary transitive verb.

Returning to the examples in (35), the presence of the object *agr* can easily be explained. It is there to tag the new object θ-role as required by (17). The θ-role is eventually assigned to a syntactic argument in the form of pro, which in turn may form an Ā-chain with an overt NP adjunct. As expected, this analysis predicts the pro to be capable of being coreferential with a c-commanding antecedent outside the binding domain (p. 322).

(39) Sak ra-tshani-s   toka   ʌ-hi-ksa-ht-a-ya'k-e'.
Sak agr$_s$-fear-hab maybe fut-agr$_{s/o}$-child-nom-$\emptyset$-hit-punc
'Sak is afraid that maybe I will slap the child.'

Since the pro in the embedded object position bears the θ-role of *ksa* 'child', which in turn receives the object θ-role of *ya'k* 'hit', it is understood to be a child that is potentially the target of hitting.[9] This pro may refer to *Sak* through coreference with the matrix subject pro, which is in an Ā-chain with *Sak*, because the two pros are located in different clauses. The incorporated noun *child* is also c-commanded by the antecedent, but this does not incur a Binding Condition C violation because *child* is interpreted at LF as a predicate, not a referential argument.

3.2.5 Possessor Raising
Another phenomenon related to NI is possessor raising. The classic Mohawk examples in (40) are from Postal 1979, 325, 319.

(40) a. I'i ri-nuhs-ohare-s   ne Shawatis.
me agr$_{s/o}$-house-wash-hab NE John
'I wash John's house.'

   b. Ro-nuhs-a-rakʌ   ne Shawatis.
agr$_o$-house-$\emptyset$-white NE John
'John's house is white.'

Semantically, Shawatis is understood to be the owner of the house. Baker at first (1988) treats these examples as a prime case of syntactic NI plus a stranded possessor, but he later (1996) argues against that analysis on the basis of the following examples (p. 341):

(41) a. *T-a-ho-hur-ʌ'-ne'   ne Sak.
cis-fact-agr$_o$-gun-fall-punc NE Sak
Intended reading: 'Sak's gun fell.'

   b. *Sak wa'-t-ho-wis-a-hri'-ne'.
Sak fact-dup-agr$_o$-glass-$\emptyset$-break-punc
Intended reading: 'Sak's glass broke.'

The verb stems are unaccusative, and such stems are otherwise capable of NI in Mohawk. If the semantically possessive NP were indeed the stranded possessor, the ungrammaticality of (41a–b) would be totally unexplainable.

As an alternative, Baker (1996) suggests that the overt NP in examples like (40a) is in fact a Benefactive argument of the verb rather than a possessive of the incorporated noun. So (40a) really has nothing to do with possessor raising at all. (40b) is the true case of possessor raising, which is limited to adjectival verbs only. For details, see Baker 1996. Here, I will concentrate on demonstrating how Baker's new insight can be accommodated in my theory to account for the phenomenon.

For Baker, the primary question is why possessor raising is *not* possible when NI is syntactically derived and can indeed strand modifiers (see (21)). The answer relies on his Condition on Agreement Relations (CAR, p. 344).

(42) *Condition on Agreement Relations*
An agreement factor X can be coindexed with a phrase Y only if Y is coindexed with a position in the argument structure of a head Z and X is adjoined to Z.

Consider Baker's structure (43) for NI with a stranded possessor.

(43)

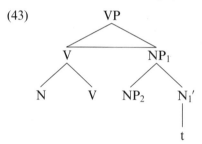

The D-Structure object, NP_1, receives a θ-role from the verb through the incorporated N. NP_2, the possessor, presumably also needs a θ-role, which N would provide as long as the MVC could be satisfied. When N is incorporated, however, this is not possible because the only available agreement belongs to the verb in this case. According to the CAR, the *agr* (= X) on V can be coindexed with an argument phrase (= Y) and hence help assign a θ-role to it only if the phrase will receive a θ-role from the θ-assigner (= Z) to which the *agr* is affixed. But the *agr* affixes to the verb, not the incorporated N. It follows that N cannot assign its possessor θ-role to NP_2 under the MVC and the CAR, thereby ruling out (43) and the examples it represents, (41a–b).

As Baker points out, this account crucially depends on banning argument structure composition in incorporation. If the incorporated noun combines its own argument structure, which contains the possessor θ-role, with that of the verb, the resulting compound verb would have the possessor role in its argument structure. Then the CAR would not be able to prevent possessor raising because the possessive NP would be receiving the θ-role from the compound verb and the *agr is* affixed to the compound verb.

Next consider (40b), the adjectival verb with NI and (presumably) true possessor raising. Baker observes that adjectival verbs in Mohawk do not bear the aspect suffix that is otherwise obligatory on verbs, seen clearly in (40a–b). For Baker, this indicates that adjectival verbs lack the Event role, a role that is bound by Asp in Mohawk but by T in other languages (see Higginbotham 1985). Furthermore, possessor raising is obviously dependent on NI (p. 341).

(44) a. Ro-nitskwara-tsher-a-hniru.
         agr_o-chair-nom-$\emptyset$-be.hard
         'His chair is hard.'
     b. *Ro-hniru ne anitskwara.
         agr_o-hard NE chair
         Intended reading: same as (44a)

While the agreement in (44a) indicates a masculine singular pro (i.e., the possessor), the same agreement (implying a possessor-like pro) is unacceptable in (44b), where NI does not take place. Apparently, the adjectival verb cannot take a Benefactive argument of its own as certain transitive verbs do. It only has *anitskwara* 'chair' as its argument, and the possessor comes into existence as the result of NI.

Still another property of NI with adjectival verbs is that the verbs consistently display object agreement with the possessor. Mohawk adjectival verbs are lexically divided into two agreement classes: some carry the object agreement form and others the subject agreement form.[10] *Hniru* 'hard' in (44a) belongs to the object agreement group, whereas *hutsi* 'black' in (45a) belongs to the subject agreement group (p. 212). But in the possessor-raising construction, they always display object agreement with the possessor. The examples in (45) show how agreement changes with *hutsi*.

(45) a. Ka-hutsi.
         agr_s-black
         'It is black.'
     b. Sa-na'ts-a-hutsi.
         agr_o-pot-$\emptyset$-black
         'Your pot is black.'

Baker's account of the data is based on the absence of the Event role in the argument structure of adjectival verbs. Essentially, the restriction on compositional argument structures is relaxed to the extent that an N-V compound may inherit either the argument structure of the verb or that of the noun, but not both at the same time. Since the adjectival verb has no Event role and its only θ-role is assigned to the NP argument, the compound can afford to inherit the Possessor role from the noun because there is no longer any need to worry about satisfying the θ-Criterion on the part of the verb. This explains why NI is so crucial for possessor raising (see (44)). Without NI, there would be no N-V compound and therefore the conditions necessary for argument structure inheritance would not even exist.

The invariable object agreement in (44a) and (45b) also has an explanation. Adjectival verbs are idiosyncratically divided between the subject and object agreement classes, which associate the θ-role of the verb with a particular choice of agreement form. As the N-V compound inherits the Possessor role from the N in possessor raising, however, the original idiosyncratic choice of agreement is no longer valid. Object agreement is chosen to be associated with the Possessor role because the latter is hierarchically lower than the R role of the same noun, under the assumption that the lower of two coarguments gets object agreement (p. 223 and sec. 8.4). Baker summarizes this predictable aspect of agreement marking as the Structural Agreement Principle (SAP). A lexicalist variant of the SAP is given in (46) to anticipate the upcoming discussion.

(46) A θ-role is marked +O if it has a thematically more prominent coargument.

A θ-role marked with +O is coindexed (tagged, in my terms; for the original definition of the +O/+A notation, see Baker 1996, 192) with an object *agr*; a θ-role not marked with +O is marked +A by default and is tagged by a subject *agr*. (See Marantz 1991 for the original idea underlying (46), and see Williams 1994 for a much more elaborate use of thematic coarguments.)

Unlike adjectives, verbs do have the Event role, which is considered part of the argument structure by Higginbotham (1985) and Baker. As a result, even when the single θ-role of an unaccusative verb is assigned to the NP complement, the Event role remains unsaturated inside VP. When the head noun of the complement NI incorporates, the N-V compound cannot inherit the argument structure of the noun at the cost of leaving the verb's Event role unsaturated (presumably owing to an extended use of the CAR). It follows that the compound can never have the Possessor role in its argument structure, and possessor raising is prohibited in the case of verbs.

Because syntactic NI is banned in principle by the theory I am proposing, an alternative account of possessor raising must be formulated. In what follows, I present a lexicalist theory of the phenomenon that takes advantage of some of Baker's insights (and is based on data from Baker 1996). The theory, as expected, rests on the composition of argument structures.

To begin with, consider another possible reason why possessor raising never happens with verbs. Mohawk verbs have a rather complex agreement system. Each example in (47) illustrates a verb type and the corresponding agreement pattern. (For many more examples, see Baker 1996, sec. 5.2.1.) The morpheme -$(h)s$, glossed as *ben*, is the applicative affix.

(47) a. T-a-hi-yena-'.   (transitive)
        cis-fact-$agr_{s/o}$-catch-punc
        'I caught him.'
     b. Wa-hiy-u-'.   (ditransitive)
        fact-$agr_{s/o}$-give-punc
        'I gave it to him.'
     c. Λ-hi-yo'tʌ-hs-e'.   (unergative
        fut-$agr_{s/o}$-work-ben-punc   plus Goal)
        'I will work for him.'
     d. Sak wa-ho-hsʌ'-s-e'   ne   owise'.   (unaccusative
        Sak cis-agr_o-fall-ben-punc NE glass   plus Goal)
        'The glass fell on Sak.' (= Sak dropped the glass.)

First compare (47a–c) with (47d). For verbs (including applicatives composed of a verb root and a Benefactive suffix) with more than one argument, the use of subject agreement correlates with an Agent argument. Since (47d) is unaccusative, no subject *agr* is possible. (47b) and (47d) represent another property that is not reflected with my notation: in the presence of two internal arguments, the Goal must be associated with object *agr* whereas the Theme is always neuter, without any phonologically overt agreement. Baker suggests that the overt subject and object *agr*s correspond to structural Cases in European languages, while the neuter form is comparable to other means for Case assignment (sec. 5.2.1).

Given the data in (47) and Baker's analysis, suppose that *only the Theme role of a verb can be tagged by the neuter form of agreement*, somewhat akin to inherent Cases. This immediately explains why verbs do not allow possessor raising. Take the NI compound *wis-a-hri'* 'glass-break' in (41b), for example.

(48) glass $\langle x \langle y \rangle \rangle$
     break $\langle a \rangle^{11}$
     glass-break $\langle x \langle y \rangle \rangle$

The noun *glass* has the R role x and the Possessor role y in its argument structure. When the compound is formed, the Theme role a of the verb *break* is assigned to *glass*. In order for the compound to allow the intended possessor raising, the Possessor role y of *glass* must remain unsaturated so as to be available in the argument structure of the compound. From the perspective of the compound, then, *glass* is used as a thematically unsaturated predicate.

Now it is a fact that no known referential NP argument contains unsaturated θ-roles, probably because of a fundamental distinction between arguments and predicates (see Stowell 1981). Technically, this means that if the R role of a nominal is automatically saturated, all its θ-roles are to be saturated at the level of representation where it functions as an argument. Since the incorporated noun *glass* in Mohawk is simply the morphological counterpart of the NP object in syntax, as the POL dictates, it must not contain any unsaturated θ-role as long as it is interpreted as an argument. Conversely, if the Possessor role of *glass* must be kept available in the argument structure of the compound, its R role cannot be automatically saturated under (18b) because automatic saturation would impose the conflicting requirement that *glass* be used referentially. In other words, if *glass* is to be used like a predicate for possessor raising as in (48), the noun must be treated as a predicate completely; no morphological component can be simultaneously a referential argument and a predicate.

But the N-V compound *glass-break* with the argument structure in (48) cannot satisfy (17) for thematic operations in morphology. First of all, the argument structure contains no Agent, making it impossible to use subject *agr* for θ-reservation. Furthermore, the argument structure contains no Theme either, x being R and y being the Possessor. Since only the Theme argument undergoes NI (see note 9), neither of the two θ-roles can be saturated through NI. For the same reason, neither can be tagged by the neuter agreement form either, given the hypothesis based on (47). What all this boils down to is that only one of the θ-roles in the compound *glass-break* can be tagged by the regular object *agr*, the other θ-role being doomed to have no legitimate means for saturation, directly in violation of (17). Consequently, no possessor raising is ever possible with such a compound. The same logic applies when V is transitive. The argument structure of such a compound would consist of the Agent role from the verb and the R role and Possessor role from the incorporated noun. Subject *agr* would be available for tagging the Agent role and object *agr* for one of the other two, say, the R role. But the Possessor role would be left unattended, just as in (47).

In this respect, possessor raising contrasts with regular NI and NI-agreement co-occurrence, discussed previously. In the latter constructions, the incorporated noun has only one θ-role, R. Whether this R role is treated referentially or predicatively is solely a matter of choice available to morphological computation. In the referential use, automatic saturation takes place and the R role is simply not represented in the argument structure of the compound. In the predicative use, the R role "replaces" the original Theme role of the verb in the compound (because Theme is assigned to N). The compound has the same number of θ-roles as the verb morpheme alone, imposing no extra burden on the agreement system.

Turning to the well-formed possessor raising with adjectival verbs (see (40b), (44a), (45b)), we may note an observation made in Baker 1996: that the phenomenon is probably not common even among polysynthetic languages (p. 388). Therefore, whatever explanation it eventually receives should be based on highly marked and/or language-specific mechanisms rather than the core principles of UG.

The argument structure of the adjectival compound *nuhs-a-rakʌ* 'house-white' in (40b) is given in (49).

(49) house $\langle x \langle y \rangle \rangle$
     white $\langle a \rangle$
     house-white $\langle x \langle y \rangle \rangle$

As in NI with a verb root in (48), the noun keeps its R role x and Possessor role y in the argument structure of the compound. The inability to saturate both x and y in the compound should be sufficient to rule out the construction, just as with (48). However, *white* in (49) is actually adjectival. Categorially, it should be represented as $[+V, +N]^{12}$ rather than as the truly verbal $[+V, -N]$. Accordingly, the whole compound is also $[+V, +N]$. This categorial difference not only sets (49) apart from (48) but also provides a marginal way to rescue possessor raising with adjectival NI.

Suppose that in an effort to interpret an otherwise ungrammatical compound like (49), Mohawk chooses to focus on the implications of $[+N]$ in the adjectival *house-white*. From this perspective, the compound is actually nominal. In fact, this is a nominal word whose R role does not have to be used predicatively. What is crucial at this point is to distinguish between the R role as part of the incorporated noun and the R role as part of the compound. The predicative nature of the noun is determined in the larger structural context of the N-A compound. In this context, the R role must be treated like the Possessor role, both unsaturated and subject to θ-assignment. And this is so because the noun must function as a predicate in order to keep the Possessor role available for future use. The N-A compound as a whole, on the other hand, can be viewed as a single word. If it contains an R role in its argument structure, it is no different from a monomorphemic noun with an R role, and there is no bigger morphological context to force the R role to be treated in one way or another.

Viewing *house-white* as a nominal word opens up the (albeit marked) possibility of treating it provisionally like a noun for θ-saturation.[13] Its R role may be automatically saturated (I return to this point shortly), and the Possessor role is marked $+O$ under (46) because it has the R role as coargument and, by hypothesis, is thematically less prominent than the latter. Several consequences follow. First, this view explains why the Possessor is always associated with the object *agr* (see (40b), (44a), (45b)). Second, treating an N-A compound as if it were a noun takes advantage of the $[+N]$ feature of the adjective and is obviously a compromise solution to possessor raising. It is therefore expected to increase the tension in the grammatical computation of the language. This explains why the phenomenon is not popular even among polysynthetic languages. Third, this marginal process represents a purely grammatical attempt to satisfy (17). It yields no absurd semantics such as a "referential adjective." This is so because a sentence like (40b) is interpreted only at LF, where constituents inside a Mohawk word are accessible to semantic principles and only semantic principles. There, *house* is understood as the Theme argument of *white*, the possessor of *house* is a male named *John*, and the R role of *house* turns into a bound variable. The fact that the R role is also part of the argument structure of the N-A compound is but a "temporary" stage of the complete derivation that matters only to the morphological component. Finally, even this marginal option is not available to an N-V compound simply because verbs are [−N] by definition. So it is not possible to treat it like any kind of nominal.

To complete this discussion, I briefly examine Baker's treatment of the possessives in (50) (p. 257) as hidden internally headed relative clauses.

(50) ake-nuhs-a' agr_o-house-suff   'my house'
      rao-'sere-' agr_o-car-suff   'his car'
      ak-kar-a' agr_o-story-suff   'my story'
      rao-wis-e' agr_o-glass-suff   'his glass'

Baker offers three arguments, the first based on Tuscarora, a Northern Iroquoian language related to Mohawk. The data in (51) are from Mithun-Williams 1976, 218–219.

(51) a. ako:-nʌhs-a-wa
       agr_o-house-$\emptyset$-belong.to(perfective)
       'her house (lit.: the house that belongs to her)'
   b. ro-tsha:r-a-wa
       agr_o-door-$\emptyset$-belong.to(perfective)
       'his door (lit.: the door that belongs to him)'

Not only is the verb *wa* 'belong to' overtly represented in these "possessive" expressions, but the agreement morpheme is in the nominal *y*-less form (Mithun-Williams 1976, 218). Within a syntactic theory of incorporation, *house* in (51a) would be the Theme argument raised to V. The other argument of *belong to* receives the θ-role with the help of the object *agr*. An empty *wh*-operator is coindexed with the NP headed by *house* and yields the reading of a relative clause. Given the Tuscarora data, it is easy to hypothesize a similar structure for Mohawk possessives provided that the verb is phonologically empty. Strictly speaking, however, this is not an argument because the data in one language can only be suggestive for another. The Tuscarora data do not force an identical structure on Mohawk.

The second argument is also based on (50): a noun with a possessor carries only one *agr* in Mohawk.[14] Since this *agr* tags the Possessor role, the R role is left unattended. But under the MVC, a θ-role lacking coindexation with an agreement morpheme is not visible to syntactic θ-assignment, ultimately leading to a θ-Criterion violation. The problem would be solved if the possessive construction were underlyingly a relative clause with an empty verb. Again assuming the verb to be something like *belong to*, the Theme argument is already incorporated and thus satisfies the MVC. The other θ-role of the verb is tagged by object agreement. The R role of the incorporated noun is saturated as in Williams's (1981a) theory (see (18) and associated text). As long as the Possessor role of the noun is optionally absent, every θ-role is properly taken care of. But as we see now, this problem is only a theory-internal one dependent on the particular formulation of the MVC. If UG allows the saturation of the R role to wait till LF, the problem never arises to begin with.[15]

The contrast between Mohawk and Spanish in (52) illustrates the third argument.

(52) a. Kikʌ Uwari ako-tya'tawi wa'-ee-ratsu-ko-'.
         this Mary agr-dress   fact-agr$_s$-tear-rev-punc
         'This dress of Mary$_i$'s, she$_i$ tore.'
     b. El libro de Juan, lo perdio.
         the book of Juan it he.lost
         'Juan$_i$'s book, he$_{*i}$ lost it.'

While *Uwari* in (52a) can be coindexed with the subject of the clause, *Juan* in (52b) cannot. According to Baker, quoting an observation made in Lebeaux 1989 and Chomsky 1993 that relative clauses don't seem to undergo reconstruction for the purpose of satisfying Binding Condition C, the contrast follows if the proper name in (52a) is embedded in a resultative clause. If Baker is correct, then Mohawk possessives may be in transition between a Tuscarora-type relative clause structure and a true nominal possessive structure. The two structures may coexist in the language. A construction like (52a) forces the relative clause structure. But all I have said so far remains valid for the other choice.

3.2.6 Complex Predicates, Argument Structure Composition, and the Condition on Agreement Relations

In this section, I examine Mohawk VI for two purposes: to illustrate how easily Baker's syntactic analysis can be converted into my more lexicalist theory, and to discuss the nature of argument composition and the CAR.

VI in Mohawk is limited in the sense that it applies only to unaccusative verb roots ((53a–b) and (54a–c) from p. 351; (53c) from p. 353).

(53) a. Wa-ha-wis-a-nawʌ-ht-e'.
     fact-agr$_s$-ice-melt-$\emptyset$-cause-punc
     'He melted the ice.'
  b. Uwari t-a-yu-hsʌ-ht-e'   ne a'share'.
     Mary cis-fact-agr$_{s/o}$-fall-cause-punc NE knife
     'Mary made the knife fall.'
  c. Sak wa-shako-ye-ht-e'   ne Uwari.
     Sak fact-agr$_{s/o}$-wake-cause-punc NE Mary
     'Sak woke Mary up.'

(54) a. *Onʌste' wa-hi-yʌtho-ht-e'   ne Sak.
     corn   fact-agr$_{s/o}$-plant-cause-punc NE Sak
     Intended reading: 'I made Sak plant corn.'
  b. *Wa'-khe-ks-ohare-ht-e'.
     fact-agr$_{s/o}$-dish-wash-cause-punc
     Intended reading: 'I made her wash the dishes.'
  c. *Wa'-te-shako-hsʌ'tho-ht-e'.
     fact-dup-agr$_{s/o}$-cry-cause-punc
     Intended reading: 'He made her cry.'

(54a–b) contain transitive verbs and (54c) contains an unergative verb.
None of them can be causativized, in contrast with the verbs in (53).

In Baker's account, the ungrammaticality of (54a–c) results from the
MVC, the CAR, and the ban against composing argument structures
in the process of incorporation. Consider the structure of (54c) shown
in (55), simplified to avoid irrelevant complications.

(55)

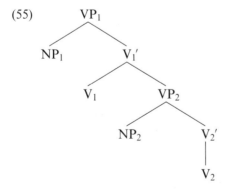

Given my (1990c) observation, no functional head may be generated
between V_1 and V_2 (see (36) of chapter 1). This immediately makes
it difficult for V_2 to assign its subject θ-role. According to the MVC,

θ-assignment happens only through agreement morphology or NI. NI is not possible because subjects do not incorporate. Agreement morphology is not available because there is no embedded AgrP. Meanwhile, the CAR prevents the matrix Agr from helping V_2 with θ-assignment: the matrix Agr cannot be coindexed with the embedded subject NP_2 because NP_2 is not coindexed with any position in the argument structure of the matrix verb V_1 to which the matrix Agr adjoins. NP_2 is indeed coindexed with a θ-position of V_2, but the matrix Agr does not adjoin to the embedded verb. The question is what is responsible for the ungrammaticality of (54)–(55). Note that the problem would disappear if V_1 and V_2 were to merge their argument structures. In that case, the whole verb cluster would have only one argument structure that contains the subject θ-role of V_2. Then the matrix Agr would be able to affect this new argument structure while still respecting the CAR, and (55) would be incorrectly permitted. Therefore, Baker concludes that no argument structure composition should be allowed.

Since this theory rules out (55) for failing to assign the embedded subject θ-role, whether the embedded verb is unergative or transitive has no effect on the result. Now consider Baker's structural representation of (53), shown in (56), in which the verb root is unaccusative.

(56)

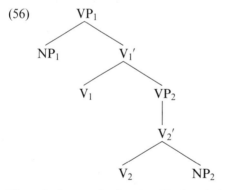

Though the matrix Agr is still of no help to V_2 in assigning its θ-roles, the internal argument NP_2 can receive the θ-role from V_2 through NI. The question is why a pro object is also permitted, as evidenced by the object agreement in (53). This is not supposed to happen if the reasoning in the previous paragraph is correct—after all, V_2 cannot carry its own *agr*.

Baker's solution is restricted argument structure composition. Assuming V_1 to be a light verb comparable to *do* in English and *suru* in Japanese (Grimshaw and Mester 1988) with the argument structure $\langle$Agent $\langle$Theme$\rangle\rangle$, Baker proposes that the Theme role of V_2 "can count as the theme of $[V_1]$" because the two argument structures are "nondistinct," meaning that they do not contain θ-roles of different types (p. 355). In effect, this operation identifies the two Theme roles and assigns them together to a single argument (i.e., NP_2 in (56)), via the matrix Agr. This satisfies the CAR because the matrix Agr is coindexed with the Theme of V_1, which in turn carries the same index as the Theme of V_2. In contrast, the Agent θ-role of an unergative V_2 in (55) is different from the Theme role of V_1, and θ-identification is impossible. Without being related to the argument structure of V_1, the Agent of V_2 cannot be properly assigned.

This account can be easily converted into my theory. To begin with, note that the argument structure Baker gives to V_1 deserves a little refinement. Crosslinguistically, causative verbs take an Event argument. Even if V_1 is a light verb, this piece of information must be part of it as long as it is treated as a causative verb. I assume that the causative affix in Mohawk, like causative verbs in other languages, has an Event θ-role. I also adopt Baker's suggestion (and Alsina's (1992); see chapter 1) that V_1 has a Theme role that must be identified with a θ-role of V_2.[16] Probably it is the nature of a light verb that at least one of its θ-roles must be identified with (or perhaps dependent on) a counterpart in the argument structure of a nonlight lexical head. In any case, when V_1 and V_2 form a V-V compound, V_2 receives the Event role from V_1, resulting in one of two possible argument structures depending on the nature of V_2.[17]

(57) a. V_1 $\langle$Causer $\langle$Theme $\langle$Event$\rangle\rangle\rangle$
     V_2 $\langle$Agent ... $\rangle$
     V_2-V_1 $\langle$Causer $\langle$Theme $\langle$Agent ... $\rangle\rangle\rangle$

  b. V_1 $\langle$Causer $\langle$Theme $\langle$Event$\rangle\rangle\rangle$
     V_2 $\langle$Theme$\rangle$
     V_2-V_1 $\langle$Causer $\langle$Theme $\langle$Theme$\rangle\rangle\rangle$

By hypothesis, θ-identification cannot happen in (57a) because the two θ-roles at issue are distinct. Under the MSMH, the compound in (57a) maps to (58) to reflect the thematic relation between V_1 and V_2. NP_2 is the Theme argument of V_1, the causative morpheme (irrelevant details are ignored).

(58)

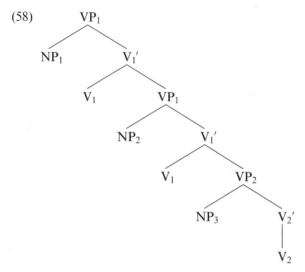

As no embedded AgrP is permitted, any *agr* on the compound can only be reflected as the matrix AgrP. Assume for the moment that the matrix AgrP can only affect the head of its own complement, that is, the matrix verb. Then the assignment of the Agent role by V_2 cannot rely on the matrix Agr. Nor can it be assigned through NI since, independently, an N-V compound requires N to be a Theme. This is sufficient to rule out (52a)/(53). Clearly, whether V_2 has its own Theme argument or not has no effect on the ungrammaticality of the construction.

The compound with an unaccusative verb root in (57b) maps to (59) if NI does not take place.

(59)

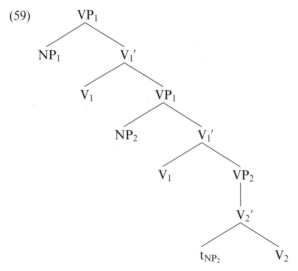

Receiving the identified Themes from the V_1-V_2 cluster, NP_2 starts inside VP_2 and raises to the Spec of the lower VP_1 (see section 1.2.2 and especially the discussion around (55) therein). The object *agr* on the compound can tag the Theme role of V_1 (or tag the identified super θ-role, depending on how one looks at it), helping assign it to the pro object in the position of NP_2. This yields the examples in (53b–c).

Logically, the NI compound *ice-melt-cause* in (53a) may have either of these two morphological structures:

(60) a. [[ice-melt-] cause]
     b. [ice- [melt-cause]]

By convention, θ-identification between *melt* and *cause* cannot happen in (60a) because *ice* would discharge the Theme role of *melt* before the cluster is further concatenated with *cause*. If *cause* does have its own Theme and must have it identified as Baker suggests, (60a) is ruled out directly. In (60b), θ-identification links the Theme roles of the two verbal morphemes, which are then assigned together to *ice*. In this compound, there are three thematic relations: θ-assignment of the Event role from *cause* to *melt*, θ-identification of the two Theme roles between *cause* and *melt*, and θ-assignment of the identified Theme roles from *melt-cause* to *ice*. According to the MSMH, each one of them should be tested for syntactic representation.

First, suppose all three relations are represented in syntax, as in (61).

(61)

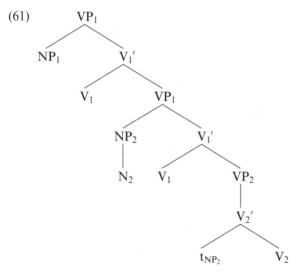

NP_1 is the subject of the causative verb and is irrelevant to the discussion. The thematic relation between *cause* and *melt* is represented as the typical head-complement relation between V_1 and VP_2, and θ-identification is reflected by placing (copies of) NP_2 inside VP_2 and the lower VP_1. One of the copies takes the form of a trace (Chomsky 1995); or, more conventionally, NP_2 first is placed inside VP_2 and then raises to VP_1. The same positioning of NP_2 also reflects the thematic relation between it and the two verb morphemes. The compound *ice-melt-cause* is to be inserted in the tree. Being categorially a verb, it cannot have N_2 as the initial point of insertion. If it starts in V_2, it can only raise to V_1 but never to N_2 owing to lack of c-command. Hence, there is no legitimate derivation for a structure like (61).

However, there is a legitimate structure, (62), that reflects only the θ-assignment relation between the two verbal morphemes (again NP_1 is the matrix subject and the lower VP_1 is not shown).

(62)

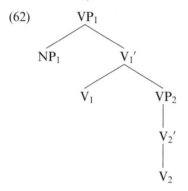

The culprit in the ungrammatical (61) is the overt representation of the incorporated N as NP_2, as we have seen many times by now. But if the nominal argument is not present in the tree, there is no syntactic means to reflect the identification of the two Theme roles. By definition, θ-identification does not involve actual assignment. Unless the recipient of the identified θ-roles is syntactically represented, the θ-roles themselves are as structurally unrepresentable as any individual θ-roles of any lexical item. It follows from the MSMH that neither of these two thematic relations should be reflected in syntax. However, the relation between *melt* and *cause* does have a legitimate structure, namely, (62). *Ice-melt-cause* is inserted in V_2 and raises to V_1, satisfying all UG principles. Needless to say, *ice* acts like a referential nominal because the morphological structure is visible to LF, as established in section 3.2.3.

Now consider the role of the CAR. Essentially a paraphrase of Baker's account for the limited VI in Mohawk, my analysis uses an idea comparable to the CAR: that the matrix Agr cannot help the embedded verb assign its own θ-roles. This contrasts with my earlier account of NI, where no similar stipulation is needed. In fact, in the limited cases of possessor raising (section 3.2.5), the CAR must not prevent *agr* from helping the Possessor θ-role of the incorporated noun to be assigned to pro when both NI and *agr* occur in the same compound. Though this may seem inconsistent in comparison with Baker's use of the CAR in both NI and VI, the asymmetry is precisely as it should be.

In essence, the CAR is an explicit statement of the local relation between Agr and V in syntax: that Agr can only facilitate θ-assignment to an argument of the verb it attaches to. One may debate whether Agr plays a role in θ-assignment in nonpolysynthetic languages, but without question it is typical of Agr, and other functional heads, to operate locally in syntax. Therefore, though a subject *agr* may tag any θ-role in the argument structure of a VI or NI compound (recall that θ-reservation respects no thematic hierarchy), this *agr* must be projected in syntax as the matrix Agr that is associated only with the matrix VP. For NI, the compound verb maps to a VP under the MSMH without an NP representation of the incorporated N. In terms of syntactic structure, the θ-role of the incorporated N *is* the θ-role of the verb and will be assigned inside the VP. So the Agr node is expected to be available for its assignment. In the case of VI, however, the verb cluster maps to two separate VPs, of which only the matrix VP is local to the matrix Agr. Hence, the CAR or the locality requirement of UG in general affects VI but not NI. To reiterate the point here, the CAR boils down to how a functional head operates in syntax; and whether it restricts the θ-operations of a compound depends on the syntactic representations of the compound.

Bearing on the status of the CAR are the ECM constructions so extensively studied in the GB framework. When the standard account of ECM is rephrased in the system with Agr, the embedded subject indeed receives Case from the matrix Agr_O, an idea that descends directly from Postal's (1974) theory of raising to object. However, the standard ECM analysis is possibly misguided in one of two ways.

First, the structural representation of the ECM construction may be wrong. Zidani-Eroğlu (1997) argues conclusively that the "embedded subject" in Turkish ECM is structurally outside the embedded clause. Lasnik and Saito (1991) draw a similar (though weaker) conclusion about

English ECM. One way to interpret these conclusions is that the so-called embedded subject NP is actually a matrix object, a possibility that becomes easy to implement when θ-identification is an option for merging, say, the subject θ-role of the embedded predicate and the object θ-role of the matrix verb under certain conditions (cf. the analyses of causatives and applicatives in this book).

Second, it may be wrong to consider the standard ECM account a core consequence of UG. Given that ECM is a rare construction not only inside a language but also crosslinguistically, it may be misleading to shape the theory of UG around it even if it proves to have the exceptional structure, as claimed. A piece of indirect evidence for the inappropriate weight given to ECM is the complexity of the GB Theory. Most of its modules—government, Case theory, binding theory—would be much simpler and much less ad hoc if it were not for ECM. Therefore, it appears more appropriate to regard regulations such as the CAR as the foundation of UG, and whatever is responsible for ECM either is some peripheral mechanism activated under specific conditions or remains to be discovered.

Finally, consider again the Mohawk applicatives discussed in section 1.2. Since the applicative affix is treated as the matrix verb, the construction is another instance of VI. Example (63) repeats example (46b) of chapter 1.

(63) Wa-hake-natar-a-kwetar-ʌ-'.
      fact-agr$_{s/o}$-bread-$\emptyset$-cut-app-punc
      'He cut the bread for me.'

With *bread* receiving the object θ-role of *cut*, and with the subject θ-roles of both *cut* and *-app* identified, the compound has the argument structure in (64), where the Goal role comes from *-app*.

(64) ⟨Agent ⟨Goal ⟨Agent⟩⟩⟩

Since the compound maps to the matrix VP and embedded VP, the *agr* can only facilitate the θ-assignment of *-app*. According to Baker, this is indeed the case, with the Agr$_S$ and Agr$_O$ always indicating the Agent and the Goal arguments of the construction. For details, see Baker 1996, sec. 9.3.

3.3   After All This Effort

Compared with Baker's specific theory of NI, the one presented in this chapter has certain empirical and/or conceptual advantages. One lies in the analysis of the coexistence of NI with agreement (see section 3.2.4). Baker's account (as well as Di Sciullo and Williams's) fails to explain why θ-identification applies regardless of thematic hierarchy in other contexts but creates a subject-object asymmetry only in NI; whereas mine not only restricts all instances of NI to the thematic object but also needs no ad hoc prohibition of argument structure composition—a process independently substantiated by Chinese resultative compounds. But more importantly, the theory in this chapter removes the mysteriousness of Baker's MVC. By replacing the MVC, (16)–(17) make it clear that the distinction between polysynthetic and nonpolysynthetic languages is simply a matter of where to draw the line of lexical opacity, the placement of morphological word formation rules being the parametric variable in the equation. Also note that (17) not only demystifies part of the MVC but also maximally generalizes the application of the θ-operations in the syntax of nonpolysynthetic languages.

In a nutshell, the theory of NI in this chapter boils down to two conclusions. First, the data Baker uses to support his syntactic approach to NI have an alternative explanation that does not require raising a nominal head to a verbal head in syntax. Second, the theory accounts for both NI and VI because it unites the characteristics of the lexicalist and syntactic approaches in a way that guarantees the right mechanisms will apply only when needed, one example being that the CAR restricts VI but not NI. The second conclusion is of course the theme of the book. The first one, however, points at a possibility that might not be easy for either side of the lexicalist-syntactic debate to accept: that NI alone may not ever be able to help distinguish the syntactic approach from the lexicalist one, because whatever data one approach can explain, the other can as well.

This possibility does not contradict my mentioning earlier the advantages that my theory has over Baker's. The advantages exist only on the basis of the particular syntactic account of NI found in Baker 1996. It is not clear to me at all, however, that any of the problems I pointed out with Baker's work are intrinsically unsolvable within the general theory of NI that primarily utilizes head movement. In fact, I would like to venture the following claim: any data about NI that one side of the debate offers an account for can, with enough effort and sincerity, be given a corresponding account by the other side. To the extent that this claim has been substantiated thus far, it indicates unequivocally the heavy redundancy inside the current P&P model of linguistics.

As disappointing as it may seem, this situation can be inspiring and motivating as well. For one thing, the continuous effort to resolve the debate through studying NI has uncovered extremely interesting facts about the phenomenon and has facilitated the refinement of both theories. For another, and more important in the long run, the heavy redundancy brings up fundamental questions: Where does the redundancy come from? Is it possible to reformulate the current theoretical model so as to reduce or remove the redundancy? If not, why not? And what would such redundancy say about the belief that UG is optimized and minimalist? This book is not meant to answer these questions, but raising them explicitly may prove to be no less significant.

Chapter 4

From X-Bar Theory to the Lexicalist Hypothesis

In the interface theory proposed here, the LH (more precisely, its requirement that words are formed independently of syntax) provides the foundation for the MSMH to operate on. It is of course entirely plausible that the LH is one of the axiomatic components of UG. As morphological structure is apparently simpler than syntactic structure—there is no evidence that there exist word-internal counterparts to such structurally defined constituents as specifiers, adjuncts, and complements—the two components may, at their core, truly employ separate sets of mechanisms for building structures. Nevertheless, in an effort to discover the organization of UG, I will explore in this chapter the possibility that the LH is a derivative of a particular theory of X-bar structure. In this theory, morphologically complex words are formed independently of syntax because the latter, in principle, forbids the merger of morphemes through head movement.

4.1 The Theory

Partially rooted in Larson's (1988) work on the internal structure of VP, Kayne 1994 explores the correlation between c-command among syntactic constituents and linear precedence among lexical terminals. Kayne's insight, like all other significant ones in this framework, is subject to multiple implementations, some of them with intriguing consequences.

At the core of Kayne's Linear Correspondence Axiom (LCA) is the asymmetric nature of linear precedence and of c-command if it is defined and applied properly. The *if*-clause in the last sentence is crucial because two constituents may indeed c-command each other. Such symmetric pairs are excluded in Kayne's definition of the LCA to achieve asymmetric c-command. But there are other intrinsic structural differences that can help define an asymmetric relation among constituents under c-command, one of them being the distinction between phrases and heads. Suppose that, instead of generating syntactic structures according to Kayne's theory, UG generates them according to (1), in which the term *morpheme* always refers to a phonetically nonempty one.

(1) Let X and Y be any two nodes in a syntactic structure such that X
    c-commands Y. Then
    a. if X is a phrase and Y is a head, every morpheme contained in X
       must linearly precede the morpheme in Y unless X and Y are
       projectionally homologous, and
    b. if a morpheme x linearly precedes a morpheme y, there must be
       an X containing x and a Y containing y such that X is a phrase
       and Y is a head unless X and Y are projectionally homologous.

Two constituents are *projectionally homologous* if they are the syntactic projections of the same head (i.e., they have the same structural origin). Since the intrinsic structural relation between projectionally homologous nodes is dominance, it is natural (though not logically necessary) that such nodes never enter the computation based on c-command, of which the standard definition is given in (2), where *inclusion* means dominance by at least a segment of the node (Chomsky 1986a).

(2) A c-commands B if neither A nor B includes the other and every
    node dominating A also dominates B.

I will refer to (1) as the *Modified Linear Correspondence Axiom* (MLCA) to highlight its conceptual origin in Kayne's LCA.[1]

4.1.1 Deriving the Lexicalist Hypothesis
The most immediate consequence of the MLCA is to impose a head-final structure as the default for all languages. Consider the two structures most commonly found in syntax, (3a) and (3b).

(3) a.

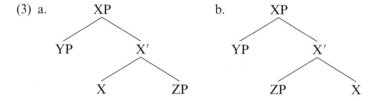

Let x be the morpheme dominated by X, y be one of the morphemes dominated by YP, and z be among the morphemes dominated by ZP. In both structures, as a phrase YP c-commands the head X and the two nodes are not homologous. According to (1), all the morphemes in YP, including y, must precede x linearly. If YP is the specifier, this conclusion forces the specifier to precede the head in both structures without constituent movement, just as Kayne's LCA does. Furthermore, YP also c-commands every head inside ZP. Since z must be dominated by one of these heads, y must linearly precede z, forcing the specifier to occur before the complement, again in both structures.

Only (3b), however, is permitted by the MLCA. As a phrase, ZP c-commands X and the two are not projectionally homologous. Under (1), every morpheme in ZP, including z, must precede the morpheme x. Since this requirement is only met by (3b), (3a) is ruled out by the MLCA. In other words, the complement must precede the head and the basic structure of languages is necessarily head-final, as is characteristic of Altaic languages and Hindi/Japanese/Korean. This is exactly the opposite of the conclusion drawn from Kayne's LCA, which forces the head-initial structure in (3a) to be the default syntactic structure.

4.1.1.1 Head-Initial Languages If the default structure of natural languages is head-final, the only way the complement can follow the head in syntax is through movement. Clearly, phrasal movement is of no help here, because phrases can only land to the left of a head in a head-final structure. Suppose, on the contrary, that a phrase X lands to the right of the head Y. If X lands in a sister position to some projection of Y through adjunction or substitution, it c-commands Y. By the MLCA, every morpheme in X must linearly precede the morpheme in Y, contradicting the initial supposition. In general, no phrase can move to the right of a (nonhomologous) head without violating the MLCA.

This leaves head movement as the only possible means to obtain a head-initial sequence. To begin with, it should be obvious that head movement in a strictly head-final structure can never place a complement after a head. This is so because heads must be raised to c-commanding head positions to satisfy the ECP. But a c-commanding head is necessarily to the right of every other constituent in its phrase. In order for head raising to yield a head-initial sequence, the landing site must be to the left of the head to be raised, as shown in (4).

(4)

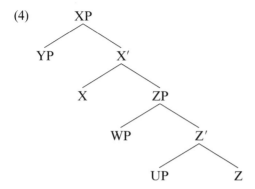

If Z moves to X, it can leave both WP and UP in post-Z positions, as is typical of Larson's (1988) analysis of double-object constructions. The question is whether such a tree is permitted by the MLCA.

The structure after head movement is given in (5), with Z adjoined to X.

(5)

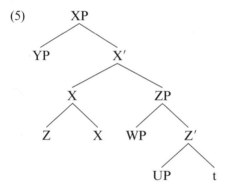

In (5), ZP c-commands two heads, the original head X and the raised head Z. Consider Z first. According to (1a), a phrase-head pair satisfying the c-command requirement must place (the content of) the phrase before (the content of) the head except when they are projectionally homologous. In (5), Z and ZP are homologous because they are projections of the same head. So they are by definition not subject to the MLCA, and ZP is not obliged to precede Z.

The same logic holds in the application of (1b) to (5). Since the morpheme in Z, call it z, linearly precedes every morpheme w contained in ZP, there should be two nodes in the tree, one c-commanding the other, such that the c-commanding one is a phrase containing z and the c-commanded one is a head containing w. This condition cannot be met in (5) because there simply is no phrase dominating z that c-commands any node, head or not, inside ZP. In all other contexts, this would be sufficient to rule (5) out as ungrammatical. However, z and w are dominated respectively by two nodes—Z and ZP—that not only c-command each other but also are projectionally homologous. Therefore, z and w are not restricted by the MLCA. In summary, raising Z to the next higher head X does create a well-formed structure in which the raised head precedes its own specifier and complement.

It may be helpful to note that the homology exception in the MLCA presumes the existence of X and Y (by referring to them) as well as the c-command relation from X to Y (which is the prerequisite for the whole condition). It follows that what can be exempted by the *unless*-clauses is limited. For (1b), for instance, the only part of the requirement that is subject to the exception involves the projectional levels of X and Y. In (5), therefore, the MLCA needs to locate Z for z and ZP for w, and to make sure that Z c-commands ZP. The projectional homology of the two nodes can only exempt them from the requirement that Z (the c-commanding node) be a phrase and ZP (the c-commanded one) a head. As it turns out, this is sufficient to permit (5).

It is also worth repeating the "intuitive" basis of the homology exception. In syntax, the default relation for projectionally homologous nodes is dominance. Since the MLCA relies on c-command, it is natural that a pair of nodes in a dominance relation are irrelevant to its application. What is required in the definition is that such a pair remains irrelevant even when one of them—say, the head—moves away. There are several technical ways to make this appear natural. For instance, UG may apply the MLCA cyclically and write off any pair of nodes already processed in the previous cycle. So within ZP in (5), the ZP-Z pair is ruled irrelevant for the computation and marked as such. Regardless of where Z moves in the next cycle, this particular pair will not be "reprocessed" by the MLCA. A less "minimalist" alternative is for the index of Z to be part of the MLCA computation. So even though the ZP-Z pair satisfies all the requirements in (1) after head movement (except the exception), Z is necessarily coindexed with its own trace inside ZP and thereby automatically invokes the ZP-trace pair, a line of reasoning frequently found in the conventional analyses (e.g., *i*-within-*i* and accessibility) of binding. Ultimately, though, these alternatives are not clearly more than terminological variations, and I will not pursue them further. What matters for now is the plausible claim that nodes bearing an intrinsically dominating relation to one another are not qualified for the MLCA that operates on c-command.

What remains to be considered in (5) is the ZP-X pair. Since the two nodes are projections of different heads, they are subject to the MLCA and should be ruled ungrammatical for occurring in the wrong linear order. However, recall that by definition, the MLCA applies only to morphemes with phonetic content. This means that if X in (5) is a phonetically empty position, it will be ignored by the MLCA, thus solving the problem. Conceptually, it is easy to justify limiting the MLCA to phonetically nonempty morphemes. By nature, the MLCA correlates c-command with linear precedence. In its most basic linguistic form, linear precedence is about the temporal sequence in which morphemes are uttered in speech. If a syntactic position is unoccupied or is occupied by a phonetically empty morpheme, it becomes irrelevant or invisible to the MLCA because nothing in it can affect the linear sequence of morphemes. For example, when there is no pronounceable morpheme under X in (5), it does not make sense for the MLCA to ask whether any morpheme dominated by X is uttered before or after the morphemes in ZP.

To summarize so far, there are two potentially problematic pairs of nodes in (5): ZP-X and ZP-Z. ZP-X satisfies the MLCA only when X is a phonetically empty position; and ZP-Z is permitted because the raised head Z is c-commanded by the homologous phrase ZP. In plain words, provided that the target position is empty, head raising can indeed generate a grammatical string of morphemes in which the head precedes its arguments.

At this point, a few clarifications are in order. First, the same logic also permits (4), the structure without head movement, provided that the higher head X is empty. In general, *the theory proposed here imposes the basic head-final structure on a phrase only when the head of the phrase dominates a morpheme with phonetic content.* If the head position is empty, the MLCA imposes no intrinsic restriction on its linear relation with its complement phrase. This makes sense: if a head is not pronounced, what empirical difference does it make whether the phrase is head-final or head-initial? Second, the notion of emptiness is at least two-ways ambiguous in the P&P model: a position can totally lack any occupant, or its occupant can totally lack any phonetic content. Throughout this chapter, it is assumed that *empty head positions are only phonetically void.* Minimally, a head position is filled with certain syntactically visible features; a totally empty head position would have no reason to exist in the first place. It follows that when a head X moves to a head Y, X always adjoins to Y; it never substitutes for Y. Third, *the nature of the MLCA determines that it only restricts overt syntax and never LF.* This is so because the MLCA operates on pronounceable morphemes. Constituents at LF, just like phonetically empty constituents in overt syntax, are invisible to the MLCA.

4.1.1.2 The Lexicalist Hypothesis With respect to head-initial languages, the previous section illustrates two properties of the MLCA: head raising yields a legitimate head-complement sequence, and the target position of head movement must be phonetically empty. If the target position is always empty, however, it is logically impossible for two overt morphemes to start in different head positions in syntax and merge into a word through head movement. This in turn means that no morphologically complex word is ever formed with head movement in syntax, contrary to what Baker's theory of incorporation claims. Rather, morphemes merge either through morphological word formation rules or in PF if they are linearly adjacent to one another. The former method embodies the defining claim of the LH; the latter simply results in PF compounds that do not necessarily reflect any syntactic constituency (see Halle and Marantz 1993). PF compounds are generally beyond the concern of this book.

Now consider head-final languages, whose structure is schematized in (6).

(6)

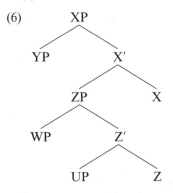

This structure satisfies the MLCA when both Z and X dominate phonetically nonempty morphemes. If Z stays in situ, the adjacency between Z and X provides the environment for phonological compounding. As Kayne (1994) points out, linear adjacency of heads also explains why strictly head-final languages are typically morphologically agglutinative: each morpheme is clearly identified with a unique function because Z and X each dominate their own morphemes in separate syntactic positions.

Next suppose that X is nonempty and Z raises to X. Left adjunction yields (7), which violates the MLCA.

(7)
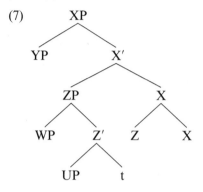

Let the morpheme dominated by X be x and the one dominated by Z be z. By (1b), there should exist a phrase containing z and a head containing x with the phrase c-commanding the head. But the phrase that does contain z is XP, which certainly does not c-command X. Note that the homology exception is irrelevant here. For the exception to take effect, there need to be a phrase and a head c-commanding each other. But XP does not c-command X (or Y for that matter). Also note that neither Z nor X c-commands the other because X includes Z. As a result, the morphemes z and x fail to meet (1b), making the raising structure in (7) ungrammatical. Obviously, adjoining Z to the right of X would run into the same problem.

On the other hand, if X is phonetically empty, both the movement-free (6) and the head-raising (7) will be permitted by the MLCA. There is not much to be said about (6) in this case—both the reasoning and the result are rather straightforward. As for (7), the structure is well formed because the problem with the morphemes x and z would never arise, anything under X being invisible to the MLCA. The ZP-Z pair is also exempted because of their homology; but for (7), this exemption is not crucial because ZP precedes Z and thus would have satisfied the MLCA anyway.

Because X must be empty when Z raises, we conclude again that two morphemes cannot be brought together through syntactic head movement; instead, they must be merged by morphological means. More generally, the MLCA defined in (1) only allows (visible) head-final structures when head movement does not take place; head movement may produce either head-initial word order as in (5) or head-final word order as in (7) under the unequivocal condition that the landing site is phonetically empty; it follows that morphologically complex words cannot be constructed through head movement in syntax. Hence, the LH is shown to be a theorem of the MLCA.

Logically, the MLCA does not restrict the formation of all morpheme clusters to the lexical module. As pointed out earlier, linearly adjacent morphemes may form PF words, a process of which agglutinative languages may be a prime example (see section 4.2). The Kʷakʷ'ala example in (8) (from Anderson 1992, 18) may be analyzed in the same fashion.

(8) Nanaqəsil-ida iʔgəl'wat-i əliwinux̌ʷa-s-is mestuwi la-x̌a   migʷat-i.
    guides-art   expert-dem hunter-instr-his harpoon prep-art seal-dem
    'An expert hunter guides the seal with his harpoon.'

Consistently, the article syntactically associated with a noun forms a PF word with the morpheme preceding the noun. So *ida* in the first word is really the subject article for the noun *iʔgəl'wat* 'expert', *s-is* signals the Case and possessor of the following noun *mestuwi* 'harpoon', and *xa* suffixed to the preposition is the object marker for *migʷat* 'seal'. As Anderson notes, the PF words in (8) are possible because of morpheme adjacency and do not correspond to syntactic structure (p. 20). PF compounds, however, are not really the concern of the lexicalist-syntactic debate.

Also worth noting is that the MLCA does permit (but does not force) a morpheme to move to another one in syntax provided the latter is phonetically empty. What this property of the MLCA implies, however, depends on independent evidence for or against the existence of phonetically empty morphemes potentially capable of occupying their own syntactic positions. Functional morphemes are not a problem because their existence and syntactic properties can typically be determined by the paradigm to which they are supposed to belong. A quick example is the zero form of the English 3rd-person-plural present tense suffix. Derivational (or lexical) morphemes without a phonetic form are a totally different matter. Ever since Generative Semantics, the mainstream practice has been to rather freely propose all sorts of zero morphemes. Justifications are sometimes loose and sometimes extremely intricate on the basis of subtle assumptions. For lack of a coherent and independently justified theory of such morphemes, I have opted to leave them aside, concentrating on phonetically nonempty ones.

To complete the derivation of the LH from the MLCA, note that head movement inevitably leaves a trace in the original position. As a trace has no phonetic content, it is not subject to the MLCA. Therefore, even though most of the tree structures given in the previous chapters contain X^0-traces in conventional head-initial positions, the discussions there remain valid under the later-defined MLCA.[2]

4.1.2 Conclusion

Up to now, the LH has been viewed by both sides of the lexicalist-syntactic debate as a claim conceptually unrelated to syntax. Whether empirically true or not, it must be stipulated; and it draws support solely from sporadic linguistic evidence. Now we see that it may in fact be a theoretical necessity, forced upon UG by a basic principle of syntax, the MLCA, which determines the well-formedness of phrasal structures. Put differently, word formation rules are needed in language because syntax is incapable of putting separate morphemes together. Also worth noting is the fact that the derivation of the LH crucially relies on examining various circumstances of head movement, the very mechanism the syntactic approach has based itself on and used to counter the lexical approach. This shows that the relation between the LH and head movement is not one of competing ideas but one of coexistence and interaction among different linguistic mechanisms. I return to the philosophical and methodological aspects of this issue later.

4.2 Other Consequences of the Modified Linear Correspondence Axiom

It is self-evident that a principle like the MLCA has a much more comprehensive influence on various phrase-structure-related aspects of language than is explored here. Equally obvious is that it takes more than a book to explore the implications of the MLCA in any sufficient manner. Admitting the magnitude of the task, I will follow the modest approach adopted by Kayne (1994) and by Fukui and Takano (1998) by studying only a few aspects of the MLCA in this section, with the hope that its full potential and problems can be investigated in the future.[3]

The most obvious distinction between the MLCA and Kayne's LCA lies in the derivational relationship between head-initial and head-final structures.[4] For Kayne, the English-like head-initial structure is the default and any head-final word order must be derived through constituent movement. For instance, to obtain a consistent head-final structure in Japanese or Korean, the object must raise to a preverbal position, then the whole VP must move to the Spec of TP, which in turn moves to the Spec of CP. This is a rather complex set of movements to achieve a word order that apparently is the most common in all human languages (Greenberg 1963; Hawkins 1983; Tomlin 1986), not to mention that no obvious motivation or justification is provided for such movement.[5] Under the MLCA, the basic typological variation in word order is simple to derive: if head movement does not take place, the language is head-final; head-initial word order takes no more than raising heads to higher positions. Since head movement is generally driven by morphology and is among the most restricted types of movement, the process is better understood and less liable to unrestricted steps of derivation.

4.2.1   To Be Head-Final or to Be Head-Initial

Ideally, it is easy to imagine that the surface location of a head is a consistent and exclusive function of head movement: if it remains in situ, a head-final structure results; if it moves, a head-initial structure is guaranteed. Here, I consider the implications of the MLCA from the viewpoint of word order typology.

Kayne's insight on this issue is that in an agglutinative language, functional morphemes are generated in their respective head positions in syntax without any subsequent head movement. This idea works well with the general theory of movement in the Minimalist Program. For instance, if a verb does not carry any inflectional morphology, there is no motivation for it to move (in overt syntax) to any functional head position for feature checking. I assume this theory of morphologically driven movement to be basically true. Obviously, if the verb stays in situ, the VP is head-final under the MLCA, as in languages of the Altaic type. In contrast, if the verb is lexically affixed with inflectional morphemes, as is typical of European languages, raising to corresponding functional head positions is required in order for morphological features to be checked, thereby setting up the necessary context for head-initial word order between the verb and its complement(s).

The complication arises from the fact that head raising does not *exclusively* produce a head-initial structure under the MLCA. Recall the structure in (7), repeated in (9).

(9)

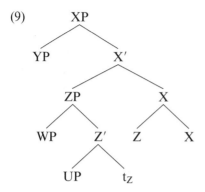

ZP c-commands Z after the latter raises to X. The pair of nodes are exempt from the MLCA because they are homologous. In other words, head raising may yield either a head-initial word order or a head-final one provided that the target position is phonetically empty.

Head raising in head-initial languages is extensively discussed and assumed. Even inside a Larsonian double-VP structure, the verb is supposed to raise at least to the upper V (or v) position. Since this upper V/v position is (phonetically) empty, the rather standard VP structure fits well with the MLCA. For head-final languages, however, solid evidence for head movement is much harder to come by, primarily because such movement is usually superficially vacuous. Certain Germanic languages may involve limited verb raising to another head-final position (Haegeman 1994 and references cited there), supplying empirical support for the MLCA's permission to generate head-final word order by means of head raising.

But there is a statistical consideration. Logically, languages may first divide according to whether they make use of head movement (which in turn may result from the bound/free distinction of inflectional morphology). Those languages with head movement may further divide according to the direction of the landing site, as discussed in the previous paragraphs. If each division is even, we predict 75% of human languages to be head-final (50% for languages without head movement + 25% for those with a structure like (9)). Judging from Greenberg 1963 and subsequent work, however, the world's languages seem to be divided evenly between head-final and head-initial.[6]

This inconsistency may be due to any of these three reasons: (i) the MLCA is wrong, (ii) the MLCA needs to be revised in such a way as to generate the right proportion of head-final languages, or (iii) the MLCA is basically correct but interacts with other factors to jointly determine the actual word order statistics.

I will ignore (i) and (ii) here largely for two reasons. First, the LH, once joining forces with the MSMH, has proven to play a crucial role in providing a unified account for a wide range of crosslinguistic morphological phenomena. The fact that the LH is a theorem of the MLCA promises a nontrivial optimization of the P&P model of linguistics. Second, the MLCA as formulated in (1) makes interesting predictions about the typology of the complementizer system and about causativization in head-final languages (see below). As a result, I will focus on (iii), fully aware that (ii) may well offer a viable route toward solving the problem of statistics.

Suppose the MLCA as defined in (1) is correct. One way to reduce the number of head-final languages permitted by the theory is to posit the performance factor in (10).

(10) Avoid vacuous head movement.

When inflectional morphology is base-generated in corresponding functional head positions, there is no need for overt head raising and typical head-final agglutinative languages result. When inflectional morphemes are affixed to lexical words, overt head raising becomes necessary. Under (10), raising to the right as shown in (9) is to be avoided because the surface sequence of the morphemes involved does not differ before and after the movement. In contrast, raising to a head position on the left is not vacuous because the raised head now occurs to the left of its complement. Put differently, head movement in (9) is permitted by the MLCA but is generally disfavored by (10). Hence, inflected languages are generally head-initial in order to compromise between obligatory head raising and (10).

I take (10) to be a performance restriction rather than part of UG primarily because it cannot yet be proven that no vacuous head movement ever takes place. In the case of morphological word formation liable to syntactic expansion under the MSMH, for instance, it is unclear whether in a head-final language, verbal causatives (or the verb-modal cluster in certain Germanic languages) indeed stay in the lower V position in overt syntax. Pending a better understanding of such constructions in head-final languages, I consider (10) comparable to the ban against center-embedded relative clauses—clearly true in some universal sense and obligatorily obeyed in certain languages but subject to different degrees of tolerance crosslinguistically.

Independently of its nature, (10) may turn out to be a quite general restriction on languages. George (1980) and Chomsky (1986a) explore the possibility that no vacuous *wh*-movement is permitted. Lasnik and Saito (1992) effectively prohibit vacuous topicalization. Combined with (10), these authors' work points to the conclusion that languages generally avoid vacuous movement regardless of whether the moved constituent is a phrase or a head.

4.2.2   The C System

Ever since Bresnan 1972, complementizers have been an important part of syntactic analysis. Probably because complementizers such as *that* and *if* take a monomorphemic form, as is also typical of words of this category in other well-studied European languages, not much attention has been paid to the fact that each of them has two conceptually different functions: to introduce an embedded clause and to signal the clause type. They are separate because there is no reason why a matrix clause cannot be overtly marked for its clause type.

That these separate functions may be represented by different morphemes is confirmed by the Chinese and Korean examples in (11) and (12), respectively.

(11) a. Li Kui lai-le   ma?
         Li Kui come-asp Q
         'Has Li Kui come?'

     b. Yan Qing zhengzai chang ge   ne.
         Yan Qing prog   sing song decl
         'Yan Qing is singing at this moment.'

     c. He   jiu ba!
         drink wine imp
         'Drink the wine!'

(12) a. John-nun Mary-lul manna-ss-ni?
         John-top Mary-acc meet-past-Q
         'Did John meet Mary?'

     b. John-nun Mary-lul salangha-n-ta.
         John-top Mary-acc love-pres-decl
         'John loves Mary.'

   c. John-nun Mary-ka   kocen   umak-lul cohaha-n-ta-ko
     John-top Mary-nom classical music-acc like-pres-decl-C
     mit-nun-ta.
     believe-pres-decl
     'John believes that Mary likes classical music.'
   d. John-nun Mary-ka   tungsan-lul   cohaha-nya-ko
     John-top Mary-nom mountain.climbing-acc like-Q-C
     mwul-ess-ta.
     ask-past-decl
     'John asked if Mary liked mountain climbing.'

In Chinese (11a–c) and Korean (12a–b), each (matrix) clause ends with a morpheme that signals the type of the clause. Even more illustrative are the Korean examples (12c–d), in which the embedded clause is introduced by *-ko and* marked by the corresponding clause-type morpheme *-ta* or *nya* (a variant of *ni*). Given these facts, the category C should really be split into two categories: C for introducing an embedded clause and C_t for clause typing. (12c–d) indicate that C takes C_tP as complement.[7] The structure without head movement is given in (13).

(13)

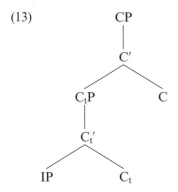

The MLCA makes an immediate prediction here: to the extent that the functions of C and C_t can be expressed either separately or with a single word, the morphologically separate expression is correlated with typical head-final languages. This is so because (13) is the only word order if C_t and C each host their own morphemes. If a single word/morpheme encodes both C and C_t, on the other hand, it will have to move from C_t to C for checking of relevant features, resulting in a head-initial word order under (10), as shown in (14).

(14)

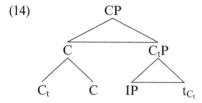

To my knowledge, this prediction seems to hold. As we have seen, Korean is head-final and the *ta-ko* 'decl-C' cluster in (12c) consists of two morphemes with separate functions. In contrast, head-initial English uses one word *that* with two functions. In other words, the C_t and C morphemes in English are merged into *that*; and with two separate sets of features, *that* must raise from C_t to C and thereby place itself ahead of IP as shown in (14).

Two clarifications are in order. First, *that* must start in the C_t position and raise to C. Inserting it in C would prevent it from lowering to C_t and therefore would fail to check the C_t features it carries. This means that *that* is of category C_t even though it carries the content of C as well. Second, like any theory that matches separate syntactic functions to corresponding syntactic nodes, the current analysis faces the question of whether *that* and *if* are morphologically decomposable into C_t and C. It is easy to postulate a zero morpheme for C, but I will take a different route. It is characteristic of inflectional languages that each inflectional morpheme simultaneously represents agreement and tense. While it has been suggested that Agr and T occupy different syntactic positions (Pollock 1989), such structural separation is not morphologically manifested. In this light, the claim that *that* and *if* each host more than one syntactic function but are not morphologically decomposable is completely compatible with how functional morphology (e.g., $-s = $ Agr+T) works in typical European languages.

This analysis differs from what Kayne's LCA would offer. In that theory, head-initial structure is the default. To the extent that some head-final languages such as Korean provide evidence for a split between C and C_t, there should be at least as many languages with overt clause-initial C_t and separately represented C-C_t clusters. This is so because head-initial structure is not derived through head movement under the LCA and there is no reason why these morphemes cannot be generated in situ. Whether this prediction is correct or not depends on further investigation. But as far as I know, no such language has been reported.

A comparison can also be made with the Merge-Demerge theory of phrase structure originated by Takano (1996) and further developed by Fukui and Takano (1998) (F&T). In spite of different technicalities, this theory shares the basic idea with the MLCA that a phrase must be pronounced temporally earlier than the head it c-commands. It follows that the default phrase structure of languages is head-final. F&T's theory differs from the MLCA in treating a raised head as a maximal projection; the authors cite Muysken 1982 and Chomsky 1995, where the notion of the maximal projection is relativized. As such, a head may be moved leftward because, as a maximal projection after raising, it can be pronounced before the constituents that have been left behind.

An immediate consequence of this theory, plus the conventional CP structure of a clause and F&T's tacit assumption that head raising targets sites outside the immediate phrase, is that *that* cannot be a head. If it were, it would occur to the right of IP, not to the left. Nor can it raise, because CP is the highest phrase in a clause and there is no place beyond it for a complementizer to move to. To account for *that*, F&T suggest that it occupies the Spec of CP and checks the $[-Q]$ feature of a phonetically empty C (p. 70).

What is unclear from this analysis is how *that* is distinguished from a *wh*-phrase occupying the same position. While both *that* and a *wh*-phrase block subject extraction (which F&T briefly discuss in the context of *that-t* effects), the two contrast sharply with respect to object extraction, as is well known from the syntactic literature. The problem does not arise for the MLCA. A head maintains its projectional status no matter where it moves to, and embedded clauses consist of CP and C_tP. Hence, *that* is fundamentally different from the *wh*-phrase in the Spec position. As the standard analysis goes, a filled Spec of CP blocks the "escape hatch" of *wh*-movement, whereas *that* in head position does not.[8]

4.2.3 Causativization in Head-Final Languages

In chapter 2, I showed that morphological causatives with an adjectival base have necessarily monoclausal structures in head-initial languages like Arabic and Hebrew. However, the same theory predicts that a causative verb of the form A-*cause* may show biclausal properties in a head-final language. As Kayne (1994) points out, typical head-final languages make it possible to have linearly adjacent morphemes each of which is generated in its own head position. The linear adjacency in turn gives rise to PF words. The tree in (15) illustrates the context.

(15)

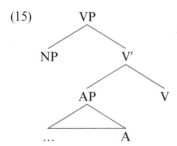

Even if no head movement takes place, the fact that A is adjacent to V is sufficient for the two morphemes to be pronounced as a word. But the tree underlying such a word still has two separate maximal projections. If a nonsubject anaphor is embedded inside AP, local binding by the subject of the adjective is expected in spite of the superficial A-V causative. This prediction is borne out in Pashto, an official language of Afghanistan (Almansour 2001).

(16) a. Shaagardan$_i$ ustaadaana$_j$ de yo   bel$._{i/j}$ mast-awi.
        the.students the.professors of one other proud-make
        'The students are making the professors proud of each other.'
     b. Zaamano$_i$ plaaraan$_j$ luh   yo   bel$._{i/j}$ na lweaney-kawi.
        the.sons   the.fathers from one other   mad-make
        'The sons are making the fathers angry with each other.'

Crucially, no such possibility should ever arise in a head-initial language, where a "wordlike" adjective-based causative can only be formed independently of syntax because heads are always separated in syntax by arguments in Spec positions.

What the theory alone cannot predict is whether morphological deadjectival causatives actually exist in a particular head-final language like Pashto. Logically, they should be possible, though other factors may be at work. For instance, if head movement is ultimately driven by morphology, then the very fact that each morpheme serves as a stand-alone head in syntax is responsible for the head-final word order of Pashto (probably with the help of (10)). But the same fact would disfavor forming deadjectival causative verbs in (presyntactic) morphology because that would require at least one of the two morphemes to function as an affix that could not fill a syntactic head position by itself. Still, idiosyncratic morphological causatives cannot be excluded in principle. Similarly, though English deadjectival causatives like *enlarge* and *lengthen* are correctly predicted to project to monoclausal structures in syntax, my theory cannot predict the fact that the language does not have morphological verbal causatives (i.e., VI).

It should be made clear that PF words based on syntactic adjacency are not confined only to head-final languages. See Lieber 1992 and Anderson 1992 for examples in head-initial languages (of which (8) is one). The examples in (17) illustrate a postverbal adverbial construction, in Chinese, that may be a dramatic case of such a phonological process in a head-initial clausal structure.

(17) a. Yan Qing chang-de feichang haoting.
    Yan Qing sing-DE   very   beautiful
    'Yan Qing sings beautifully.'

   b. Dai Zong pao-de teibie   kuai.
    Dai Zong run-DE extremely fast
    'Dai Zong runs extremely fast.'

The predicative phrase after *de* describes the manner in which the action is carried out. On the surface, this construction resembles the resultative V-*de* discussed in the appendix, both constructions being formed with *de* attached to the matrix verb and introducing a predicate.

The examples in (18) illustrate a puzzling difference between the two constructions.

(18) a. Yan Qing chang-de (*ger) feichang haoting.
    Yan Qing sing-DE   song very   beautiful
    'Yan Qing sings (*songs) beautifully.'

   b. Ger, Yan Qing chang-de feichang haoting.
    song Yan Qing sing-DE very   beautiful
    'Songs, Yan Qing sings beautifully.'

   c. Yan Qing chang-de feichang haoting de ger
    Yan Qing sing-DE very   beautiful DE song
    'the songs that Yan Qing sings beautifully'

   d. Yan Qing chang ger   chang-de feichang haoting.
    Yan Qing sing   song sing-DE very   beautiful
    'Yan Qing sings songs beautifully.'

When *de* is understood as introducing the manner adverbial, the object of the matrix verb must not occur after the V-*de* cluster. Instead, the object must be preverbal, either in the form of topicalization as in (18b) or through VP reduplication as in (18d) (see Li 1990b). The object may also take the form of a *wh*-trace, as in the relative clause construction in (18c).

The data in (18) contrast with the resultative V-*de* in which the object of V_c occurs postverbally without any problem. The example in (19) repeats (62a) of chapter 1, where *guan-bing* 'government soldier' is the thematic object of V_c *gan* 'chase'.

(19) Li Kui gan-de   guan-bing   sichu   bentao.
     Li Kui chase-DE government-soldier everywhere ran.away
     'Li Kui chased the soldiers off to all directions.'

To explain why the *de*-adverbial disallows the postverbal NP, Li and Ting (1999) suggest that *de* is a semantically bleached verb that takes a clausal complement.[9] In the resultative, *de* functions as V_r and thus in effect forms a resultative compound with V_c. As a result, the clausal complement of *de* becomes the complement of the compound through argument structure composition. If V_c happens to have its own NP object, the compound is basically like *gaosu* 'tell' (see (2b–c) of the appendix) with respect to its internal arguments, one of them being NP and the other a clause. Hence, (19) results.

On the other hand, Chinese independently does not allow V-V compounds in which the second verb morpheme functions adverbially with respect to the first.[10] It follows that V-*de* is not a legitimate lexical compound when *de* introduces a manner adverbial. At the same time, suppose that the "lightness" of *de* requires a verbal host. Chinese resolves this dilemma by forcing any other postverbal constituent out of the place so as to create linear adjacency between the matrix verb and the adverbial *de*. This happens when the object is topicalized, relativized, or introduced by the duplicated verb—anything goes as long as the overt NP does not intervene between the verb and *de*. Note that the trace of the object has no effect on this process of PF compounding. For details of this analysis, see Li and Ting 1999.

4.2.4 Cliticization and the Modified Linear Correspondence Axiom

Cliticization in Romance has been studied extensively from different angles (e.g., Belletti and Rizzi 1981; Kayne 1984, 1991, 1994; Burzio 1986; Cinque 1990; Li 1990a, 1997b; Rizzi and Roberts 1990; Roberts 1991; Chomsky 1995; Uriagereka 1995; Sportiche 1996). While many scholars analyze the phenomenon by means of head movement to a functional head position, the real nature of clitics is far from clear with regard to the projectional level of a clitic and the landing site.

Consider first the head movement analysis. In (20), the clitic is taken to be of category D and the landing site is simply marked as a functional category F.

(20)

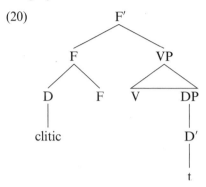

F must be phonetically empty because of the MLCA. For the same reason, the raised D is ruled out because VP c-commands D but linearly follows D. There is an easy solution to this problem, however. Recall that the MLCA includes an exception in terms of projectional homology. If V had raised to F rather than D in (20), the VP would c-command the raised V without violating the MLCA since VP and V are homologous. In section 4.1, where the MLCA was introduced, I reasoned that this exception of homology could be traced to the fact that the intrinsic relation between V and its phrase VP is dominance, exempting the pair of nodes from the MLCA's computation based on c-command. If the notion of homology is replaced with D-Structure dominance, (20) will be permitted by the MLCA: VP c-commands D, but their D-Structure relation is really dominance; thus, the VP-D pair qualifies as an exception for the MLCA for the same reason that a raised V is permitted even though it is c-commanded by a temporally later VP.

This minor modification of the MLCA would cause no change at all in the analyses of the previous chapters because projectional homology is properly included in D-Structure dominance. If any case of incorporation and inflection involves head movement at all, it is local movement to the next higher head, guaranteeing that the resulting structure only contains the (stricter) homologous X-XP pair. What is prohibited in principle is for the clitic and another phonetically overt head X to land in the same position, as illustrated in (21).

(21)

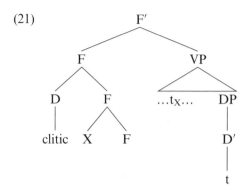

Since D precedes X and there is no homologous (or D-Structure dominance) relation between them, the pair violates the MLCA because D is not a phrase. In other words, (21) will be ruled out by the MLCA whether X is the verb itself or another clitic. This result may be theory-internal evidence for the multiple functional heads advocated in Cinque 1999. Only in such a structure does it become possible that each clitic adjoins to a unique and phonetically empty functional head. Since the precise number of functional heads, as well as their functions, is yet to be determined, I leave the assessment of this possibility to future investigation.

An alternative analysis of Romance clitics is that they are actually phrasal pronouns. The idea is partially implied by Kayne (1991), who argues that at least in some cases, the clitic adjoins to F′, not F. In the standard theory of movement in which heads only adjoin to heads (Baltin 1982), the ability to adjoin to F′ may be interpreted as a sign that the clitic is projectionally more than a head. Pursuing a different line of reasoning, Chomsky (1995) suggests that the clitic, when raised, acquires the status of a maximal projection that is responsible for the clitic's ability to undergo limited long-distance movement, namely, clitic climbing.

It also must be pointed out that the prima facie arguments that motivated treating Romance clitics as moved heads in earlier literature are mostly subject to reevaluation in the more recent framework. The landing site, for instance, used to be limited to the I position because that is the only one available between the subject and an overt verbal morpheme occupying I. Once I splits into multiple heads, there are not only new head positions but also new Spec and adjunct positions, the latter being characteristically phrasal. A priori, a clitic could well be a phrasal pronoun occupying one such phrasal position in the I system. To be sure, clitics appear to attach to a verbal head. But this fact alone does not say anything about the projectional property of the clitic. Descriptively, the clitic must raise (e.g., for feature checking); and from the landing site, it must be attached to another head because of its phonological lightness (as is commonly assumed in the literature on clitics; see Kayne 1975). But an analysis covering these properties would apply equally well whether the clitic is a head or a phrase.

Suppose, then, that clitics move as DPs and adjoin to some functional F' position. The schematic structure of this analysis is given in (22), where F_j is the proper functional head in the split-I system that attracts clitics.

(22)

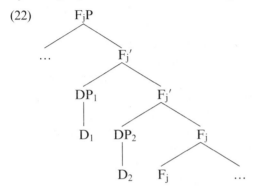

As a phrase, DP_1 c-commands all the heads to its right, satisfying the MLCA as expected. Suppose there is another clitic, DP_2 (as, e.g., in French *Je le lui donne* 'I it him give (I give it to him)'). Like DP_1, DP_2 c-commands all the heads to its right. But DP_2 does not c-command D_1 because there is an F_j' dominating DP_2 but not DP_1 (see the definition of c-command in (2)), effectively licensing the D_1-D_2 sequence under the MLCA.

The immediate advantage of phrasal clitics is their potential for long-distance movement. Combined with a proper implementation of feature checking between such adjoined clitics and the functional head F_j, it is also easy to restrict the distance of clitic movement. Furthermore, taking a clitic adjoined to the intermediate projection of F_j to be a phrase also maintains the essence of Kayne's (1991) account of Romance cliticization while avoiding his unconventional assumption that a head may adjoin to X'.[11] It is clear that many details still need to be worked out before such an analysis can be adopted comfortably. The task is too immense to be undertaken here because the generative literature on nominal clitics is on the whole conceived around the belief that they are dislocated heads. However, there is so far no systematic proof in the current framework of syntax that treating them as phrases is necessarily inferior to the main-stream theory of head movement.

4.2.5   Adjuncts and the Modified Linear Correspondence Axiom

Another question regarding the consequences of the MLCA (or any prin-ciple of the same nature) is how it deals with adjuncts. Kayne's (1994) theory essentially obtains any word order not directly generated by the LCA through constituent movement. Fukui and Takano (1998) do not really address this issue. In the rest of this chapter, I sketch an alternative to Kayne's approach.

The discussion about (22) indicates that adjuncts are permitted as long as they are to the left of the node they adjoin to. (I leave it to the reader to prove that adjunction to the right violates the MLCA.) What this means is that a phrasal adjunct must always occur before the head of the phrase it adjoins to. In head-final languages like Korean and Japanese, this is precisely what happens: all adjuncts precede the head. In many VO languages, Chinese being one of them, adjuncts obligatorily precede the verb as well, again lending support to the MLCA's prediction.

But there are also languages like English in which adjuncts may occur to the right of the head they modify and like Mohawk in which argu-ment-like adjunct NPs can occur to the right of the clause they adjoin to (see section 1.2). Logically, posthead adjuncts may be easy to derive in a theory based on the MLCA. For instance, if V raises all the way to C, as in VSO languages, most adverbials are automatically stranded to the right of V. The difficulty arises with languages like English, in which V-raising is highly local (Pollock 1989) and the complements nonetheless stay with the verb. To get posthead adjuncts in position through move-ment in English would necessarily involve ad hoc operations. Just to get a taste of what such operations would entail, imagine that we want the AdvP to end up on the right of VP in (23) in order to generate *examine the patient carefully* in English.[12]

(23)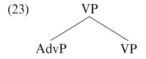

There are two ways to place both the verb and the object before the AdvP. Either the whole lower VP segment raises to a higher position, or the verb and the object move separately to positions left of AdvP. Both options raise the question of where the lower VP segment moves to outside the upper VP segment, while the second option also runs the risk of separating the verb and the object—after all, they target different locations and it would take extra stipulations to keep them together in that particular word order. To make matters worse, certain VP adverbs seem to occur rather freely on either side of V: *to carefully write the paper* versus *to write the paper carefully* (see the next paragraph). Even if movement of V and NP were a plausible means to derive the second example, the reason for such movement would remain unclear.

A simpler alternative is (24).

(24) *Adjunct Parameter*
     Languages vary in whether adjuncts respect the MLCA.

In Chinese and Korean, the value of this parameter is "yes," forcing all adjuncts to occur to the left of the heads they modify. In English and Mohawk, adjuncts are not subject to the MLCA, leaving their actual linear position to other factors such as phonological heaviness (which obviously is at work in English, where heavy adjunct phrases typically occur after the head (and its complement)) and discoursal considerations. The free word order of adjuncts is best illustrated with *carefully*-type adverbs in English (see Bowers 1993).

(25) a. Sam carefully evaluated the situation.
     b. Sam evaluated the situation carefully.

(26)

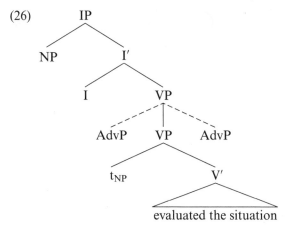

The alternations in (25) follow naturally from generating *carefully* optionally on either side of VP,[13] indicated by dashed lines under the upper VP node in (26).

Also worth pointing out is that if the notion of adjunct in the Adjunct Parameter (24) means adjuncts "by nature" (i.e., constituents that never occupy the Spec or complement position throughout derivational history), then this parameter does not apply to arguments that happen to move to adjoined positions. It follows immediately that overt argument topicalization (see Baltin 1982; Lasnik and Saito 1992) and multiple cliticization in (22) are always adjunction to the left even in languages where true adjuncts can or must occur after the head, as in English and French. Since these constituents are generated as arguments, they must be subject to the MLCA no matter where they move to. This seems to be a welcome result considering their linear locations.

That adjuncts may differ fundamentally from arguments according to how they are restricted by UG principles is not a new idea. Rizzi (1990) proposes that only true adjuncts incur minimality effects on $\bar{\text{A}}$-movement; arguments QR-ed to an adjunct position do not. Lasnik and Saito (1992) argue that the argument-adjunct asymmetry in the context of *that-t* is attributed to the fact that UG principles only require arguments to leave traces during overt movement. Since moved adjuncts have no trace at S-Structure, they are not subject to the ECP until LF, at which point *that* can be deleted to avoid the *that-t* effect. At the least, these proposals raise the possibility that arguments and adjuncts are not created equal in the eyes of UG principles. At the most, they might even be unified with the Adjunct Parameter in (24). There may be a more general parameter on the visibility of adjuncts to (certain) UG principles applying in overt syntax. For instance, adjuncts in English are not visible to, say, the MLCA and the ECP, giving rise to free word order and lack of the *that-t* effect. In Chinese and Korean, they are visible and must be linearly distributed just like arguments. Such a theory also predicts that traces of overt adjunct movement in Chinese and Korean will show the *that-t* effect. In addition to obligatory prehead adjuncts, the language to test this prediction with must have overt adjunct movement and an overt counterpart of *that* $(= C+C_t)$ that independently creates a *that-t* effect for the subject. Since none of the languages I have access to has this cluster of properties (which itself may or may not be a coincidence), at present I cannot assess the possibility of a more general visibility parameter.

Under different assumptions, Ernst (2002) also pursues the possibility that the word order of adjuncts is parameterized. According to his Directionality Principles (p. 166), the linear direction between the Spec and the head is a constant, with the former preceding the latter, whereas the direction between the head and its complement is parametric. The location of an adjunct is a function of these two factors. If a language has Spec-head and complement-head word order (i.e., it is purely head-final), the adjunct can only pick up the same directionality, yielding languages like Korean and Turkish. If a language has Spec-head but head-complement word order, however, the adjunct has a mixed directionality to reflect the more basic difference between the Spec and the complement.

It is obviously beyond the scope of this book to fully evaluate or even introduce Ernst's theory. But two points are worth making. First, allowing the directionality of adjuncts to be computed separately from that of the core components like the Spec and complement does have the potential to simplify the syntactic structures. To get *carefully* to the right of the verb and its object, one wouldn't need to rely on the sheer theory-driven proliferation of phrases whose existence has no independent support. Second, the essence of Ernst's Directionality Principles can be adapted to LCA-style theories of phrase structure, especially the ones in this book and in Fukui and Takano 1998 that have the head-final structure as the default. Since in these theories, head-initial word order comes about only when a head raises to a higher position, a double-VP structure is sufficient for deriving both head-initial and head-final languages. Within this minimal structure, the hierarchical location of an adjunct can remain stable and predictable, while its directionality with respect to the head is determined by reference to the (superficial) linear locations of the Spec and the complement.

Chapter 5

Philosophical Thoughts on
Linguistic Research

The goal of this book has been to propose and defend a theory of the morphology-syntax interface that merges the two conflicting approaches in the field, the lexical and the syntactic. This new approach, while inevitably based on the accumulated knowledge and insights of previous research, differs philosophically from mainstream modern linguistic practice. The difference is not due to any lack of previous attempts to integrate (part of) morphology with syntax. On the contrary, such attempts have been made throughout the history of the morphology-syntax debate, from Generative Semantics to more recent theories such as those of Scalise (1984) and Lieber (1992), where (some version of) the X-bar schema is explicitly argued to apply to morphology. What sets these previous theories apart from the one I propose here is that mine does *not* try to extend the mechanisms of one component to the other. Rather, it recognizes the separation and autonomy of syntax and morphology and constructs their interface as the synthesis of both components.

The synthesis takes place at multiple levels of UG. Its most straightforward manifestation is to unite the central technical claims of both the syntactic and the lexicalist literature into the Morphology-Syntax Mapping Hypothesis. On the one hand, the mapping between the two components is based on the lexicalist view that morphemes are always concatenated into words with nonsyntactic word formation rules. This premise plays a vital role in preventing uncontrolled, and often empirically wrong, representations of morphologically complex words as multiphrasal structures. On the other hand, the MSMH also forces, in effect, the thematic relation between two verb morphemes of a word W to be mapped to a biclausal structure in which W undergoes head movement from the embedded V to the matrix V, as is characteristic of the syntactic theory of VI. This property of the MSMH makes it possible to encompass the well-supported foundation of the syntactic approach: that not every word maps to the same monophrasal structure. Empirically, the MSMH correctly predicts the syntactic behaviors of various types of morphologically complex words. Theoretically, it achieves this goal with the least ad hoc means: let UG decide how a thematic relation between two morphemes is to be represented in syntax.

The synthesis also lies in reevaluating the Lexicalist Hypothesis. As it is formulated in the literature, the LH prevents both transformational operations such as movement and interpretive rules such as coindexation from affecting any component of a morphologically complex word. In this book, however, the two parts of the LH are treated separately. Words are formed with nonsyntactic morpheme-concatenating operations as a matter of principle (regardless of whether this is derivable from the Modified Linear Correspondence Axiom). Throughout the book, this position on word formation is loosely referred to as the LH. On the other hand, depending on the setting of the Parameter of the Lexicon, the constituents inside a morphological construction may or may not be subject to the same LF interpretation as the constituents in a syntactic construction are. Specifically, I have argued that in polysynthetic languages a word-internal nominal morpheme has the same interpretation as the bare NP in many nonpolysynthetic languages. As I showed in chapter 3, allowing word-internal structure to be parametrically visible to LF operations is one of the steps toward demystifying Baker's Morphological Visibility Condition.

Finally, and in a more global sense, the synthesis of syntax and morphology at their interface may be achieved through the two components' interdependence with regard to their respective operations. Morphology depends on syntax because, if the content of chapter 4 proves tenable, the very existence of word formation rules is forced on UG by the MLCA, the mechanism for constructing syntactic structures. Meanwhile, syntax also depends on morphology because the proper syntactic representation of a morphologically complex word is determined by the MSMH, which uses certain word-internal information to help build corresponding syntactic structures. It is through this mutual dependence between syntax and morphology that a unified explanation is provided for the wide-ranging data that have fueled the opposing sides of the debate.

Because the interface is where syntax and morphology meet, the two components have been viewed as opposing forces and research has focused on deciding which side should take over. The theme of this book is that the two forces, different as they are, actually interact smoothly at the interface and collectively produce the linguistic facts as we know them. That an entity/phenomenon consists in the proper balance of two opposite factors is not strange to science: an atom consists of an equal number of protons and electrons, to achieve balance between the positive and negative electric charges. More often than not, however, this fact of the universe does not get abstracted from specific instances and become an active part of the general analytical methodology. In practice, researchers typically assume that when two theories conflict, only one of them promises to represent the truth; moreover, they assume that the solution to the conflict lies in modifying the "right" theory so as to attain a dominating status in the field and at the same time to annex the empirical basis of the "wrong" one. Certainly, there is nothing intrinsically wrong about such an approach. But when the two opposing theories happen to correctly capture different aspects of the subject matter, failure to remember the inner workings of atoms will only serve to block understanding.

Remarkably, Chinese philosophy has always considered it intrinsic to the universe that everything is made up of opposing components. The following quotation is from *Lao Zi*, the classic of Taoism written at least 2,400 years ago:[1]

Tao begets one; one begets two; two beget three; three beget everything in the universe. (*Lao Zi*, verse 42)

The interpretation of this verse by Wei Yuan (1794–1857) of the Qing Dynasty is representative:

One refers to Qi; two refers to Yin and Yang;[2] three refers to the Qi of the combination of Yin and Yang. (*Lao Zi Ben Yi*)

Concepts like Tao, Qi, Yin, and Yang have no direct counterparts in Western philosophy. Loosely speaking, Tao is the ultimate law, determining the existence, structure, and behavior of everything (in and beyond the universe). At the most fundamental level, Qi is the essence/energy that may either exist by itself or take the form of "things" under Tao. The essence/nature of a specific thing is also referred to as its Qi. Yin and Yang are the abstractions of all pairs of opposing factors.

Details aside, *Lao Zi* depicts the beginning of the universe as homogenous Qi polarizing into two opposing components, Yin and Yang (i.e., one begets two). When Yin and Yang combine, a third entity forms; this entity is composed of Yin and Yang but different from either of them (two beget three). It is Yin, Yang, and their proper combination that underlie everything in the universe (three beget everything). In such a theory, finding opposing factors in a single phenomenon is not a reason for making choices but a reflection of the norm of the universe.

Such is the philosophy underlying the theory of the morphology-syntax interface in this work: the real mechanism operating at the morphology-syntax interface is neither syntax nor morphology, but an organic combination of both whose interaction generates all the relevant phenomena. The approach does not mean that one should abandon efforts to explore the potential of the syntactic theory or the lexicalist theory. On the contrary, since we do not know a priori which morphological facts are best accounted for in syntax and which in morphology, it is methodologically necessary to adopt a divide-and-conquer strategy and pursue a (sometimes arbitrarily) isolated portion of the phenomena. Nonetheless, it is important to bear in mind that successful methodology is not equal to the truth, and that the final answer may lie in a synthesis of apparently conflicting ideas. To the extent that the interface theory presented here fares better than either the syntactic or the lexicalist approach alone, it indicates that the ancient Chinese philosopher's view of the world is more than philosophical contemplation. The world is so composed indeed.

I conclude this book with a quotation from Ernst Mayr, a world-renowned biologist:

That the ultimate answer in a long-lasting controversy combines elements of the two opposing camps is typical in biology. Opponents are like the proverbial blind men touching different parts of an elephant. They have part of the truth, but they make erroneous extrapolations from these partial truths. The final answer is achieved by eliminating the errors and combining the valid portions of the various opposing theories. (Mayr 1997, 158)

Mayr's observation refers to the two-centuries-old debate between the epigenesist and preformationist theories in developmental biology, which ultimately resulted in modern genetics. How well it echoes the philosophy and theme of this book on the morphology-syntax interface!

Notes

Introduction

1. Unless otherwise stated, all the Arabic data in this book are from Abdullah Al-Dobaian, Abdulrahman Almansour, and the native speakers Al-Dobaian consulted to confirm the judgments. I thank them for their time and patience. My special gratitude goes to Abdulrahman Almansour for an accurate transcription of all the Arabic examples.

That the verb in (4) is deadjectival is assumed in Benmamoun 1991 and is also the perception of the ten Arabic speakers consulted. Dustin Cowell (personal communication) points out that such verbs might be derived from nouns instead. As will become clear in chapters 1 and 2, the theory proposed in this book predicts the same syntactic behavior for causativization whether the root is nominal or adjectival. So all the discussion in the text remains valid as long as the verb in (4) is not derived from verbal stems.

2. The term *biclausal* is based on Baker's (1988) original account of verb incorporation, where the matrix causative verb indeed takes a CP complement containing the verb root. Since Li 1990c, however, it is generally accepted that a necessary condition for verb incorporation is for the complement to be a bare VP (see, e.g., Baker 1996; Bošković 1997; Hale and Keyser 2002), which is sufficient to derive various facts that Baker (1988) accounts for with the biclausal structure. In other words, *biclausal* actually refers to a "double-VP" structure. But because *double-VP* may be misinterpreted as referring to a Larsonian VP structure, *biclausal* will be used in this book.

Chapter 1

1. The notation for the argument structure is from Grimshaw 1990. Except for discussions directly involving Grimshaw's work, however, I will use angled brackets "$\langle \ldots \langle \ldots \rangle\rangle$" rather than parentheses to represent the hierarchy of the θ-roles, following my own notation in Li 1990b, 1993, 1995, 1999.

2. The definition (p. 209) has *c-command* rather than *th-command*. That must be a typographical error, since (i) c-command is not a relation among θ-roles, at least not in Williams's theory, and (ii) of all Williams's definitions, that of th-binding is

the only one that refers to any notion of command—if th-command were not part of th-binding, it would not be incorporated anywhere in the theory at all.

3. It has been proposed that the stranded trace could be rescued if the lowered compound moves back to V_1 at a later stage of the derivation. But there are many ways in the current model to exclude such an operation. Proper binding is one (Fiengo 1977; Lasnik and Saito 1992); extra cost in comparison with raising from V_2 to V_1 is another (Chomsky 1995).

4. Baker (1988) suggests that different dialects of Chichewa choose type I or type II, whereas Alsina (1992) provides evidence that the same language simultaneously allows both. My analysis is independent of exactly how the alternations are distributed. Since I have already discussed type II in section 1.1.3, I concentrate here on type I.

5. The specific UG principles at work will be illustrated shortly. Note that this logic deviates from the more recent representation of the upper V as v because, presumably, V and v belong to different categories and therefore the selection of vP is not interchangeable with the selection of VP.

6. Any analysis of unaccusative verbs inevitably incurs questions regarding the possibility of the postverbal NP and its particular semantics. The issue is clearly not just a matter of Case assignment, involving the role of expletives such as *there* and chains (Safir 1985, 1987; Lasnik 1992, 1999; Chomsky 1981, 1995) as well as various aspects of syntax-sensitive semantics (Diesing 1992). Discussions on various aspects of the phenomenon can also be found in Reuland and ter Meulen 1989. Since the available data on VI do not bear on this aspect of the unaccusative verb root, the possibility is not examined here.

7. Whether NP_2 indeed rejects promotion to the subject in passivization is not clear, and is at least partially dependent on a better understanding of the double-object construction. For the sake of discussion, I pick the worst-case scenario, namely, that it cannot become the subject. If it could, (26) would be totally indistinguishable from (25).

8. Larson (1988) takes the dative construction as basic and the double-object construction as derived.

(i) Sam gave a gift to Pam.

(ii) Sam gave Pam a gift.

In (ii), the NP *a gift* is demoted to an adjunct and *Pam* is raised to carry accusative Case. But there are plenty of reasons to conclude that Larson's analysis, if correct in spirit, should be reversed, with (ii) being the basic structure and (i) being derived by demoting *Pam* to an adjunct.

9. One obvious difference between the two analyses is that Alsina's adopts a single-VP structure and mine a multiple-VP structure. As evidence against the analysis in Li 1990c, Alsina offers these examples from Kichaga:

(i) Ndesambulro n-a-i-zrem-ilr-a   mana muinda.
    1name   foc-1s-pres-cultivate-cause-fv 1child 3farm
    'Ndesambulro is causing the child to cultivate the farm.'

(ii) Muinda u-i-m-zrem-ilr-o.
    3farm   3s-pres-1o-cultivate-cause-pass
    'The farm is caused to be cultivated by him.'

The word order of (i) indicates a type II causative. In (ii), the thematic object of the verb root *zrem* 'cultivate' becomes the syntactic subject of the passive sentence, whereas the phonetically empty thematic subject of the verb root triggers object agreement on the verb. Given Alsina's presentation of (i)–(ii), these examples raise a problem for my current theory as well: if the compound *zrem-ilr-a* in (ii) must be mapped to a multiple-VP structure as required by the MSMH, the embedded object *muinda* 'farm' is not expected to become the matrix subject, as we saw with Arabic in section 1.1.3 and with Chimwiini in (28). On the other hand, if VI projects to a single-VP structure in a typical lexicalist manner, (ii) becomes easy to explain.

However, Alsina (1992, 540 n. 13) notes that (ii) becomes "less acceptable" if the remaining object is not expressed through object agreement but with an overt NP. Without access to Kichaga speakers, I cannot speculate on how much "less acceptable" the example becomes, but as we already know, the very fact that it is not fully acceptable is actually predicted by the current theory if (i)–(ii) have double-VP structures. In other words, at least when all NP arguments are overtly represented, Kichaga VI is just like its Arabic counterpart in (15b) and (16b).

The question remains why (ii) is acceptable at all. Without a systematic investigation of Kichaga, many possibilities exist and it would be pointless to speculate. Worth noting is that Alsina's (1992) analysis is otherwise based on Chichewa, which has two dialects according to Baker (1988, 163–165).

(iii) *Chimanga chi-na-kolol-ets-edw-a   mwana wake ndi Catherine.
    corn   agr$_s$-pres-harvest-cause-pass-asp child   her   by Catherine
    'The corn was made to be harvested by her child by Catherine.'

(iv) Ana   a-na-meny-ets-edw-a   kwa buluzi (ndi anyani).
    children agr$_s$-past-hit-cause-pass-asp to   lizard by baboons
    'The children were made to be hit by the lizard (by the baboons).'

(iii) is a passivized type II causative from a dialect of Chichewa. It is unacceptable, as my theory predicts. What is interesting is (iv), which Baker claims to be from another dialect of Chichewa. The optional presence of *ndi anyani* 'by baboons' indicates that the sentence is a type I causative, in which the embedded object *ana* 'children' can indeed become the matrix subject. This raises the possibility that (ii) is actually not the passive form of (i) but a type I variant of (i). I leave the question for future study.

10. The same ban against lowering in (37) can be achieved in the Minimalist Program by invoking cost of derivation. Compared with A-to-V raising, which takes one step of movement, V-to-A lowering would either result in an unbound trace or, if the compound moves back to V afterward, take two steps of movement. The more costly derivation is ruled out by the existence of less costly ones, which themselves are ungrammatical for reasons discussed in the text. Another alternative is to generate syntactic structures with strictly enforced cycles. See Chomsky 1995.

11. Note that there is also an account of (36) in Lexical Phonology: that morphemes as the material of word formation fall into different classes and that different classes participate in word formation at different levels arranged in a specific order (Siegel 1974; Kiparsky 1982a,b). Whether or not it is possible to establish a crosslinguistic sequence of levels, it is generally the case that inflectional morphology applies after derivational morphology and compounding. This accounts for the contrast in (i) and (ii).

(i) baby-boom, house-decorating, ...

(ii) *babies-boom, *houses-decorating, ...

By the same logic, the nonexistent VI causative of the form [affix-V_2]-V_1 is also ruled out, the verb root V_2 being inflected prior to causativization by V_1. Such an account is trivially compatible with the LH and the MSMH since the derived word would never have a chance to exist in the lexicon.

12. The possibility of Y receiving an external θ-role from X, apparently nonexistent, will be discussed in detail in chapter 3 when noun incorporation and the issue of redundancy are examined.

13. The other possibility is for -*app* to have no external θ-role (i.e., for it to be a "double-object" raising verb). I am not aware of empirical reasons to choose between these two alternatives, so the following discussion takes up the theoretically more difficult one: that -*app* has three θ-roles. It will be much simpler, in fact easy, to implement the raising -*app* alternative.

14. Marantz (1993) also argues for a similarly truncated structural representation when two verb morphemes share the subject. Specifically, he assumes (i) that the Agent θ-role is compositionally assigned by the verb and its complement(s) and (ii) that the subject is always generated outside VP. As a result, neither the embedded VP (headed by the verb stem) nor the matrix VP (headed by the applicative affix) contains a subject. Rather, they collectively assign the Agent role to an argument generated outside the matrix VP.

There is no intrinsic syntactic incompatibility between this analysis and my theory of the morphology-syntax interface, since the V-*app* complex can still be formed and project to Marantz's structure as long as there is a thematic relation between the two morphemes.

What the two theories disagree on is whether the subject θ-role is indeed compositional. The data on Chinese resultative compounds in the appendix seem to favor the presence of the external θ-roles in the lexicon in order to derive all the interpretations of such compounds. But the final decision depends on too many alternative supporting assumptions to be made at the moment.

It is also worth noting that Marantz's two assumptions regarding the subject are logically unrelated. In particular, a compositional Agent role may be assigned by VP if the latter never contains the subject, or it may be assigned by V′ under the VP-Internal Subject Hypothesis. So evidence in favor of compositional subject θ-roles, if there is any, cannot be used in itself to support the assumption that the subject is generated outside VP.

15. But it must be pointed out that the chain [NP$_1$, t] in (55) is not identical to a typical A-chain of which a member receives a "whole" θ-role. In (55), both members of the chain contribute toward obtaining a full thematic interpretation by holding a relation with a "segment" of the θ-role of the applicative compound. Put differently, [NP$_1$, t] in (55) has the same thematic function as a single member of the regular A-chain. Since neither Relativized Minimality nor its more recent successors are designed for this context, it is not obvious that (55) is automatically ruled out.

16. By treating the applicative NP as affected, Marantz (1993) proposes that the optional word orders in (50)–(51) result from the independent requirement that an affected argument must occupy the Spec of VP, regardless of the thematic content of the argument. The idea that arguments are ranked both thematically and aspectually and that the aspectual ranking overrides the thematic ranking when the two conflict is explicitly formulated in Grimshaw 1990 and Li 1995 as well. But Marantz's notion of affectedness is both vague and different from that of the other two authors. In addition, his theory seems incompatible with what is found in Chinese.

As I show in note 3 of the appendix, the morpheme *ba* can quite reliably identify the affected argument in a clause. However, it is unequivocal that neither the Benefactive nor the Instrument argument can ever be introduced by *ba*.

(i) a. Li Kui gei-le   Lin Chong yiba fuzi.
        Li Kui give-asp Lin Chong an   ax
        'Li Kui gave Lin Chong an ax.'
    b. Li Kui ba yiba fuzi gei-le   Lin Chong.
        Li Kui BA an   ax give-asp Lin Chong
        Same as (ia)
    c. *Li Kui ba Lin Chong gei-le   yiba fuzi.
        Li Kui BA Lin Chong give-asp an   ax

(ii) a. Li Kui na   fuzi kan shu.
         Li Kui with ax   chop tree
         'Li Kui chopped the tree with an ax.'
     b. Li Kui na   fuzi ba shu kan-le.
         Li Kui with ax   BA tree chop-asp
         Same as (iia)
     c. *Li Kui ba fuzi kan shu.
         Li Kui BA ax   chop tree

(ia–c) illustrate the double-object verb *gei* 'give'. While the Theme argument *yiba fuzi* 'an ax' can be introduced by *ba* in (ib), the B/G argument *Lin Chong* cannot in (ic). Similarly, the Instrument argument *fuzi* is incompatible with *ba* in (iia–c). If B/G and Instrument could be affected arguments, it is not clear at all why *ba* must always skip them and pick up the Theme.

Given these examples, I do not treat the applicative argument as affected and consequently do not adopt Marantz's account of the word order options in (50)–(51).

17. Strict linear adjacency in syntax may not be a necessary condition for PF words in the theory of Distributive Morphology as articulated by Halle and Marantz (1993). I will not explore this possibility here, but there is no fundamental incompatibility between it and my interface theory.

18. For a proposal regarding the interaction between prosody and morphology in Chinese, see Feng 1997.

Appendix

1. *Lian* and *dou* may be analyzed separately. See Huang, Li, and Li, to appear, for a theory of *lian . . . dou*. Also see Lin 1996 for a theory of *dou*. What is relevant here is simply the descriptive usage of the expression.

2. Huang and Tang (1991) later formulate this generalization in terms of subcommand, a relation that also applies to anaphor binding in Chinese.

3. The morpheme *ba* is the most natural way to introduce the object NP when the latter is an affected participant of the event. There is much discussion in Chinese linguistics on this morpheme. But its occurrence in these examples is not relevant to the current discussion on the nature of V_r. See section A.2.3 for the Case-assigning aspect of *ba*.

4. I thank the audience at the Chinese Department, Fudan University, for feedback on the judgments reported in these examples.

5. Collins's (1997) major argument for treating the embedded phrase in SVCs as VP rather than V′ (as in Baker 1989) rests on an optional postposition *yi* in Ewe. ((i)–(iii) are from Collins 1997, (30), (32), (35).)

(i) E   wɔ   ɖokoe-wo fiɛ   (yi).
    you make yourself   king P
    'You have made yourself a king.'

(ii) Kofi zɔ   efiɛ-tɔ   (yi).
    Kofi walk king-like P
    'Kofi walked regally.'

(iii) Me nya   ɖevi-ɛ   dzo (yi).
    I   chase child-def leave P
    'I chased the child away.'

The logic goes as follows. *Yi* is used in Ewe to introduce (i.e., Case-mark) an NP argument that otherwise does not receive a Case (see (i)–(ii)). Hence, there must be a covert NP argument in (iii), which functions as the internal argument of the unaccusative verb *dzo* 'leave'. Since the theory forces this covert NP to be pro bound by the matrix object *ɖevi-ɛ* 'child-def', the embedded phrase headed by *dzo* needs to be a VP to host this pro argument, which Baker's V′ leaves no room for.

There is a gap in Collins's analysis: he provides no proof that *yi* must exclusively introduce an NP argument. In all his examples (e.g., (i)–(ii)), the phrase before *yi* borders on being used as an embedded bare predicate (small clause?) in a structure with a single I. One naturally wonders if this is also the case with the SVC example in (iii), where some projection of *dzo* functions as the embedded predicate of a single-I structure. If so, *yi* would no longer constitute evidence for pro.

Also note that Collins uses the following examples (his (51a–b), (52)) to argue against treating the covert NP before *yi* as an Ā-trace:

(iv) *Kofi tsɔ ati-ɛ *f*o Yao ku.
     Kofi take stick hit Yao with
     'Kofi took the stick and hit Yao with it.'

(v) Kofi tsɔ ati-ɛ *f*o Yao (yi).
    Kofi take stick hit Yao P
    Same as (iv)

(vi) ?tati   xe   me to   fufu ku
     pestle which I   pound fufu with
     'the pestle that I pounded the fufu with'

Preposition stranding is marginally acceptable with Ā-movement in (vi), but the same preposition cannot be stranded in the SVC in (iv). Hence, whatever the complement of P is in SVCs, it is not an Ā-trace. Then why is there a contrast between (iv) and (v), both of which are supposed to contain a P taking a pro complement? Collins suggests that *ku* 'with' assigns inherent Case, which pro cannot accept, whereas *yi* does not assign inherent Case. This account is valid to the extent that *yi* can be shown to introduce nominal arguments. If it is associated with embedded predicates of certain kinds, the contrast between (iv) and (v) may have a totally different source.

Overall, Collins's analysis of SVC requires many extra assumptions to handle the data in question. It is not clear to me whether it indeed has an advantage over Baker's analysis.

6. The problem with binding does not disappear even when the thematic subject of V_r happens to be the object of V_c so that V_r indeed projects to a TrP-less bare VP as in (29b). On the basis of a three-way contrast among Chinese resultative compounds, V-*de*, and English resultatives, I show in Li 1999 that the binding domain for an anaphor A is in fact the smallest XP in which all thematic/ grammatical relations of the head governing A are satisfied (cf. Chomsky's (1986b) complete functional complex). It follows that, if the object of V_r is an anaphor, the binding domain is actually the bare VP of V_c without the matrix TrP because it is this VP that is the smallest phrase containing all thematic arguments of V_r. Again, one would not expect the embedded anaphor to take the subject of V_c as its binder. For a brief review of the evidence given in Li 1999, see section 2.3 of this book.

7. A more interesting comparison, though beyond the scope of this book, is between the resultative SVC and the V-*de* construction, as both are syntax-based. Recall from section 1.3.1 that the V-*de* construction shows no obligatory object sharing either.

(i) Yan Qing chang-de jinpilijin.
    Yan Qing sing-DE be.totally.exhausted
    'Yan Qing was totally exhausted from singing.'

This is expected if the embedded clause contains a pro argument. In the absence of the matrix object (V_c being unergative), pro is expected to be bound by the subject. Since the structural properties of the V-*de* construction are rather straightforward, examples like (i) cast doubt on Collins's pro-/PRO-oriented structure of SVCs. If the embedded VP contains a pro/PRO argument as in his structure (29b), it becomes mysterious why Ewe does not have a resultative SVC corresponding to (i). On the other hand, Baker's (1989) SVC structure without the embedded pro/PRO may be tailored into a Larsonian shell to account for both the Ewe resultative SVC and English resultatives. See Li 1999 for details. Also see note 5 above for other problems with Collins's theory.

Another point worth mentioning is this: though Chinese has V-V compounds corresponding to the resultative SVC, there are no V-V compounds matching the so-called instrumental SVC in (ii) (from Collins 1997, 461).

(ii) Kofi tsɔ ati-ɛ   ƒo Yao.
    Kofi take stick-def hit Yao
    'Kofi took the stick and hit Yao.'

Within the P&P model, (ii) is assigned the same kind of structure as the resultative SVC, with the (probably correct) assumption that the shared internal argument is the Theme for *take* and the Instrument for *hit* (see Baker 1989; Collins 1997). The effort to unify all the SVCs could be misguided, though, considering that Chinese uses the same (surface) form as (ii) for instrumentals but uses compounds or a full biclausal V-*de* construction for resultatives. If instrumentals are essentially the same as resultatives, why would Chinese use totally different forms for the two? I leave this question to future investigation.

Chapter 2

1. When the verb root is transitive, native speakers' judgments seem to become controversial with some examples. (i) is adapted from Borer and Grodzinsky 1986.

(i) Sara her'a   la-tinoket   'et 'acma ba-re'i.
    Sara made.see (show) to-the.baby acc herself in-the.mirror
    'Sara showed the baby herself in the mirror.'

Some informants believe that *'acma* 'herself' is bound by *tinoket* 'the baby', but one thinks that the matrix subject *Sara* may also serve as a binder. A possibility is that *her'a* 'made see' is regarded by some as a truly lexicalized verb and, despite its surface form, not as the product of active morphological processes. In other words, there may be a more fundamental reason why English has a monomorphemic verb *show* meaning 'make see', but no monomorphemic verb meaning 'make write'. Another possibility is that Hebrew morphological causatives are type I causatives like those in Chichewa. When the verb root is transitive, its thematic subject is demoted and the thematic object raises into the matrix VP. From there, it can be locally bound by the matrix subject. (See section 1.1.4.) While the controversial status of (i) deserves careful investigation, causatives with an intransitive verb root like (4a) seem to behave consistently like a biclausal construction. This is expected because intransitive verb roots do not undergo subject demotion. So any anaphor inside the embedded VP must be bound by the thematic subject of the verb root.

The examples in (4c) and (i) also resemble the possessive dative construction in the Case-marking patterns. See Borer and Grodzinsky 1986 and Landau 1999 for analyses of this construction in Hebrew and more references. In Landau's analysis, the dative NP *la-yeladim* 'the boys' in (4c) would originate as the possessor of the noun *sipur* 'story' and raise to the Spec of the lower VP. But typical examples given by these authors do not involve the causative form of the verb, not to mention that the semantics would seem wrong for (4c)—to make the boys' story written does not mean that the boys would be the authors of the story. Similarly, it is not clear how *tinoket* 'the baby' in (i) is generated as the possessor of *'acma* 'herself'. In any case, (4a–b) would illustrate a biclausal structure because they do not contain possessive datives.

2. Because English does not have morphological causatives that are clearly derived from verbal stems, however, the language provides only partial support for the current theory. Still, the same question should be asked of English in the light of Arabic and Hebrew: is it accidental that the rather large number of deadjectival verbs like *lengthen* and *popularize* can, as far as we know, only project to a monoclausal structure?

3. I am grateful to Abdullah Al-Dobaian for bringing Borer's work to my attention.

4. I thank Ray Jackendoff for discussing these examples with me. He tentatively suggests that the subject of *turn* may be treated as an Actor on the Action tier in his theory of lexical semantic structure (Jackendoff 1990).

5. The idea presented here occurred to me during a meeting with Abdullah Al-Dobaian. I thank him for inspiring discussions and for his feedback.

6. See Levin and Rappaport 1986 and Cinque 1990 for discussion of whether the θ-argument of an adjective is internal or external, a distinction that clearly should affect the syntactic structure of AP.

7. In fact, Baker's analysis of (24) has a more fundamental problem that essentially falsifies it completely. In the same section where the analysis is presented, he assumes that moving a lexical head (e.g., V) to a functional one (T) results in a complex functional head (p. 67) that, like any other functional head, fails to license a trace. In this theory, no verb could ever move to T (or T to C or N to D) because the trace of the moved head could never be c-commanded locally by a lexical head. It does not help to invoke coindexation (e.g., by claiming that a coindexed c-commanding head, possibly through movement, also counts as a "lexical governor"; see Rizzi 1990). In (26a), the clitic *ne* moves to T. If the index it carries percolates to the whole complex T node and somehow makes the latter a "lexical licenser," then the trace of *ne* would satisfy Baker's ECP and (24a) would be wrongly ruled grammatical.

8. See Jackendoff 2002 for the speculation that the subject existed prior to the advent of functional categories in the course of linguistic evolution. This idea, if

proven true, is consistent with treating Pred as a lexical category because by the time the subject-predicate came into being, functional words did not yet exist. One possible way to test the combination of Jackendoff's idea and mine is to check the ontogenetic order in which the subject, the adjective, and functional morphemes such as tense and agreement emerge.

9. Personally, I think the contrast between (29) and (30) suggests an old objection to Generative Semantics: one may decompose a lexical item L into its conceptual-semantic components to one's heart's content, and may even achieve a deeper understanding of certain properties of L, but whatever structure is used to represent such decomposition is "submorphemic" and not operative at the syntactic level. This is ultimately why the practically identical structures in (28) and (31) yield different patterns of binding depending on whether a separate adjective is present or not: the decompositional structure of the matrix verb is simply *invisible* to the adjective. In this sense, Hale and Keyser (1993) are not only right but in fact wise to call their structures *l-syntax*, which sets the stage for distinguishing it from the "syntax syntax."

10. Note that my analysis of applicatives in section 1.2 only employs a relative correspondence between the thematic hierarchy and the syntactic hierarchy, without abiding by the UTAH. In fact, if the UTAH were fully implemented in these structures, more than two VP copies would be needed to maintain absolute syntactic positions for Goal, Theme, Instrument, and so on.

Chapter 3

1. Baker's original gloss shows no object agreement in this example. But as he clarifies later, Agr_O is always present in such a case, though it happens to be a null form.

2. This claim begs the question of whether the *wh*-chain needs a Case, especially considering (i)–(ii).

(i) *Who does it seem [t to be happy]?

(ii) Who does he believe [t to be happy]?

The only difference between these sentences would seem to be whether the trace of *who* is in a Case-marked position. Indeed, Kayne (1984) discusses examples of the following kind:

(iii) *He said [Sam to be a good candidate].

(iv) Who did he say [t to be a good candidate]?

The ungrammaticality of (iii) is attributed to lack of Case for *Sam*, so the original trace of *who* in (iv) should be Caseless as well, apparently in support of Baker's analysis of Mohawk. But Kayne observes that the matrix verb *say* could assign Case to the intermediate trace of *Sam* in the embedded Spec of CP position. While such a scenario may be more exceptional than ECM, it is at least consistent with (i)–(ii). I leave this issue open for future investigation.

3. The model in (16) differs from Halle and Marantz's (1993) Distributive Morphology in placing the morphological module "before" syntax rather than "after"

it. In reality, the difference is not as fundamental as it appears. For compounding and derivational morphology, we saw ample evidence in chapter 2 that lexical morphemes do not merge in syntax. It follows that such processes can only happen either before syntax as in (16) or after syntax if they form PF words through pure linear adjacency. As far as I know, morphological phenomena such as NI are not the result of PF word formation and therefore should happen prior to syntax. As for inflectional morphology, it is easy to imagine a lexical morpheme picking up certain grammatical features F (T, Agr, Num, etc.) in the morphological module in (16), having F checked in syntax or LF, and spelling out the morphophonological form of F in the "distributed" postsyntactic portion of morphology.

4. See Pesetsky 1989 for the idea that certain principles must be satisfied at the earliest stage of derivation.

5. A question facing Baker's theory (and consequently mine) is what it means for *agr* to receive Case. The answer may lie in the role that agreement plays in Case assignment. In the Minimalist Program, Agr actually collaborates with another head (say, V) to assign Case. Following this logic, an *agr* does not really receive Case from another head. Rather, the only thing it can do to affect regular Case assignment is to lose its own Case-assigning capability. More study is called for on this problem.

6. A rare exception is Pesetsky 1985, which explores LF raising of derivational morphemes with a view to resolving the "bracketing paradox" in English.

7. In fact, under Chomsky's (1995) theory of bare phrase structure, Baker's bare nominal argument would be just N because it consists of no other constituent.

8. If this idea of LF movement is indeed desirable, one detail to be worked out is why overt movement apparently does not apply to morphemes inside a compound in Mohawk. Various possibilities arise. At the moment, I am inclined toward the following approach. Movement does not happen in morphology because bonding between morphemes is (obviously) relevant and visible in this module. Movement in syntax does not split a morphologically complex word because syntax does not alter morphological structures, the MSMH being the only mapping principle between the two autonomous modules. LF, on the other hand, is not simply a covert extension of syntax. At this level, the internal structure of every construction not considered by the language to be a lexical unit (i.e., an item from the lexicon defined under the POL) is visible to LF operations. In English, that means syntactic structures; in Mohawk, it includes both syntactic structures and morphological structures.

9. Both Baker's theory and mine (and for that matter, all theories) face an unanswered question: if there are two different options for NI (no matter exactly how they are analyzed), why don't languages have "double NI," with the first taking a new argument (i.e., the agreement-friendly NI) and the second being the incorporated argument? Different solutions are imaginable. For instance, since both options of NI happen in the same morphological module in my theory, conceivably some kind of (processing?) rule against repetitive operations (probably comparable to the Obligatory Contour Principle in phonology) disfavors two

instances of NI within a single compound. That such a rule is at work in overt syntax can be seen in these English examples:

(i) Sam keeps talking.

(ii) ??Sam is keeping talking.

On the other hand, Baker treats one option as lexical and the other as syntactic. Since the two modules are opaque to each other, appeal to any Obligatory Contour Principle–style rule becomes much harder. Another possible explanation is that somehow, only the Theme argument can incorporate, as Di Sciullo and Williams (1987) suggest. As long as the R role of N is not considered the Theme by UG under all circumstances, no noun receiving it from the N-V compound can incorporate, period. Once more, such a solution is more difficult to implement in Baker's account, which would likely place the NP with the R role in a complement position to the N-V compound, from which incorporation-style head movement is expected to happen.

Another question is why English compounds such as *car-driving* do not have the option of treating *car* as a predicate (e.g., **the car-driving of my new Ford Taurus*). The same question arises in Baker's theory but in slightly different terms: if an N may undergo lexical θ-identification with a V in Mohawk, why can't the same process happen in English? I have no answer to offer except to note the possible relevance of lexical opacity.

10. Baker (1996, 195–196 and sec. 5.4) shows convincingly that this difference in agreement classes has nothing to do with the unergative/unaccusative distinction, as both classes of adjectival verbs allow incorporation, which applies only to internal Theme arguments.

11. I ignore the issue of more accurately representing the argument structure of unaccusative verbs. Grimshaw (1990) and I (Li 1993) argue that the argument structure should reflect the fact that the θ-role of these verbs is hierarchically lower than, say, Agent. Such information is largely irrelevant to the current discussion.

12. That a form of category [+V, +N] can directly function as a predicate without the help of a copula is best illustrated in Chinese.

(i) Li Kui hen   gaoxing neng gensui Song Jiang.
    Li Kui quite glad   can follow Song Jiang
    'Li Kui was glad to be able to work for Song Jiang.'

(ii) Li Kui dui zhege jieguo hen   gaoxing.
     Li Kui to this result quite glad
     'Li Kui was glad about this result.'

(iii) *Li Kui hen   gaoxing zhege jieguo.
      Li Kui quite glad   this   result
      Intended reading: same as (ii)

The fact that a clausal complement follows *gaoxing* 'glad' as in (i) while an NP complement must precede it with the help of the preposition *dui* 'to' is characteristic of adjectives that are incapable of assigning a Case to their object (cf.

of-insertion in English), indicating that *gaoxing* is of category A. Crucially, no copula is used in this context. See Li 2002 for a comparison of Chinese and English adjectives.

13. Compounds like *house-white* also can be analyzed as nominal predicates headed by the noun (here, *house*) and modified by the adjective (here, *white*) (Marianne Mithun, personal communication).

14. The examples in (50) actually do not show this clearly because the R role of these nouns takes the neuter agreement, which would be realized as $\emptyset$ in the presence of another *agr*. But even nouns with nonneuter *agr* for their R role resist multiple agreement. See Baker 1996, 266.

15. Following this logic, the agreement prefix in the following NPs (from Baker 1996, 245) must not be signaling a pro argument to receive the R role:

(i) ka-nuhs-a'   agr-house-suff   'house'
    o-kar-a'   agr-story-suff   'story'

According to Baker, *agr* links the R role of each N to a pro inside the NP to satisfy the MVC. If the referentially used R role waits till LF to be automatically saturated, then *agr* in these examples is nothing more than a marker like English determiners such as *the* and *a* in Heim's (1982) theory. Theories about the distribution of the nominal *agr* system can be devised but quickly become extremely complicated, again owing to our insufficient understanding of the R role. I leave the matter to subsequent work.

16. For the purpose of my theory, it is sufficient for the causative suffix V_1 to have an optional Theme—all undesirable outcomes will be ruled out automatically. But for reasons of space, the discussion assumes the presence of the θ-role.

17. Again, I ignore the precise representation of the argument structure, opting for using names to refer to θ-roles.

Chapter 4

1. I am grateful to Jim Huang and the audience at the 1997 LSA Summer Institute for feedback on earlier versions of this principle. A brief comparison between the MLCA and Fukui and Takano's (1998) Linearization appears in section 4.2.

2. Logically, it is even possible that the driving force for head movement among lexical head positions is not morphological factors or feature checking but the MLCA. Suppose a language can set the head parameter as either head-final or head-initial, as is usually believed. A head-final VP structure automatically satisfies the MLCA and therefore provides no reason for the lexical verb to move anywhere, yielding a typical agglutinative language. A head-initial setting, however, violates the MLCA unless the verb moves to the higher V and the original V position contains only an MLCA-exempted trace. Conceptually, such lexical head movement is comparable to NP-movement, in which the NP is generated in a position illegitimate for the Case Filter and thus must be saved through raising. I leave this possibility for future investigation.

3. Though proposed for different reasons and formulated in different terms, at the most fundamental level the MLCA shares much with Fukui and Takano's (1998) theory of Merge-Demerge. It follows that much of what one can say about one theory directly applies to the other.

4. See Fukui and Takano 1998 for a comparison between Kayne's LCA and their theory that, like mine, takes head-final structure to be the default.

5. Kayne (1994) associates this complement-to-Spec movement with two typological facts: that head-final languages are typically agglutinative and *wh*-in-situ (see Bresnan 1972). As mentioned in section 4.1, the first association can be obtained with a default head-final structure generated by the MLCA. What matters here is not any particular type of movement (or lack of it), but the fact that heads end up adjacent to one another. So the agglutinative languages cannot be used to distinguish Kayne's theory from its competitors like the one presented here. The second association is inspiring but nonetheless suffers from inconsistent logic. Kayne's reasoning is this: if the whole IP occupies the Spec of CP in, say, Japanese, no *wh*-phrase can move to that position anymore, resulting in the typical in-situ phenomenon. But Kayne's theory also intrinsically allows a constituent adjoined to whatever phrase occupies the Spec of CP to c-command C and trigger Spec-head agreement with it, a property he uses to explain an apparent problem with (i).

(i) Whose book did you borrow?

Here, the phrase carrying [+wh] is not the NP in the Spec of CP, *whose book*, but the possessor of this NP, *whose*, which in Kayne's theory adjoins to the NP headed by *book*. Following this reasoning, a *wh*-phrase inside the Japanese IP can still adjoin to IP (or to a phrase in the Spec of the Spec ... of IP) overtly and trigger Spec-head agreement on C once IP raises to the Spec of CP. So Kayne's theory cannot really explain why head-final languages are usually *wh*-in-situ.

6. For a substantial investigation of word order typology with a sample of over 400 languages, see Tomlin 1986.

7. Shlonsky (1992) discusses the possibility of splitting CP into CP and AgrP. A similar idea is proposed by Haegeman (1994) on the basis of West Flemish. Whether Shlonsky's AgrP corresponds to C_tP is yet to be determined. Also see Shlonsky 1997 on treating Top as a C.

8. Exactly how *that-t* should be analyzed is a completely different question that, as far as I can see, awaits an answer. Various proposals utilizing UG principles such as the ECP have been made (see, e.g., Chomsky 1981; Pesetsky 1982; Kayne 1984; Aoun et al. 1987; Rizzi 1990; Lasnik and Saito 1992; Watanabe 1993; Browning 1996). However, examples like (i), provided by Culicover (1993), complicate the data to be accounted for.

(i) This is the tree that I said that *(just yesterday) had resisted my shovel.

It is unclear why the presence of an adverbial can exempt the subject *t* from an ECP violation. Attempts have been made to account for (i) in terms of extra licensing heads (Culicover 1993; Browning 1996). But fieldwork by DeMerit (1995) indicates that there may be more than a black-or-white UG violation involved:

(ii) *This is the tree that I said that had resisted my shovel.

(iii) ?This is the tree that I said that yesterday had resisted my shovel.

(iv) (?)This is the tree that I said that just yesterday had resisted my shovel.

(v) This is the tree that I said that just the day before yesterday had resisted my shovel.

After consulting ten native speakers, none of whom was a linguist, DeMerit found that although differences in judgments can be subtle and vary from person to person, the acceptability of a *that-t* sentence is generally proportional to the length of the intervening adverbial phrase up to 5–6 words, beyond which it starts to decline again. If this result can be independently confirmed, it will suggest that processing factors are involved.

9. There may be two different *de*s for the resultative and the manner adverbial, and the latter may take less than a full clause as its complement. However, such details do not affect the analysis presented here.

10. The only examples where an adverbial relation holds between V and V are *zuo-dai* 'sit-await', *sheng-chi* 'raw-eat', and so on. In all of them, the first verb modifies the second. Examples like (i) are indeed composed of V_1-V_2, with V_2 modifying V_1.

(i) Ta zou   man le.
     he walk slow LE
     'He walked (too) slowly.'

But see Ting and Li, in preparation, for arguments that *man* 'slow' is actually a modifying phrase rather than forming a compound with *zou* 'walk'.

11. In the Minimalist Program, the boundary between a head and a phrase is blurred so that a bare head may also be (functionally) a phrase. But then a clitic both is D and functionally serves as a phrase. And adjoining it to F' under Kayne's (1991) analysis qualifies it as a phrase by the same logic. Hence, cliticization at least *can* be treated as phrasal movement.

12. Alternatively, it is suggested that adjuncts adjoin to X' rather than XP (Freidin 1991; Bowers 1993). The basic argument in the text is independent of which node is the adjunction site.

13. Bowers (1993) notes that English adverbs such as *poorly* can only occur postverbally.

(i) Sam learned Chinese poorly.

(ii) *Sam poorly learned Chinese.

He places this type of adverb in the lower VP of a Larsonian structure, a structural position he argues to be responsible for making *poorly* consistently postverbal, regardless of which side of the lower VP/V' the adverb adjoins to.

Chapter 5

1. Whether the actual author of *Lao Zi* is Lao Zi himself has always been controversial. Here, I adopt the tentative conclusion in *Ci Hai* 1979. I am immensely grateful to Professor Tsai-fa Cheng for locating the precise source of the quotations here and for discussing them with me.

2. It should be noted that the typical English pronunciation of *Yin* and *Yang* makes these terms totally unrecognizable to a native speaker of Chinese. The English forms perceptually closest to *Yin* and *Yang* are *yean* and *young*, respectively.

References

Al-Dobaian, Abdullah. 1998. Arabic verbal and de-adjectival causatives. Ms., University of Wisconsin-Madison.

Almansour, Abdulrahman. 2001. Pashto causatives. Ms., University of Wisconsin-Madison.

Alsina, Alex. 1992. On the argument structure of causatives. *Linguistic Inquiry* 23, 517–556.

Alsina, Alex, and Sam A. Mchombo. 1993. Object asymmetries and the Chichewa applicative construction. In Sam A. Mchombo, ed., *Theoretical aspects of Bantu grammar*, 17–45. Stanford, Calif.: CSLI Publications.

Anderson, Stephen. 1982. Where's morphology? *Linguistic Inquiry* 13, 571–612.

Anderson, Stephen. 1992. *A-morphous morphology.* New York: Cambridge University Press.

Aoun, Joseph, Norbert Hornstein, David Lightfoot, and Amy Weinberg. 1987. Two types of locality. *Linguistic Inquiry* 18, 537–577.

Aoun, Joseph, and Yen-hui Audrey Li. 1989. Constituency and scope. *Linguistic Inquiry* 20, 141–172.

Aronoff, Mark. 1994. *Morphology by itself.* Cambridge, Mass.: MIT Press.

Baker, Mark. 1985. The Mirror Principle and morphosyntactic explanation. *Linguistic Inquiry* 16, 373–415.

Baker, Mark. 1988. *Incorporation: A theory of grammatical function changing.* Chicago: University of Chicago Press.

Baker, Mark. 1989. Object sharing and projection in serial verb constructions. *Linguistic Inquiry* 20, 513–553.

Baker, Mark. 1996. *The polysynthesis parameter.* New York: Oxford University Press.

Baker, Mark. 2002. Building and merging, not checking. *Linguistic Inquiry* 33, 321–328.

Baker, Mark. 2003. *Lexical categories: Verbs, nouns, and adjectives.* Cambridge: Cambridge University Press.

Baltin, Mark. 1982. A landing site theory of movement rules. *Linguistic Inquiry* 13, 1–38.

Belletti, Adriana. 1988. The Case of unaccusatives. *Linguistic Inquiry* 19, 1–34.

Belletti, Adriana, and Luigi Rizzi. 1981. The syntax of *ne*: Some theoretical implications. *The Linguistic Review* 1, 117–154.

Benmamoun, Elabbas. 1991. Causatives in Moroccan Arabic. In Bernard Comrie and Mushira Eid, eds., *Perspectives in Arabic linguistics III*, 173–195. Amsterdam: John Benjamins.

Benmamoun, Elabbas. 2000. *The feature structure of functional categories: A comparative study of Arabic dialects.* New York: Oxford University Press.

Bobaljik, Jonathan David. 1995. Morphosyntax: The syntax of verbal inflection. Ph.D. dissertation, MIT.

Bonet, Eulàlia. 1991. Morphology after syntax: Pronominal clitics in Romance languages. Ph.D. dissertation, MIT.

Borer, Hagit. 1988. On the morphological parallelism between compounds and constructs. *Yearbook of Morphology* 1, 45–66.

Borer, Hagit. 1991. The causative-inchoative alternation: A case study in parallel morphology. *The Linguistic Review* 8, 119–158.

Borer, Hagit, and Yosef Grodzinsky. 1986. Syntactic versus lexical cliticization: The case of Hebrew dative clitics. In Hagit Borer, ed., *The syntax of pronominal clitics*, 175–217. Orlando, Fla.: Academic Press.

Bošković, Željko. 1997. *The syntax of nonfinite complementation.* Cambridge, Mass.: MIT Press.

Bowers, John. 1993. The syntax of predication. *Linguistic Inquiry* 24, 591–656.

Bresnan, Joan. 1972. Theory of complementation in English syntax. Ph.D. dissertation, MIT.

Bresnan, Joan, and Jonni Kanerva. 1989. Locative inversion in Chicheŵa: A case study of factorization in grammar. *Linguistic Inquiry* 20, 1–50.

Bresnan, Joan, and Lioba Moshi. 1993. Object asymmetries in comparative Bantu syntax. In Sam A. Mchombo, ed., *Theoretical aspects of Bantu grammar*, 47–91. Stanford, Calif.: CSLI Publications.

Browning, M. A. 1996. CP recursion and *that-t* effects. *Linguistic Inquiry* 27, 237–255.

Burzio, Luigi. 1986. *Italian syntax: A government-binding approach.* Dordrecht: Reidel.

Carrier, Jill, and Janet H. Randall. 1992. The argument structure and syntactic structure of resultatives. *Linguistic Inquiry* 23, 173–234.

Carrier-Duncan, Jill. 1985. Linking of thematic roles in derivational word formation. *Linguistic Inquiry* 16, 1–34.

Chafe, Wallace. 1970. *Seneca morphology and dictionary.* Washington, D.C.: Smithsonian Institute.

Chapin, Paul. 1967. The syntax of word-derivation in English. MITRE Corporation Information System Language Studies 16. Bedford, Mass.: MITRE Corporation.

Chomsky, Noam. 1970. Remarks on nominalization. In Roderick Jacobs and Peter Rosenbaum, eds., *Readings in English transformational grammar*, 184–221. Waltham, Mass.: Ginn.

Chomsky, Noam. 1981. *Lectures on government and binding*. Dordrecht: Foris.

Chomsky, Noam. 1986a. *Barriers*. Cambridge, Mass.: MIT Press.

Chomsky, Noam. 1986b. *Knowledge of language*. New York: Praeger.

Chomsky, Noam. 1993. A minimalist program for linguistic theory. In Kenneth Hale and Samuel Jay Keyser, eds., *The view from Building 20*, 1–52. Cambridge, Mass.: MIT Press.

Chomsky, Noam. 1995. *The Minimalist Program*. Cambridge, Mass.: MIT Press.

Chomsky, Noam. 2000. Minimalist inquiries: The framework. In Roger Martin, David Michaels, and Juan Uriagereka, eds., *Step by step*, 89–156. Cambridge, Mass.: MIT Press.

Ci hai. 1979. Shanghai: Shanghai Dictionary Press.

Cinque, Guglielmo. 1990. Ergative adjectives and the Lexicalist Hypothesis. *Natural Language and Linguistic Theory* 8, 1–41.

Cinque, Guglielmo. 1999. *Adverbs and functional heads: A cross-linguistic perspective*. Oxford: Oxford University Press.

Collins, Chris. 1997. Argument sharing in serial verb constructions. *Linguistic Inquiry* 28, 461–497.

Collins, Chris, and Höskuldur Thráinsson. 1996. VP-internal structure and object shift in Icelandic. *Linguistic Inquiry* 27, 391–444.

Culicover, Peter. 1993. Evidence against ECP accounts of the *that-t* effect. *Linguistic Inquiry* 24, 557–562.

Davidson, David. 1967. The logical form of action sentences. In Nicholas Rescher, ed., *The logic of decision and action*, 81–95. Pittsburgh: University of Pittsburgh Press.

Déchaine, Rose-Marie. 1986. *Opérations sur les structures d'argument: Le cas des constructions sérielles en Haitien*. M.A. thesis, Université du Québec à Montréal.

DeMerit, Jean. 1995. *That-t* and the length of the intervening adverbial. Ms., University of Wisconsin-Madison.

Diesing, Molly. 1992. *Indefinites*. Cambridge, Mass.: MIT Press.

Di Sciullo, Anna Maria, and Edwin Williams. 1987. *On the definition of word*. Cambridge, Mass.: MIT Press.

Dowty, David. 1979. *Word meaning and Montague Grammar*. Dordrecht: Reidel.

Dowty, David. 1987. Thematic proto-roles, subject selection, and lexical semantic defaults. Paper presented at the annual meeting of the Linguistic Society of America.

Dowty, David. 1991. Thematic proto-roles and argument selection. *Language* 67, 547–619.

Emonds, Joseph. 1978. The verbal complex V'-V in French. *Linguistic Inquiry* 9, 151–175.

Ernst, Thomas. 2002. *The syntax of adjuncts*. Cambridge: Cambridge University Press.

Evans, Nicholas. 1991. A draft grammar of Mayali. Ms., University of Melbourne.

Fabb, Nigel. 1984. Syntactic affixation. Ph.D. dissertation, MIT.

Falk, Yehuda. 1985. Semantic representation and the dative alternation. Paper presented at the 1st annual conference of the Israel Association for Theoretical Linguistics, Tel Aviv University, 9–10 June.

Fassi Fehri, Abdelkader. 1993. *Issues in the structure of Arabic clauses and words*. Dordrecht: Kluwer.

Feng, Shengli. 1997. Prosodically determined word-formation in Chinese. *Social Science in China* 4, 120–137. Beijing.

Fiengo, Robert. 1977. On trace theory. *Linguistic Inquiry* 8, 35–62.

Foley, William. 1991. *The Yimas language of New Guinea*. Stanford, Calif.: Stanford University Press.

Foley, William. 1997. Polysynthesis and complex verb formation: The case of applicatives in Yimas. In Alex Alsina, Joan Bresnan, and Peter Sells, eds., *Complex predicates*, 355–396. Stanford, Calif.: CSLI Publications.

Foley, William, and Mike Olson. 1985. Clausehood and verb serialization. In Johanna Nichols and Anthony Woodbury, eds., *Grammar inside and outside the clause*. Cambridge: Cambridge University Press.

Freidin, Robert. 1991. *Foundations of generative syntax*. Cambridge, Mass.: MIT Press.

Fukui, Naoki, and Margaret Speas. 1986. Specifiers and projections. In Naoki Fukui, Tova R. Rapoport, and Elizabeth Sagey, eds., *Papers in theoretical linguistics*, 128–172. MIT Working Papers in Linguistics 8. Cambridge, Mass.: MIT, Department of Linguistics and Philosophy, MITWPL.

Fukui, Naoki, and Yuji Takano. 1998. Symmetry in syntax: Merge and Demerge. *Journal of East Asian Linguistics* 7, 27–86.

George, Leland. 1980. Analogical generalization in natural language syntax. Ph.D. dissertation, MIT.

Gibson, Jeanne. 1980. Clause union in Chamorro and in Universal Grammar. Ph.D. dissertation, University of California, San Diego.

Greenberg, Joseph. 1963. *Universals of language*. Cambridge, Mass.: MIT Press.

Grimshaw, Jane. 1979. Complement selection and the lexicon. *Linguistic Inquiry* 10, 279–326.

Grimshaw, Jane. 1990. *Argument structure*. Cambridge, Mass.: MIT Press.

Grimshaw, Jane. 1993. Extended projection. Ms., Rutgers University.

Grimshaw, Jane, and Ralf-Armin Mester. 1988. Light verbs and θ-marking. *Linguistic Inquiry* 19, 205–232.

Gruber, Jeffrey. 1965. Studies in lexical relations. Ph.D. dissertation, MIT.

Haegeman, Liliane. 1994. *Introduction to Government and Binding Theory*. Oxford: Blackwell.

Hale, Kenneth, and Samuel Jay Keyser. 1993. On argument structure and the lexical expression of syntactic relations. In Kenneth Hale and Samuel Jay Keyser, eds., *The view from Building 20*, 53–109. Cambridge, Mass.: MIT Press.

Hale, Kenneth, and Samuel Jay Keyser. 2002. *Prolegomenon to a theory of argument structure*. Cambridge, Mass.: MIT Press.

Halle, Morris, and Alec Marantz. 1993. Distributive Morphology and the pieces of inflection. In Kenneth Hale and Samuel Jay Keyser, eds., *The view from Building 20*, 111–176. Cambridge, Mass.: MIT Press.

Hawkins, John. 1983. *Word order universals*. New York: Academic Press.

Heim, Irene. 1982. The semantics of definite and indefinite noun phrases. Ph.D. dissertation, University of Massachusetts, Amherst.

Higginbotham, James. 1985. On semantics. *Linguistic Inquiry* 16, 547–593.

Hoekstra, Teun. 1988. Small clause results. *Lingua* 74, 101–139.

Huang, C.-T. James. 1982. Logical relations in Chinese and the theory of grammar. Ph.D. dissertation, MIT.

Huang, C.-T. James. 1988. *Wo pao de kuai* and Chinese phrase structure. *Language* 64, 274–311.

Huang, C.-T. James. 1989. Pro-drop in Chinese: A generalized control theory. In Osvaldo Jaeggli and Kenneth Safir, eds., *The null subject parameter*, 185–214. Dordrecht: Kluwer.

Huang, C.-T. James. 1993. Reconstruction and the structure of VP. *Linguistic Inquiry* 24, 103–138.

Huang, C.-T. James, Yen-hui Audrey Li, and Yafei Li. To appear. *The syntax of Chinese*. Cambridge: Cambridge University Press.

Huang, C.-T. James, and Jane Tang. 1991. The local nature of the long-distance reflexives in Chinese. In Jan Koster and Eric Reuland, eds., *Long-distance anaphora*, 263–282. Cambridge: Cambridge University Press.

Jackendoff, Ray. 1972. *Semantic interpretation in generative grammar*. Cambridge, Mass.: MIT Press.

Jackendoff, Ray. 1987. The status of thematic relations in linguistic theory. *Linguistic Inquiry* 18, 369–411.

Jackendoff, Ray. 1990. *Semantic structures*. Cambridge, Mass.: MIT Press.

Jackendoff, Ray. 1998. The architecture of the language faculty: A neominimalist perspective. *Syntax and Semantics* 29, 19–46.

Jackendoff, Ray. 2002. *Foundations of language: Brain, meaning, grammar, evolution.* Oxford: Oxford University Press.

Jelinek, Eloise. 1984. Empty categories, Case, and configurationality. *Natural Language and Linguistic Theory* 2, 39–76.

Jelinek, Eloise. 1989. The Case split and argument type in Choctaw. In Lazlo K. Maracz and Pieter Muysken, eds., *Configurationality: The typology of asymmetries*, 117–141. Dordrecht: Foris.

Jensen, John. 1990. *Morphology: Word structure in generative grammar.* Amsterdam: John Benjamins.

Julien, Marit. 2000. Syntactic heads and word formation. Ph.D. dissertation, University of Tromsø.

Jung, Dukkyo. 1999. Korean V-V compounds. Ms., University of Wisconsin-Madison.

Kayne, Richard. 1975. *French syntax.* Cambridge, Mass.: MIT Press.

Kayne, Richard. 1984. *Connectedness and binary branching.* Dordrecht: Foris.

Kayne, Richard. 1991. Romance clitics, verb movement, and PRO. *Linguistic Inquiry* 22, 647–686.

Kayne, Richard. 1994. *The antisymmetry of syntax.* Cambridge, Mass.: MIT Press.

Kimenyi, Alexandre. 1980. A relational grammar of Kinyarwanda. Berkeley: University of California Press.

Kiparsky, Paul. 1982a. From cyclic morphology to lexical phonology. In Harry van der Hulst and Norval Smith, eds., *The structure of phonological representations*, 131–175. Dordrecht: Foris.

Kiparsky, Paul. 1982b. Lexical morphology and phonology. In Linguistic Society of Korea, ed., *Linguistics in the morning calm*, 3–19. Seoul: Hanshin.

Kiparsky, Paul. 1988. Agreement and linking theory. Ms., Stanford University.

Kisseberth, Charles W., and Mohammad Imam Abasheikh. 1977. The object relationship in Chi-Mwi:ni, a Bantu language. In Peter Cole and Jerrold Sadock, eds., *Syntax and semantics 8: Grammatical relations*, 179–218. New York: Academic Press.

Kitagawa, Yoshihisa. 1986. Subjects in Japanese and English. Ph.D. dissertation, University of Massachusetts, Amherst.

Koopman, Hilda, and Dominique Sportiche. 1991. The position of subjects. *Lingua* 85, 211–258.

Kung, Hui-yi. 1993. The Mapping Hypothesis and postverbal structures in Mandarin Chinese. Ph.D. dissertation, University of Wisconsin-Madison.

Kuroda, S.-Y. 1988. Whether we agree or not. *Lingvisticæ Investigationes* 12, 1–47.

Landau, Idan. 1999. Possessor raising and the structure of VP. *Lingua* 107, 1–37.

Lapointe, Steven. 1980. A theory of grammatical agreement. Ph.D. dissertation, University of Massachusetts, Amherst.

Larson, Richard. 1985. Bare-NP adverbs. *Linguistic Inquiry* 16, 595–621.

Larson, Richard. 1988. On the double object construction. *Linguistic Inquiry* 19, 335–391.

Lasnik, Howard. 1991. On the necessity of binding conditions. In Robert Freidin, ed., *Principles and parameters in comparative grammar*, 7–28. Cambridge, Mass.: MIT Press.

Lasnik, Howard. 1992. Case and expletives. *Linguistic Inquiry* 23, 381–405.

Lasnik, Howard. 1999. *Minimalist analysis*. Malden, Mass.: Blackwell.

Lasnik, Howard, and Mamoru Saito. 1991. On the subject of infinitives. In Lise M. Dobrin, Lynn Nichols, and Rosa M. Rodriguez, eds., *CLS 27*. Vol. 1, *The General Session*, 324–343. Chicago: University of Chicago, Chicago Linguistic Society.

Lasnik, Howard, and Mamoru Saito. 1992. *Move α*. Cambridge, Mass.: MIT Press.

Lebeaux, David. 1989. Relative clauses, licensing, and the nature of the derivation. Ms., University of Maryland, College Park.

Lee, Gun-soon. 1996. From referentiality to syntactic dependencies. Ph.D. dissertation, University of Wisconsin-Madison.

Legate, Julie. 2002. Warlpiri: Theoretical implications. Ph.D. dissertation, MIT.

Levin, Beth, and Malka Rappaport. 1986. The formation of adjectival passives. *Linguistic Inquiry* 17, 623–662.

Levin, Beth, and Malka Rappaport Hovav. 1995. *Unaccusativity: At the syntax–lexical semantics interface*. Cambridge, Mass.: MIT Press.

Li, Yafei. 1988. The characteristic θ-role and θ-operations. Ms., MIT.

Li, Yafei. 1990a. *Conditions on X^0-movement*. Ph.D. dissertation, MIT.

Li, Yafei. 1990b. On V-V compounds in Chinese. *Natural Language and Linguistic Theory* 8, 177–207.

Li, Yafei. 1990c. X^0-binding and verb incorporation. *Linguistic Inquiry* 21, 399–426.

Li, Yafei. 1993. Structural head and aspectuality. *Language* 69, 480–504.

Li, Yafei. 1995. The thematic hierarchy and causativity. *Natural Language and Linguistic Theory* 13, 255–282.

Li, Yafei. 1997a. Chinese resultative constructions and the UTAH. In Jerome Packard, ed., *Word formation in Chinese*, 285–310. Berlin: Mouton de Gruyter.

Li, Yafei. 1997b. Head-government and X′-theory. *The Linguistic Review* 14, 139–180.

Li, Yafei. 1997c. An optimized Universal Grammar and biological redundancies. *Linguistic Inquiry* 28, 170–178.

Li, Yafei. 1999. Cross-componential causativity. *Natural Language and Linguistic Theory* 17, 445–497.

Li, Yafei. 2002. Of categorial features. Ms., University of Wisconsin-Madison.

Li, Yafei, and Jen Ting. 1999. Grammar can be a superficial thing. Ms., University of Wisconsin-Madison.

Lieber, Rochelle. 1980. On the organization of the lexicon. Ph.D. dissertation, MIT.

Lieber, Rochelle. 1992. *Deconstructing morphology*. Chicago: University of Chicago Press.

Lin, Jo-Wang. 1996. Polarity licensing and *wh*-phrase quantification in Chinese. Ph.D. dissertation, University of Massachusetts, Amherst.

Marantz, Alec. 1984. *On the nature of grammatical relations*. Cambridge, Mass.: MIT Press.

Marantz, Alec. 1991. Case and licensing. In Germán F. Westphal, Benjamin Ao, and Hee-Rahk Chae, eds., *ESCOL '91*, 234–253. Columbus: Ohio State University, Department of Linguistics.

Marantz, Alec. 1993. Implications of asymmetries in double object constructions. In Sam A. Mchombo, ed., *Theoretical aspects of Bantu grammar*, 113–150. Stanford, Calif.: CSLI Publications.

Mayr, Ernst. 1997. *This is biology: The science of the living world*. Cambridge, Mass.: Harvard University Press.

McCawley, James. 1988. Review of Chomsky, *Knowledge of language*. *Language* 64, 355–365.

Mithun, Marianne. 1984. The evolution of noun incorporation. *Language* 60, 847–895.

Mithun, Marianne. 1986. On the nature of noun incorporation. *Language* 62, 32–38.

Mithun, Marianne. 1987. Is basic word order universal? In Russell Tomlin, ed., *Coherence and grounding in discourse*, 281–328. Amsterdam: John Benjamins.

Mithun-Williams, Marianne. 1976. *A grammar of Tuscarora*. New York: Garland.

Mohanan, K. P. 1989. On the representation of theta role information. Ms., Stanford University.

Muysken, Pieter. 1982. Parametrizing the notion of "Head." *Journal of Linguistic Research* 2, 57–75.

Nakamura, Masanori. 1997. Object extraction in Bantu applicatives: Some implications for minimalism. *Linguistic Inquiry* 28, 252–280.

Newmeyer, Frederick. 1980. *Linguistic theory in America*. New York: Academic Press.

Nishiyama, Kunio. 1998. V-V compounds as serialization. *Journal of East Asian Linguistics* 7, 175–217.

Ouhalla, Jamal. 1998. Possession in sentences and noun phrases. Ms., Queen Mary-London University.

Pesetsky, David. 1982. Paths and categories. Ph.D. dissertation, MIT.

Pesetsky, David. 1985. Morphology and Logical Form. *Linguistic Inquiry* 16, 193–246.

Pesetsky, David. 1989. Language-particular processes and the Earliness Principle. Ms., MIT.

Pesetsky, David. 1995. *Zero syntax*. Cambridge, Mass.: MIT Press.

Pollock, Jean-Yves. 1989. Verb movement, Universal Grammar, and the structure of IP. *Linguistic Inquiry* 20, 365–424.

Postal, Paul. 1974. *On raising*. Cambridge, Mass.: MIT Press.

Postal, Paul. 1979. *Some syntactic rules of Mohawk*. New York: Garland.

Pustejovsky, James. 1995. *The generative lexicon*. Cambridge, Mass.: MIT Press.

Reinhart, Tanya, and Eric Reuland. 1993. Reflexivity. *Linguistic Inquiry* 24, 657–720.

Reuland, Eric, and Alice G. B. ter Meulen, eds. 1989. *The representation of (in)definiteness*. Cambridge, Mass.: MIT Press.

Rizzi, Luigi. 1982. *Issues in Italian syntax*. Dordrecht: Foris.

Rizzi, Luigi. 1986. Null objects in Italian and the theory of *pro*. *Linguistic Inquiry* 17, 501–557.

Rizzi, Luigi. 1990. *Relativized Minimality*. Cambridge, Mass.: MIT Press.

Rizzi, Luigi, and Ian Roberts. 1989. Complex inversion in French. *Probus* 1, 1–30.

Roberts, Ian. 1991. Excorporation and minimality. *Linguistic Inquiry* 22, 209–218.

Roeper, Thomas. 1983. Implicit arguments. Ms., University of Massachusetts, Amherst.

Rosen, Sara. 1989. Two types of noun incorporation: A lexical analysis. *Language* 65, 294–317.

Ross, John. 1967. Constraints on variables in syntax. Ph.D. dissertation, MIT.

Runner, Jeffrey. 2002. When minimalism isn't enough: An argument for argument structure. *Linguistic Inquiry* 33, 172–182.

Sadock, Jerrold. 1980. Noun incorporation in Greenlandic. *Language* 56, 300–319.

Sadock, Jerrold. 1985. Autolexical syntax: A proposal for the treatment of noun incorporation and similar phenomena. *Natural Language and Linguistic Theory* 3, 379–439.

Sadock, Jerrold. 1986. Some notes on noun incorporation. *Language* 62, 19–31.

Sadock, Jerrold. 1991. *Autolexical syntax: A theory of parallel grammatical representations*. Chicago: University of Chicago Press.

Safir, Ken. 1985. *Syntactic chains*. Cambridge: Cambridge University Press.

Safir, Ken. 1987. So *there*! A reply to Williams' analysis of *there*-sentences. In M. A. Browning, Ewa Czaykowski-Higgins, and Elizabeth Ritter, eds., *The 25th anniversary of MIT linguistics*, 239–263. MIT Working Papers in Linguistics 9. Cambridge, Mass.: MIT, Department of Linguistics and Philosophy, MITWPL.

Sag, Ivan. 1976. Deletion and Logical Form. Ph.D. dissertation, MIT.

Saussure, Ferdinand de. 1974. *Cours de linguistique générale*. Critical edition, prepared by Tullio de Mauro. Paris: Payot.

Scalise, Sergio. 1984. *Generative morphology*. Dordrecht: Foris.

Shlonsky, Ur. 1992. Resumptive pronouns as a last resort. *Linguistic Inquiry* 23, 443–468.

Shlonsky, Ur. 1997. *Clause structure and word order in Hebrew and Arabic*. New York: Oxford University Press.

Siegel, Dorothy. 1974. Topics in English morphology. Ph.D. dissertation, MIT.

Smith, Carlota. 1991. *The parameter of aspect*. Kluwer, Boston.

Soh, Hooi Ling. 1998. Object scrambling in Chinese: A close look at post-duration/frequency phrase positions. In Pius Tamanji and Kiyomi Kusumoto, eds., *NELS 28*, vol. 2, 197–211. Amherst: University of Massachusetts, GLSA.

Sportiche, Dominique. 1996. Clitic constructions. In Johan Rooryck and Laurie Zaring, eds., *Phrase structure and the lexicon*, 213–276. Dordrecht: Kluwer.

Sproat, Richard. 1985. On deriving the lexicon. Ph.D. dissertation, MIT.

Stowell, Tim. 1981. Origins of phrase structure. Ph.D. dissertation, MIT.

Takano, Yuji. 1996. Movement and parametric variation in syntax. Ph.D. dissertation, University of California, Irvine.

Tenny, Carol. 1994. *Aspectual roles and the syntax-semantics interface*. Dordrecht: Kluwer.

Ting, Jen, and Yafei Li. In preparation. Resultative V-*de*, manner V-*de* and distributive morphology in Chinese. Ms., Taiwan National Normal University, Taipei.

Tomlin, Russell. 1986. *Basic word order: Functional principles*. London: Croom Helm.

Travis, Lisa. 1984. Parameters and effects of word order variation. Ph.D. dissertation, MIT.

Uriagereka, Juan. 1995. Aspects of the syntax of clitic placement in Western Romance. *Linguistic Inquiry* 26, 79–123.

Vendler, Zeno. 1967. *Linguistics in philosophy*. Ithaca, N.Y.: Cornell University Press.

Watanabe, Akira. 1993. Agr-based Case theory and its interaction with the A-bar system. Ph.D. dissertation, MIT.

Williams, Edwin. 1977. Discourse and Logical Form. *Linguistic Inquiry* 8, 101–139.

Williams, Edwin. 1980. Predication. *Linguistic Inquiry* 11, 203–238.

Williams, Edwin. 1981a. Argument structure and morphology. *The Linguistic Review* 1, 81–114.

Williams, Edwin. 1981b. On the notions "lexically related" and "head of a word." *Linguistic Inquiry* 12, 245–274.

Williams, Edwin. 1994. *Thematic structure in syntax*. Cambridge, Mass.: MIT Press.

Zaenen, Annie. 1994. Unaccusativity in Dutch: Integrating syntax and lexical semantics. In James Pustejovsky, ed., *Semantics and the lexicon*, 129–161. Dordrecht: Kluwer.

Zhu, Dexi. 1982. *Yufa jiangyi*. Beijing: Commercial Press.

Zidani-Eroğlu, Leyla. 1997. Exceptionally Case-marked NPs as matrix objects. *Linguistic Inquiry* 28, 219–230.

Index